D1165861

Be
Exceptional

ALSO BY JOE NAVARRO

What Every BODY Is Saying

Louder Than Words

Dangerous Personalities

Three Minutes to Doomsday

The Dictionary of Body Language

Be Exceptional

MASTER THE FIVE TRAITS
THAT SET EXTRAORDINARY
PEOPLE APART

Joe Navarro

with Toni Sciarra Poynter

WILLIAM MORROW
An Imprint of HarperCollins*Publishers*

BE EXCEPTIONAL. Copyright © 2021 by Joe Navarro. All rights reserved. Printed in the United States of America. No part of this book may be used or reproduced in any manner whatsoever without written permission except in the case of brief quotations embodied in critical articles and reviews. For information, address HarperCollins Publishers, 195 Broadway, New York, NY 10007.

HarperCollins books may be purchased for educational, business, or sales promotional use. For information, please email the Special Markets Department at SPsales@harpercollins.com.

FIRST EDITION

Library of Congress Cataloging-in-Publication Data has been applied for.

ISBN 978-0-06-302539-4 (hardcover)
ISBN 978-0-06-311347-3 (international edition paperback)

21 22 23 24 25 LSC 10 9 8 7 6 5 4 3 2 1

In loving memory of my father, Albert

Mind your thoughts—for thoughts become words.

Mind your words—for words become actions.

Mind your actions—for actions become habits.

Mind your habits—for habits become character.

Mind your character—for character shapes destiny.

—Adapted from Lao Tzu

Contents

Be
Exceptional

Before We Begin

Do not think that what is hard for you to master is humanly impossible; and if it is humanly possible, consider it to be within your reach.

—MARCUS AURELIUS

What makes people exceptional? For a long time, I pondered that question, and perhaps you have also. Over the course of more than forty years studying human behavior—including twenty-five years of service in the FBI, as a founding member of the FBI's elite National Security Behavioral Analysis Program, conducting more than ten thousand interviews in the field, and years of consulting with multilevel organizations worldwide, as well as researching and writing more than a dozen books on behavior and performance—nothing has captivated me more than those individuals who display exceptional characteristics. These people make you feel special. They draw you in instantly with their kindness and caring. They energize with their wisdom and empathy. They leave you feeling better than when you arrived. You want them to be your friend, neighbor, workmate, or coach. You certainly would want them to be your teacher, manager, community leader, or candidate for office.

What is it that makes them who they are—so influential, effective, worthy to model, and worthy to lead? The qualities that make them stand out aren't related to their level of education, income, or talents—say, in athletics or art or even business. No, these individuals excel in the ways that really matter: they seem to know what to say and what to do to earn trust, command respect, and positively influence and inspire even the most jaded among us.

My research for this book began more than a decade ago, quite unintentionally, when I was working on *Dangerous Personalities*. In that book, I explored the characteristics of those who let themselves and others down because of their abhorrent behavior, the decisions they made, the priorities they neglected, lack of emotional control, or because of their lack of caring or conscientiousness.

It was serendipitous that in researching these flawed individuals, their polar opposites—those individuals who have such remarkable positive traits that they make life better for everyone around them—effervesced in front of me with such clarity. It was that transparency, coupled with the thousands of observations that I had made in the FBI and in my international consulting work, that crystallized into this book.

What makes people exceptional? As it turns out, there are just five traits that set exceptional individuals apart from everyone else. Just five, but they are such powerful traits. I call them the Five Domains of the Exceptional.

The Five Domains of the Exceptional

Self-Mastery: The Heart of the Exceptional

By crafting our own apprenticeships, understanding ourselves through honest reflection, and cultivating key habits that lead to personal achievement, we lay the foundation for an exceptional life.

Observation: Seeing What Matters

By increasing our ability to observe the needs, preferences, intentions, and desires of others, as well as their fears and concerns, we are better prepared to be able to decode people and situations with speed and accuracy, gaining the clarity to do what is best, what is right, and what is effective.

Communication: From Informative to Transformative
By embracing both verbal and nonverbal skills, we can express ideas more efficiently and intentionally, appealing to the heart and mind and establishing bonds that build trust, loyalty, and social harmony.

Action: Make It Timely, Ethical, and Prosocial
By knowing and applying the ethical and social framework for appropriate action, we can learn, as exceptional people do, to "do the right thing at the right time."

Psychological Comfort: The Most Powerful Strength Humans Possess
By grasping the foundational truth that what humans ultimately seek is psychological comfort, we can discover what exceptional people know: that whoever provides psychological comfort through caring wins.

In the chapters that follow, I will combine field-tested insights, examples, and anecdotes from my decades of experience in behavioral analysis and business consulting with examples from history, current events, and everyday life to explore these Five Domains and explain how you can use them to improve and enhance your life, differentiate yourself, and most of all to positively influence others in your pursuit of a more empathetic, ethical life—the kind of life the truly exceptional live every day.

One cannot help but learn from and be influenced by studying exceptional individuals who daily demonstrate that to be exceptional, one must do exceptional things. These five life-changing traits are all that is needed to set you apart. They will immediately reward you the moment you begin to incorporate them into your daily routine. They will increase your capacity to positively influence others and no doubt will make you a better person. They will also make you a better leader—not just ready to lead when or if the opportunity arises, but worthy to lead.

So join me on this journey of discovery of who we are and who we can be. Let's explore that special realm shared by those few we call honorable, trustworthy, purposeful, and stalwart, but above all: exceptional.

CHAPTER I

Self-Mastery

THE HEART OF THE EXCEPTIONAL

By crafting our own apprenticeships, understanding ourselves through honest reflection, and cultivating key habits that lead to personal achievement, we lay the foundation for an exceptional life.

> Everybody thinks of changing humanity, and nobody thinks about changing himself.
>
> —Leo Tolstoy

One of the toughest decisions I ever had to make as a SWAT team commander took place before the operation even began.

As a team commander, you're responsible for the operational plan and the skilled and safe execution of that plan. Once you receive the "green light" for the operation to begin and are fully geared up, weapons locked and loaded, and you say over the headset, "I have control, I have control, I have control," many people are counting on you to have your head in the game. The public expects it. So do your superiors. And your fellow SWAT team members need you to have laserlike clarity of thought, as their safety and the success of the operation depend on it.

Events were unfolding fast in this particular operation—an armed fugitive holding his girlfriend hostage in a run-down motel outside Haines City, Florida, vowing never to be taken alive. Normally the hostage negotiators can deal with events like this, but this hostage was in need of medicine and her life was in peril. With little time to lose, the heat of the day making tempers even more testy, and the suspect unwilling to cooperate in any way, the last thing I needed was to have one of our FBI SWAT operators not up to the task. This particular operator wasn't as quick with his questions, nor was he finessing the final plans as swiftly as he usually would. Issues that he would normally raise—such as building construction (to determine how far a stray bullet might penetrate); whether the hinges on the door faced out or in (to help us determine how to open the door and what kind of breaching tools we might need); how close we could place an ambulance without it being seen; the location of the nearest hospital with a Level I Trauma Center, and so on—weren't coming up. His head, I could tell, wasn't in the game. Finally, I told myself: *You have to address this, and quickly.* We didn't have time to explore the cause. I just knew something was going on with him, and I had to take action.

My superiors, in the heat of the moment and busy with decisions that needed to be made by management—dealing with FBI Headquarters, last-minute changes, and making sure local law enforcement was aware of what we were about to do—hadn't noticed, though we'd been in the same room. But as team commander, I couldn't ignore it. This SWAT operator was not himself. It was the worst of times to have to deal with a personnel issue—and perhaps no one would notice, so long as I kept it to myself and nothing went amiss in the operation—but I had noticed, and it was on me to resolve. I couldn't have someone like that going into an operation where the potential for a firefight in an urban environment was high and decisions would have to be made quickly. As a leader you cannot put others at risk if you can easily avoid it, no matter how badly someone wants to be a part of something important or, as in this case, had been critical to the planning of this intricate operation to make a fugitive arrest and rescue a young woman with medical issues who, according to her family, was being held against her will.

I went to the Special Agent in Charge, who was on the phone updating FBI Headquarters on unfolding events, and said, "I need to take one of our operators out of this mission." As I said the words, I realized that in my two decades on SWAT, this had never happened before.

"You do what is best," was all he said, his trust in me having been well established over the years. Then, as if sensing I had more to say, he signaled to me with a nod. That's when I said, "I need to take myself out of this operation, sir."

At first he just stared at me for a second to make sure he had heard right, his hand covering the phone receiver, putting Washington on hold. He scanned my face, and in that brief moment, I believe, he began to realize what I had been experiencing that day.

He asked if I was sure. I said yes. "Do what you need to do. Do what is best," he repeated, without hesitation. "I trust your judgment."

And with that, I took myself out of a major SWAT operation. This was not easy to do, as my second-in-command now had the burden of assuming my role, and I knew some of the SWAT operators would wonder what was going on. Regardless, it was what was needed, and as team commander, it had been my duty to make the call.

The operation went down without incident and no one got hurt.

What had been affecting me? In the end, with some introspective prodding, what should have been immediately obvious eventually percolated to the surface. My grandmother had passed away a week earlier, and I was still under the effects of that profound loss. I was still grieving, still in pain—even though I thought I could just work my way through it. To others perhaps I looked a little more stoic than usual, maybe joking less, but when we're busy, it's easy to overlook what others are experiencing emotionally. My emotions were affecting my thinking. Fortunately, I recognized it in time.

That Special Agent in Charge said something important: "Do what is best." But how do we know what is best to do? And then how do we do it? It begins with self-mastery.

Self-Mastery Defined

We often equate mastery with skill. Skill, we say, is what underlies the ability to build a Stradivarius-quality violin or chisel a magnificent statue. But mastery and skill are two different things.

To become skilled at something requires dedicating yourself to whatever the challenge may be, no matter how difficult—but more importantly, it requires self-mastery: focus, dedication, industriousness, curiosity, adaptability, self-awareness, and determination, to name just some of self-mastery's skills.

I start with self-mastery because it is foundational to mastering the other four traits that set exceptional individuals apart. The good news is that self-mastery is not an impossible quest. We can actually rewire our brains to bring better versions of ourselves to the small and large things we do every day.

If, as I believe, our lives are defined by what we think—the mindsets and attitudes we adopt and the knowledge we acquire—what we feel, and the things we choose to do each day, then we cannot achieve our full potential without self-mastery.

Self-mastery may not conquer mountains, but a mountain cannot be conquered without self-mastery. The fastest human to ever live, Usain Bolt, did not achieve that status merely on athletic ability. He achieved it through self-mastery: he learned, he sacrificed, he worked hard, he remained diligently focused. Michael Jordan, the greatest basketball player of all time, did the same thing. This is what it takes to achieve that elite level shared by the exceptional.

But there's another side to self-mastery that includes knowing our emotions, our strengths, and more importantly our weaknesses. By knowing ourselves, we know when others should take the lead, when today is not our day (as happened to me on that SWAT operation), when we need a dose of humility, need to confront our demons, or take some other action to call forward the power of our better selves. That is what self-mastery allows for—a conscious and honest appraisal of ourselves that can compel and support us to strive and try harder, and to grasp the nuances of awareness that can make the difference between failure and success.

In this chapter, we'll explore how to take command of your life through your daily habits and behaviors by focusing on how to build the scaffolding essential to self-mastery, ending with a series of self-assessment questions to help you in your journey toward this most essential capacity. You want to reach your potential, grow your influence, grow your brand? Self-mastery is the only way.

Apprenticeship: The Scaffold of Knowledge

Sometime during high school, I had a sobering self-reckoning. It was not imposed on me. No one sat down to talk to me about it or suggested it. It was a very private conversation I had with myself, because it was abundantly clear to my young mind that things needed to change.

Fleeing to the United States at the age of eight as a refugee after the Cuban Revolution had left me at a tremendous disadvantage. Coming to the United States abruptly, not speaking English, not understanding this totally new environment with different rules, customs, and norms had left me bewildered and lagging. I was several steps behind and always trying to catch up in my new world. We arrived in America with no money (Cuban soldiers at the airport made sure of that) and traumatized, having survived a very violent communist revolution in Cuba. As a new arrival I had to fit in, yet the only thing I had in common with the children around me was that, like them,

I loved to learn and play sports. They did not speak Spanish and I did not speak English. They had not been through a bloody revolution. They had not been there on the street during the Bay of Pigs Invasion as I had, nor heard the gunshots of the *paredón* (the wall) where soldiers would line up citizens and summarily execute them for being anti-Castro. They knew Tinkerbell, Bugs Bunny, Road Runner, Disneyland, and the Mouseketeers; to me these were names with no meaning. I was used to wearing a uniform to school; they wore jeans and T-shirts. I went from being in a classroom with one teacher all day to changing classrooms every fifty-five minutes—why, I wasn't sure. I knew the rules of baseball but had never seen a basketball. I loved this new game I was introduced to called dodgeball, but I hated to be called up to the board to do math problems.

It was culture shock as defined by Alvin Toffler. I tried hard to learn all the social rules: no talking in line, hold hands while crossing the street but don't touch otherwise, don't stand too close, don't gesture too much, don't talk too loud, raise your right hand if you need to pee, make more eye contact with the teacher when being reprimanded (the exact opposite of what I had been taught, which was to look down, avoid eye contact, and look contrite). There were endless differences I had to learn and overcome to fit in. But there was also the matter of the schoolwork. During the revolution it was not safe to attend school and frankly it was scary, so I was already behind academically when we fled Cuba. Now, on top of that, nothing the teacher said made any sense because it was in English.

Somehow, through sheer persistence and out of necessity, I became fully fluent in English in about a year. There is nothing like immersive socializing for learning a language. I had been put back a grade so I could catch up academically, and in time I made up two years in one. But that was only the beginning.

There was the issue of my accent. I had to work hard to get rid of it because one thing I learned was that if you speak with an accent in America, you stand out, and I so wanted to fit in. Eventually I was able to overcome my accent, but there was always the reality that there was so much to learn that my classmates knew that I didn't know: all the things we learn from toddlerhood on, on the playground, while watching TV, by attending the same schools, and through years of culture and socialization.

I knew no nursery rhymes. I did not know any playground songs and never quite figured out what "London Bridge Is Falling Down" was about. (Why would such a calamitous event be described in a singsong children's rhyme?) We had no radio or television at home for about a year, and so the only song I learned was the national anthem, which we sang each morning.

As I entered high school, my classmates knew Shakespeare; I knew Miguel de Cervantes. They read Steinbeck and I Federico García Lorca. They knew Bob Hope; I knew Cantinflas. I knew every island in the Caribbean; most of my classmates could not locate the Gulf of Mexico. The communists in Cuba had indoctrinated us about the "proletariat and the bourgeoise," terms I readily recognized. My schoolmates thought I was making up those words—but then, I didn't know what it meant to be "blue collar."

For a long time, I erroneously thought other kids were smarter than I was. In time I came to understand that they were no more intelligent than I; they just knew things I didn't know because I hadn't been exposed to them. It bothered me that I had missed out on so many things. And at the pace we were going in school, I wasn't going to catch up anytime soon.

School, I realized, could only teach me what was in the curriculum. It could not teach me what I lacked, nor what I most wanted to learn—which went further afield than the Dade County school system allowed for. I wasn't going to wallow in self-pity, but I somehow knew that I had to take action on my own. I had to face my own reality. And so, in my teenage years, I started my own program of self-apprenticeship.

Take a moment to think about the exceptional people you've known, or those you've read about or studied. Who wouldn't appreciate the breathtaking athletic artistry of American gymnast and Olympic gold medal winner Simone Biles or basketball legend Michael Jordan? How about the investment genius of Warren Buffett, known as the Oracle of Omaha? It would be nice to be a legendary singer like Frank Sinatra or Adele, whose voices can fill or break a heart. They are all exceptional in their own ways. But what about us? I will never be an elite athlete, nor likely helm a billion-dollar business, and my singing only offends resting animals. But we can be exceptional in other ways—the most important of ways—including the number one business we're all in: the people business. How do we achieve that level of performance, where our actions are truly exceptional?

We do it by self-apprenticeship: investing in our own knowledge, growth, and potential, just as great achievers do.

Some people find it easier to value and take care of others than themselves. But just as we support others in bettering themselves, so too we have that same responsibility to ourselves. Once you accept that the best way to value yourself is through your own commitment to become a better version of yourself, you're on your way to becoming an exceptional individual.

Every time I read about someone in their eighties who graduates from high school or like Giuseppe Paternò who at the age of ninety-six finally graduated from college, I'm reminded that here is a person whose plans may have been derailed by work, responsibilities, or misfortune but who remained committed to investing in their education; even late in life, because they valued themselves. And what a beautiful example they set for all of us.

It's never too late to take mastery over yourself and pursue your full potential, to acquire those traits and behaviors of exceptional individuals. Not only will you lead a better, fuller life, but when and if the time comes, you can become not just a leader, but *worthy* to lead.

Often, we're told to seek out mentors—admirable individuals who serve as guides on the path to wherever it is we want to go. Mentors are great to have. But they can be difficult to come by, and often they have limited time to instruct us.

To be exceptional and to achieve self-mastery, I have found, we must take responsibility for mentoring ourselves.

History offers a useful model in the form of the Renaissance, that vibrant period between the fourteenth and seventeenth centuries when science and art flourished throughout Europe. To learn a trade, young men such as Michelangelo, who went on to paint the Sistine Chapel, were apprenticed to experts in the field—in his case, master artists and sculptors to bootstrap their learning. Artistic guilds brought together the best practitioners in drawing, sculpting, drafting, painting, calligraphy, paint mixing, pottery casting, architecture, needlecraft, woodworking, metalworking, gold smelting, et cetera.

These were no summer camps. Apprentices followed rigorous schedules to learn and master skills through days filled with disciplined focus on specific tasks. Many were apprenticed at very young ages, earning their keep through their labor while acquiring skills and an appreciation for being responsible for their own lives and work. In time, they perfected their abilities, adding their own expertise and nuance. Thus, through the arduous annealing process of an apprenticeship, a new generation of masters was assured, and we of course are the beneficiaries of that process.

The concept of a formal apprenticeship is for the most part lost today, except for a few trades and professions. Medical doctors in essence enter into a twelve- to sixteen-year apprenticeship to learn the mind-bendingly complex process of diagnosing and healing human illness. One of my editors described learning her craft in the publishing world as an apprenticeship, in which she first watched her boss work with authors to edit and shape books; then participated in the process under supervision; then finally was entrusted to acquire and edit projects on her own. Apprenticeships still exist in certain trades such as plumbing and electrician's work, though these tend to be for a short period of time and are very narrowly focused.

But if you look closely at exceptional individuals, as I have, you see that they create apprenticeships for themselves. While they may seek help, advice, or expertise from others, they actively take responsibility for their own improvement. They know what we were never taught: that to be exceptional, you must apprentice yourself.

This self-education process may take a variety of forms—some formal, some informal; some undertaken out of necessity or from a burning desire. And in each case, through patience, force of will, trial and error, and hard work, sandwiched between other duties, or even between jobs or after work—a way is found.

For me, interested in human behavior, I began to keep a journal of behaviors I observed that I did not understand. In time, through experience and research, I would decipher these behaviors, becoming a better observer. At about the same time, I trained for and got my pilot's license before I graduated from high school. Why? I can't give you a reason beyond being profoundly curious. I thought these activities and skills would later help me in life and they did, though at the time I did not know how. Those behavioral observations I made as a fifteen-year-old later saved my life in the FBI when dealing with criminals, and that pilot's license allowed me to serve as a pilot-in-command to conduct aerial surveillance on terrorists. I didn't know any of that was in my future, but my self-apprenticeships certainly helped me years later.

Without exception, in every case I studied, exceptional individuals made it a lifelong habit to carve out the time to work on themselves. They treated the drive to do better, to learn and experience more, as a worthwhile and essential enterprise.

Now famous for her work for the humane treatment of animals, in particular cattle destined for the slaughterhouses, Mary Temple Grandin was diagnosed with autism (autism spectrum disorder) at an early age. Long before this malady was understood, it was often the case that people with Grandin's condition were relegated to menial jobs or forfeited a higher education because they were seen as not a good fit for the rigors of academia.

Grandin created her own apprenticeship program to meet her special learning needs and satisfy the depth and breadth of her interests.

She taught herself as she wanted to be taught, in her own way, at her own pace, eventually earning a college degree and ultimately a doctorate. But Grandin wanted to be a force for change, and for that she had to go beyond the classroom. She had a vision for what she wanted for herself, what she deemed she needed to learn, and she crafted the program to achieve that. She dug deep into animal behavior and physiology. She researched autism so she could understand her own affliction, which also led to a greater understanding of others and animals. She studied psychology, even delving into how colors affect humans and animals. She learned about drafting and engineering so she could design more humane environments for cattle. She honed her observational skills to the point where she could arrive on a property where cattle were about to be slaughtered and immediately see things that were problematic in their handling and treatment. There was no end to her self-mentorship. She went above and beyond out of necessity to reach out and influence others by studying marketing, social engineering, salesmanship, media relations, negotiations, branding, and on and on.

Over a lifetime Grandin apprenticed herself not to a mentor or school of thought but rather to herself. She sculpted her own path as many exceptional individuals have—no matter how many hurdles were in their way. In doing so, she became a champion for not just the humane treatment of cattle, but also for people on the autism spectrum.

More than two hundred years before Grandin carved out an influential niche for herself, a young boy in Boston began his journey of influence. Before this nation was a nation, America's first and most notable entrepreneur and the greatest influencer not only of his era, but for generations thereafter led the way by showing us what you can achieve, no matter your circumstances, if you apprentice yourself.

Benjamin Franklin's father wanted him to be a minister, but from a young age, Benjamin wanted more. Ever observant even as a child, Franklin watched the world around him and saw how things got done and what it took to be successful. He understood that education was key, but no school in America could teach him everything he wanted or needed. So he created a self-apprenticeship program to learn in that unforgiving laboratory we call life.

He read voraciously and became such a good writer that he succeeded in getting himself repeatedly published in local newspapers by passing himself off as an adult, using a number of pseudonyms, including that of a middle-aged spinster.

He was formally apprenticed to his brother James at age twelve, under whom he learned the printing trade, including typesetting, bookbinding, marketing, and publishing. He wasn't just a laborer learning a trade for making a living—he was learning how to master the most influential communicative platform of his time. He learned to expertly set type, formulate inks, work with printing presses of all types, edit manuscripts, write pithy articles, and generate what we now call "trending" subjects to change minds and challenge the political order. He read everything that came into the print shop and thus honed his reading and writing skills. Back then printed books were expensive, so he bartered and traded for any and all reading material he could get his hands on. No one assigned him things to read; he did this on his own—the very definition of self-apprenticeship. Interestingly, it was that difficulty as a youth in having access to reading material that led him later, as an adult, to create the first lending library in the United States.

After five years, Franklin had learned enough to continue in that trade, but he yearned for more. As the story goes, with fifteen cents in his pocket he left for Philadelphia, where other printing houses eagerly sought not his labor—they could find that anywhere—but rather his skills. Labor in those days was abundant, but skill and knowledge, Franklin learned early, were highly valued and not all that common.

Franklin also understood the power of what we now call networking and access—including the importance of adopting the traits and habits of those who wielded power, influence, or authority in order to fit in and be welcomed among them (what we now call *mirroring*—something we'll discuss in later chapters). Similar to how my behavioral study as a teenager helped me immeasurably in the FBI, Franklin's awareness of customs and manners would serve him well many years later as America's first ambassador to France.

With his abundant curiosity, skills, and will, he grew his circle of influence to the point that while still a young man he so impressed the governor of Pennsylvania that the governor arranged for him to study in England to further his self-apprenticeship. Franklin had found the secret to success: that knowledge, curiosity, adaptability, hard work, and a yearning for more knowledge can make your life better.

By the time Franklin died in 1790 at the age of eighty-four, this person whose formal education had ended at age ten had been and done so many things that it staggers the mind. He was an original signing member of the Declaration of Independence. He shaped the drafting of the Constitution. He counseled Thomas Jefferson on the founding principles that helped create the United States. As ambassador to France during the American Revolution, he mastered the delicate nuances of French customs and diplomacy, eventually persuading the French to risk war with England by financing these newly minted Americans struggling for independence. These contributions would have been more than enough. But he achieved so much more.

Beyond being an author, a newspaper editor, a printer, a champion for independence, a diplomat with few equals, and the man who "harnessed lightning," he was a humorist, satirist, Freemason, scientist, inventor, educator, civic activist, researcher, spokesperson, founder of the first fire department in Philadelphia and the University of Pennsylvania, a statesman, and the architect of the first national communications network to keep the colonies and people connected through what we now call the postal system. As Walter Isaacson said in his biography of Franklin, he "was the most accomplished American of his age and the most influential." He was America's first thought leader, influencer, and self-help guru—and if TED Talks had been available back then, you would have needed to carve out a few months to binge-watch.

The only way he could have accomplished all that was through self-mastery: creating a scaffold of knowledge, building strength upon strength, through a program he created for himself based on his boundless curiosity. Many more educated people had better access to what Franklin sought to learn, yet he stands out because of his determination to embrace it all, to construct that eclectic and robust scaffolding through his self-apprenticeship that allowed him to achieve everything he did. No school, then or now, could possibly teach all the things he is known for.

Franklin was a legend in his own lifetime and the world owes him much. But perhaps his greatest legacy is the example he set for all of us: that no matter how humble your beginnings, you can take control of your own life, of your own passions, of your own learning, and never stop.

Once we take on the responsibility to reshape our lives through self-apprenticeship, something quite marvelous begins to happen.

When Joseph Campbell spoke of following "your bliss" in his landmark book with Bill Moyers entitled *The Power of Myth*, he didn't mean it would come without effort, that it would just appear. He meant that if you have a love, a yearning, or a passion, you go after it, no matter what difficulties you may encounter. When you do, as Campbell said, you "put yourself on a kind of track that has been there all the while, waiting for you and the life that you ought to be living."

If you're willing to serve that self-apprenticeship, Campbell says, you start a momentum that builds and gathers force: "you begin to meet people who are in the field of your bliss." Things begin to go your way. "I say, follow your bliss and don't be afraid," Campbell exhorts us, "and doors will open where you didn't know they were going to be." They certainly did for Franklin and Grandin. They did for me, too—and they will for you. Someone once said that luck is the residue of hard work, but I would argue that luck is the residue of the hard work we put into our self-apprenticeship.

In 1971, when I was a freshman at Brigham Young University, there were only a few books on body language. The field was barely recognized. There were certainly no majors in the subject. But it was my passion, as I knew how useful it can be for relating to others—something I had discovered in my youth when I arrived in the US without knowing any English. I promised myself that when I graduated, I'd teach myself everything there was to know about nonverbal communication.

On graduation day, I celebrated by, of all things, getting a library card at the city library. Away from the university, now there was time to read whatever I wanted, not just what was required. I created my own apprenticeship in nonverbals, learning about the body language of Trobriand Islanders in the Pacific one day and about greeting gestures among the first people of Alaska the next. The nonverbals the conquistadores observed when they arrived in the New World were just as fascinating to me as the mandated color of clothing King Henry VIII allowed his nobles to wear. The body language Sir Richard Burton observed in Africa while seeking to find the origins of the Nile was every bit as interesting as the customs and mannerisms the medieval explorer Ibn Battuta found over a thirty-year period and seventy-five thousand miles traveling across Africa, the Middle East, India, and Asia. What no class could teach me, I sought to teach myself.

I apprenticed myself to study everything I could about body language and nonverbal communication from psychologists, zoologists, ethologists, anthropologists, clinicians, ethnographers, artists, photographers, primatologists, sculptors, and anatomists. This self-apprenticeship went further afield than I ever could have anticipated—and changed my life in the process. It has assisted me in my multiple careers, helped me to grow a global enterprise, helped me make the most interesting of acquaintances in so many varied fields, greatly enriched my life, and given me treasured insights into human nature.

When I got that library card and started my self-apprenticeship on nonverbal communication, I never dreamed I would meet the giants in the field: Paul Ekman, Bella DePaulo, Judee Burgoon, Mark Frank, David Givens, Joe Kulis, Amy Cuddy, and many others. I couldn't imagine that I'd be recruited by the FBI and use my knowledge to catch spies, terrorists, and kidnappers. I never foresaw that I would write more than a dozen books on human behavior, give yearly lectures at the Harvard Business School, do educational videos that would receive over thirty-five million views, and consult for organizations and governments all over the world. I had no idea that in apprenticing myself, following my own bliss, doors would in time open to me, as Joseph Campbell had forecast, where I didn't even "know they were going to be."

It was hard work. I had to make a total commitment to learn about nonverbal communication—something I still pursue every day. But hard work is the price of this gift we give ourselves of choosing to follow our bliss.

Perhaps best of all, when we find that bliss, we are not the only ones who benefit.

You don't have to be aiming to improve or save the world or its creatures to mentor yourself to a better state of being and living. I think of the young man in the lane next to mine at the local pool who has practiced to perfection the low-silhouette "combat swim"—on one's side, arms kept below the waterline to eliminate splash, gliding between strokes, only the mouth pops up out of the water for a breath—based on a video he downloaded from the internet, because he aspires to be a US Navy SEAL. Or of William, a man in his early forties, who recognizes that when he's excited about something, he talks too fast. He knows it, his wife certainly knows it, but so do his senior managers, who want him to "take it down a notch." So, on Saturday afternoons, he practices speaking into a recorder, reciting a speech in cadence, almost like a preacher, teaching himself to pace his delivery so that when he shares his thoughts, others have time to absorb them. He is a successful manager, but he wants to be better. While his friends are watching Formula One races on TV on their day off, he is improving himself, one speech at a time.

Self-apprenticeships fill our well of knowledge. They give us resources for weighing options and making decisions, skills for finding and gathering information or pursuing new ventures, and confidence that whatever we need to learn to move forward in life, we can resolve to learn.

Self-apprenticeships take time, but not necessarily money. For years, the local library was my greatest resource in my self-mentoring in nonverbal communication. The internet brings a universe of information within easy reach—from easy-to-follow video tutorials to authoritative articles to engaging podcasts. You can also get leads on resources simply by telling people on social media what you're pursuing.

What will your apprenticeship be? It's a question that should stir excitement and one we can ask ourselves at any time in life. Self-mentorship is a gift you give yourself. With it you create your own momentum, one discovery leading to the next as you chart your own path, form your own character, and decide who you will be and what you stand for.

If you truly want to be exceptional, then begin your apprenticeship today. Make a start to build your personal scaffold of knowledge. Take a step. Take control! Enjoy the project of designing what you want and need to know, and how you'll get there. There are so many ways to learn: reading on your own, talking to others knowledgeable about what you seek to learn, podcasts, checking out video tutorials, signing up for a class, joining organizations or online groups. Delight in where your learning quest takes you. Trust, as Joseph Campbell said, in doors opening where you didn't know they existed. Create that apprenticeship for yourself. When you do, the exceptional will welcome you, because they understand and respect the commitment you have made.

Emotional Balance: The Scaffold of Stability

One of the best FBI agents I ever worked with was Terry Halverson Moody. The office could be in turmoil—prosecutors demanding this and that, incessant calls from headquarters, media queries that might expose sensitive operations, micromanaging bosses, interviews piling up—yet she was ever calm. I admired her for that and for her ability to balance her life. As a wife, mother, FBI Special Agent, and my partner (that alone was no easy task), she seemed to have embraced early on in her life the one powerful and important component all exceptional individuals share. That secret? Emotions must be kept in balance at all times. Either you control emotions or emotions will rule over you.

Although Special Agent Moody was my junior in the FBI by a decade, she was my senior by decades when it came to dealing with the demands and stresses of the office. Those everyday events in a high-pressure environment that keep our emotions ever-ready so we can act can also cause us to be irritated, testy, or inconsiderate.

Ironically, it was during the truly high-pressure situations that I became calmer. In SWAT operations, I became more composed and focused, reliant on my training—emotions were pushed aside. Plane engine on fire at three thousand feet? No problem: turn off fuel pump, switch to guard frequency (121.5), declare emergency, kill the master power switch, look for an emergency landing field, maintain a proper glide angle, place extinguisher near legs (where fire will most likely come through), navigate to nearest airport, keep updating alternate landing sites (highways, sugarcane fields), unlock doors in case we need to be rescued, avoid other aircraft, look for light signals from airport clearing our approach—and aviate (fly the plane as best you can) to a powerless landing. That I could do and did do in Puerto Rico during one harrowing nighttime flight. It was the stress of daily work—the inconveniences, interruptions, distractions, exacting demands—that would set me off emotionally. Emotions were changing who I was, overriding my own standards of good behavior, causing me to be less gentle, giving sharp verbal ripostes when challenged, being less patient. Just knowing that Headquarters was calling was enough to get me riled up. It was taking a toll on me and on my relations with others.

Fortunately, Agent Moody came along just at the right time. Sitting across from me, she would say, "Exhale before you pick up that call." "Stay focused on fixing the problem even if the person calling is an 'asshole.'" *Lower your voice*, she would signal with her hand as I grew more agitated by yet another unreasonable demand. When the call was over she would say, "Exhale slowly. Repeat, this time longer." She would then say, "Now, do it again." And as I began to recount the call, she would admonish me: "Don't swear or curse," "Stand up and stretch," or "Let's go for a walk before we talk."

If she sensed I was getting more upset, she would give me a much-needed maternal look and say, "Joe, go for a run. I'm not going to talk to you until you come back." And I would. I would come back much tamer. Even during lunch, she would sense my urgency to get back to work and insist I slow down: "Your mouth is for eating. It's not a woodchipper."

On those days when I wasn't paying attention to her advice, she would remind me that if I had a heart attack, she would not resuscitate me because I hadn't listened to her—a tough bargain, and so I would slow down.

I knew my emotions were getting the best of me and that it was unhealthy, unproductive, and I was beginning to make life difficult for those around me. Yes, I was working one of the most important espionage cases in the history of the United States, one that ultimately turned into a ten-year ordeal, but I could not continue to be off-balance emotionally. There would be a price to be paid, and eventually that happened, as I recounted in my book *Three Minutes to Doomsday*. Three days after making the first arrest on this spy case, my body broke down. My immune system was compromised, I came down with the Epstein-Barr virus, I had to be hospitalized, and I went into a state of anxiety and depression that lasted nearly a year.

Why am I telling you this? It's a cautionary tale and a reminder that we may be involved in something that is important, exciting, can save lives or change the world—but if emotions are not in check, emotions will at best negatively affect us or at worst destroy us. We all could use an Agent Moody to coach us and catch us before we go off the rails. That experience that put me in the hospital wasn't my first wake-up call—Agent Moody had done plenty of that—but it was that singular event that told me: you need to reconstitute yourself in a better way emotionally.

So much of our life revolves around emotions that I'm surprised we don't spend more time on the subject, especially when it comes to the two areas that consume us most: interpersonal relations and work.

When we are young, if not checked, emotionally boorish behaviors can shape us, and not in a good way. We have all known a spoiled brat or an inconsiderate person with little emotional control. Temper tantrums, grudges, petty jealousies, impulsive behaviors, intentional meltdowns to garner attention, and other toxic acts that impose on others can become routine. Over time they can become even more noxious, leading to harassment, bullying, even to acting out violently.

I'm sure you or someone you know has remarked that someone at work is acting like a child. They are not. They are acting like adults who have not learned to self-regulate their emotions. The pettiness, lashing out, bullying, or impulsive behaviors we are seeing in adulthood are simply because they lack self-regulation.

Most of us learn by the time we reach adulthood to rein in our emotions, thanks to our parents, caregivers, teachers, and others. Even so, they can percolate to the surface if we don't actively manage them and can get the best of us if we aren't careful—even when we instinctively know better. They can and will affect us mentally and physically, as well as impact our interpersonal relationships and our performance and relationships at work.

What makes emotions exert such a powerful pull? Our responses to the outside world and even to our own thoughts or predicaments are usually handled first by the *limbic system* in our brain—the same area responsible for our emotions as I noted in my book *What Every BODY Is Saying*. This exquisitely elegant system that assesses and responds to the world quickly, without our giving much thought, is hardwired in us to keep us alive. As a more primitive area of the brain that we share with all mammals, it is highly responsive to immediate threats but has long-term limitations.

In the face of a threat, the emotional or *limbic brain* kicks in, freezing our movements to make us less noticeable to predators, while simultaneously allowing us to assess our situation so we can go into defense mode, protective mode, flight mode, or fight mode.

These tense states, be they from a predator, someone scaring us, hearing bad news, or having to deal with a toxic boss, subconsciously muster our physiological resources in seconds through the sympathetic nervous system. In an instant, adrenaline is released for quick action, glucose surges through our body for energy, and cortisol, which coagulates blood if we're bitten or injured, goes to work. We don't have to think about it. It just happens. This system also conjures up our ability to scream, yell, rant, and fiercely fight—in a heightened emotional state.

For hundreds of thousands of years we humans have relied on the limbic system to keep us alive, because anger, apprehension, fear, and even fury, when confronted by a predator and applied at the right moment, have helped us to manage a world full of threats.

This legacy inscribed in our DNA is always with us, but in a world where we're not likely to have to spear a charging bear or beat back a large feline, the limbic system can work against us. Too much adrenaline or too much cortisol due to stress or emotional upheaval over time wears us down and affects our immune system—which is what happened to me. But perhaps more importantly, during emotional arousal—whether by a predator, an argument, a missed flight connection, an upsetting phone call, "our" candidate not getting elected, or pressure to complete a project—we pay a heavy price, and that price is rational thinking and even recall.

When this happens, there is *"emotional hijacking"*—a phenomenon in which the supremacy of emotions so useful for survival overwhelms our ability to think logically. Not so good when conducting business or socializing. This is why when we are stressed, we forget assignments or appointments, go blank during a test, can't remember phone numbers, or can't find our keys anywhere.

Over time, if we're not mindful to regulate our emotions and take control of ourselves when stressed, emotions can overwhelm logic, rationality, and common sense and become, unfortunately, our default response. Like a child, we break down; have a tantrum; do impulsive, ridiculous, unhealthy things; or lash out at others. This then causes others to avoid us, not respect us, or lose their trust in us.

Take impulsiveness, for instance. Essentially, it's the inability to regulate our desires and step in with logic to say "That is a bad idea" when our impulsive act may in fact hurt us as well as others. Just look at what happened to the stock market price of SpaceX when its founder, Elon Musk, decided to smoke marijuana during a podcast. Overnight, investors lost confidence as they wondered if he was capable of regulating himself. After all, if you invest tens of millions in one individual's vision, you want the person to at least know better than to go on a public forum and take a toke. An impulsive act may, unfortunately, tell the world to watch out, this person may be lacking in emotional control.

Perhaps like you, I've had experience with people unable to govern their emotional impulses. I've had bosses who screamed at us when things didn't go their way. I've had workmates who turned into bullies when work got stressful, picking on the most fragile. I've seen grown men throw a leg-kicking, foot-stomping temper tantrum because a flight attendant told them to put their luggage in an overhead bin, and I've heard verbal arrows launched so indiscriminately and so out of proportion to the situation that one can't help but think that it was intended to hurt others, not to correct a situation.

As a SWAT team commander, one of the things that I always looked for in team members during the selection process was the ability to stay calm under pressure—especially once an operation had been planned and approved. It's challenging enough to keep an eye on the objective while talking to the command post, the surveillance pilots overhead, unseen SWAT operators beyond a wall, and snipers at the ready, knowing they're aiming at a spot, measured in mere inches, just in front of my face as I stand ready to breach that "lethal funnel" where so many agents have died, otherwise known as the front door—all on one crowded frequency in my headset, while civilians are screaming in the distance—without having someone on my own team who is hyperventilating, asking rapid-fire questions, wondering aloud whether there isn't a better way to do this at this late stage, and otherwise letting everyone know that he is unraveling under pressure. As General Patton famously said, "The time to take counsel of your fears is before you make an important battle decision. That's the time to listen to every fear you can imagine. When you have collected all the facts and fears and made your decision, turn off all your fears and go ahead." If you are controlled by your fears, you are out of control. We would all do well to channel the outlook of a good SWAT team operator: be smart, ask questions, be deliberative, be conscientious—and then, once the decision has been made and the pressure is on, let go of any doubt and find your inner calm.

I recognize in myself those times when emotions have gotten the best of me or are about to, and it is something that I personally work on all the time. I'm introspective enough to know when my emotions did me in, and frankly, I hate when it happens. I've learned to think about what I've said or done, consider how to prevent it next time, and, with my tail between my legs, apologize with deep regret for my thoughtless or hurtful behavior.

Stress may be the explanation for failure to self-regulate, but it is not an excuse. What sets the exceptional apart is not that they don't have emotional responses—they're human like the rest of us—but that they do a lot of self-regulating of their emotions. Like a muscle, they've conditioned this capacity and are always working to keep it in top form so it's there for them, even (especially) on the stressful days. Mastering our emotions is a challenge for many of us, certainly for me, and maybe for you as well. That's why I've included it in the first chapter of this book, because failure to regulate emotions is something that can keep you from ever being exceptional.

We're all subject to emotional upheaval at times, of course, whether from relentless unreasonable work demands, pressures at home, or catastrophes happening. But it's continual impulsivity, lack of consideration, and emotional outbursts that can put us on a fast track to losing credibility and the respect of others. And it can undermine and derail even the most creative or skilled individuals among us.

Bobby Knight, a gifted basketball player who later famously coached at Indiana University, was one of the most innovative, successful coaches in the history of the game. But there was a dark side to Bobby Knight. He could not control his emotions. The brilliant coach who popularized the "motion offense" that opened up opportunities for dynamic plays and winning seasons—because it drove defensive players crazy with the impossible task of trying to move faster than a passed ball—was also the person who was accused of assaulting a police officer in Puerto Rico during the Pan Am Games, who threw a chair across the court at a Purdue game, who head-butted a player at another game, and who repeatedly cursed and berated players, coaches, referees, students, and faculty administrators.

Eventually, Knight's behavior could no longer be excused. His legacy was cut short when Indiana University president Myles Brand had had enough. He fired Knight in 2000 because of his combative nature and a "pattern of unacceptable behavior." In other words, he was tired of a coach who could not control his emotions. Period.

Some say this was too little, too late and that most of us would have been fired if we did anything close to what he did at work. No doubt. It's a lesson for all of us that unchecked emotions eventually undermine us. Lack of emotional self-regulation can kill a career or a relationship.

Why should anyone follow or respect an adult who throws tantrums, who is emotionally unstable or out of control? We shouldn't. When I've worked for people who have screamed and yelled when things didn't go their way, my colleagues and I had no respect for them, we began to question their instincts, and our productivity suffered as a result.

The first key to emotional regulation is to acknowledge that emotions can and will affect us and learn to recognize when we feel our emotions surging up. Start with some simple questions about your emotional habits:

> What emotions do I find most challenging to manage (worry/fear, sadness, anger)?

> What tends to "set me off" (too many tight deadlines, not enough sleep, when x person does or says y, when a certain combination of things happens)?

> When I'm emotionally hijacked, how do I behave (yelling, saying mean things, sulking, banging things around, withdrawing, unhealthy eating/drinking/drugs)?

Once you have a sense of what sets you off emotionally and how you tend to react, raise your threshold against emotional hijacking by looking for strategies you can implement to deal with stress. This could be an excellent self-apprenticeship, as there's a great deal of scientific study and literature on stress reduction. Or start closer to home:

> Think about those people you know who handle things well—they don't lose their cool; they stay focused and decisive under pressure; they deal respectfully with others even when their patience is tested.

> What do they do in these situations? Really observe and be specific here.

> › How might you adapt their strategies to the situations that challenge you emotionally?

> › Look for blog posts, books, and videos that deal with emotional regulation or anger management.

> › Seek professional help in anger management—it can only be beneficial.

I was lucky along the way to have parents, leaders, and yes, an Agent Moody who could help me. Sometimes we need help from professionals, be it a therapist, a clinician, an anger management specialist, or a religious leader. There's no shame in this. It takes courage to say, "I need to find a better way," and then seek healthy, sustainable ways to deal with it.

Distancing ourselves from emotions doesn't mean not feeling them. It means applying our rational skills to take our internal temperature and channel our emotions productively. For eleven weeks in 2018, Brigham Young University's women's volleyball team was number one in the nation. When their star setter, Lyndie Haddock-Eppich, was asked about the team's remarkable success, she attributed it to a "Very strong work ethic across the team"—and to this, which caught my eye: "We're a very no drama team. We get to work and do what we need to do. I think that is what has made us so strong."

It's not that the players don't have emotions. They do—they are *über*passionate. It's that their emotions are channeled into something productive.

We must distance ourselves from our emotions so that we can think clearly, sort out the issues, and, as NASA flight director Gene Kranz famously said to the engineers during the *Apollo 13* space flight, "work the problem" so the problem doesn't work us.

Be it the admonitions of an Agent Moody, walking away so that you can think, listening to music, praying, calling a friend, exercising, or doing yoga—whatever your strategy is, make sure that it is ready and handy. As the BYU team found, when you suppress the drama, there is efficiency, harmony, and, with hard work, success.

For me it can be anything from distancing myself physically from someone who confronts me, to turning to humor, to exhaling repeatedly, to going for a long walk, to talking to a friend, to writing my response on paper where I let it all out; but I make sure it never gets mailed. I learned that last hack from no less a figure than Thomas Jefferson, who would vent his bile on paper, let it sit overnight, then was grateful the next day that he never mailed it. So go ahead, draft that nastygram—but don't hit send for at least twenty-four hours. You'll be glad you waited and can delete it before letting the situation that riled you do you greater harm. I know—because of how often it has saved me.

Another strategy I have learned and used to avoid being derailed by emotions is to immediately channel emotions into constructive action. Midway through my career, Sue Adams, a fantastic FBI Special Agent and famous instructor at the FBI Academy in Quantico, called me and said, "We want you to come and teach here permanently." I said that I would love to. But then three weeks later, she called apologetically to say she was retracting the offer because I didn't have a master's degree.

This was a golden opportunity and I could feel my blood boiling. But I had the example of exceptional individuals—don't wallow, don't whine—take focused, constructive action. And I did. Within two days I was talking to the Registrar's office at Salve Regina University in Rhode Island, which has one of the nation's finest International Relations graduate programs. And by just taking that positive action, I was able to put away all that disappointment. It led to many doors that later opened to me in and out of the FBI.

Over the years I had watched the great Michael Jordan play basketball, and I learned from him that when things did not go his way, he just came back the next time around with a better game: more focused, even more enthused, he played better, harder, smarter, singularly dedicated to achieve his goal of outscoring and personally outperforming the other team. The greatest basketball player to ever play did it by focused, constructive action.

Emotional control doesn't mean being a robot where you aren't sensitive to setbacks or other emotional events. It's about managing those emotions and impulses. I've had indignities flung at me and my family because we were refugees and couldn't speak English, or because of the work I was doing. I have been called every imaginable name. I've cried at the funerals of fellow agents killed in the line of duty. I've felt disgust and fury as I was taunted by a serial child predator after the judge gave him a light sentence. But I learned to turn away, to focus on what I could do or what needed to be done to make this turn out differently next time. Importantly for my self-mastery, I learned that I *could* let it go by focusing on what's next. The key is to have a plan—a focused, constructive plan of action. Perhaps this is what Mark Twain was talking about when he admonished us not to get drawn in when we are taunted—or trolled, as we say now—which more than ever merits repeating: "Don't wrestle with pigs; the pigs enjoy it, and it gets you dirty." Move on. Focus on something positive and constructive.

Especially when you're dealing with personal losses or major setbacks, self-mastery is recognizing when you're not completely on your game and stepping back briefly to work on yourself before you work the problem. If you can take some time to regroup, do so. If you need twenty-four hours to think over a decision, say so. Not everything can wait, but many things can. Being strong means knowing how to handle yourself when you're stressed so it doesn't negatively impact your work and relationships.

Agent Moody and her husband, a fellow agent, eventually moved away, and I foolishly went back to many bad habits. But then I'd catch myself—with the help of good friends, family, and role models in my life and in history—and I'd regroup, rethink, and rededicate myself to having a plan for managing my emotions.

I haven't always succeeded, but I have tried through my own self-apprenticeship to mirror those even-tempered individuals I admire so that I can master my emotions. I can report that I am much better at it now than I was thirty years ago. It is—and I am—a work in progress.

The sections to come will help you increase your capacity for calm by engaging the enormous cognitive capacities of your brain, providing alternatives to the limbic response when losing emotional control won't serve you. Whatever it takes, the exceptional will do because they know that no one wins when you lose it emotionally—in fact, you can be the one with the most to lose.

Conscientiousness: *The* Key Success Indicator

You can be an extraordinary artist, businessperson, or scientist, but that doesn't make you an exceptional *person*. Exceptional individuals aren't just masterful at what they do or for what they know. They are exceptional because of how they live their lives and how they treat others. They are influential in the ways that matter most: by how they make us feel, how they behave toward others, how they care and make sacrifices for the benefit of others. Self-mastery is about who we are as people, apart from what we do. Much of that boils down to what we call conscientiousness.

In personality theory, conscientiousness is considered one of the "Big Five" traits that, along with extraversion, agreeableness, neuroticism, and openness to experience, helps determine how well suited someone is to succeed socially, at school, and in the workplace. But of all the success indicators researchers have studied, from IQ to family background, conscientiousness towers above the others.

Conscientious people have the ability to toggle between empirical and emotional realities. They can blend their knowledge, technical skills, and the facts of the situation with understanding of the added dynamics of their own and others' feelings. This ability makes them exquisitely insightful and enormously effective, able to harness their own full potential and encourage it in others.

One way to understand conscientiousness is to look at how conscientious people behave:

> They accomplish tasks while being mindful of their responsibilities toward others, the community, and the environment.

> They're aware of the consequences of their actions.

> They can delay gratification when other things take precedence.

> They have the humility to know they're not always right.

> They are dependable, disciplined, persistent, and well-intentioned.

Before going further, take another look at the list above and ask yourself these two questions:

1. Which of these areas am I strong in?
2. Which ones could I improve on?

Taken together, these traits allow conscientious individuals to be deliberative in their planning and actions. They are able to apply themselves to learning and study and take pleasure in being prepared and organized. They have the ability to start and finish projects, persisting regardless of the obstacles. For them the future is full of possibilities, and they often have a life plan of things they'd like to achieve, do, or see—frequently from a young age. They tend to care about how they appear, exercise good manners, and are empathetic toward others. Their reliability and organization have a positive effect not just on them but on those around them.

Notice I haven't mentioned how intelligent they are. That's because conscientiousness isn't about intelligence or what school you attended. It's about delivering on your promises and responsibilities to yourself and to others by living a purpose-filled life.

Many business experts and venture capitalists have told me that promising businesses often fail not for lack of good ideas or a worthy product, but because of their leaders' lack of conscientiousness; including the inability to stay on task, giving in to impulsive or rash acts, or pursuing selfish needs that interfere with meeting commitments. As one investor told me, "The big box I have to check for myself and my fellow investors when it comes to venture capital is: How well do I think this person or group of people will be able to fulfill their objectives? When I sense there is a hint of lack of conscientiousness—and that includes whether they are on time for our meetings—I begin to hesitate. I begin to doubt."

Conscientiousness, then, is not just a trait of good character or a moral imperative—it's also a business necessity.

This is a reality check. If you are failing frequently, it may not be about this, that, or the other. It may be about your level of conscientiousness. If your answers to the questions above revealed areas where you could use some improvement in the conscientiousness department, be assured you're not alone. You'd be surprised how many people don't finish tasks—smart, talented people who get derailed all too easily. They start out with good intentions, but then become distracted. This isn't a modern problem caused by the hectic pace and stress of contemporary life. It has always plagued mankind. If Leonardo da Vinci were alive today, I wonder what his online ratings would be. An indisputable genius with arguably no equal in the world of art, he was also an easily distracted perfectionist famous for not finishing commissioned projects, to the consternation of the many patrons who were after him to complete jobs, return their money, or justify multiyear delays. It took him more than ten years to finish the *Mona Lisa*. That would be unacceptable today. Between his perfectionism and his near-compulsive, darting curiosity that compelled him to explore everything from principles of how water eddies behave near the shoreline to dissecting one more human cadaver to studying how birds fly to ascertaining the length of a woodpecker's tongue, he simply was incapable of staying, as we would now say, on task. Yes, he was brilliant beyond measure and his talents carried him far. But even so, people reached their limit when dealing with him.

The ability to stay on task, deliver on one's promises and to expectation, and not be distracted by the insignificant or the need to indulge personal whims is critical. There's little patience for the person who can't get it together, is always late, fails to answer calls or emails, derails projects with analysis paralysis or pedantic perfectionism, creates delays or drama, or wields power abusively. To accomplish anything—from starting a business to farming to child-rearing to management at the highest levels—conscientiousness is an essential trait when it comes to being exceptional. Focusing on the Five Domains will help you develop and internalize habits that support a conscientious life.

Untethered: Challenging the Limits Others Place on Us

On a business trip to San Francisco, the car service driver asked me if we could listen to the news about a runner from East Africa who had just won a marathon. When the winner's name was announced, the driver said, "I am from the same tribe as this runner."

"You must be very proud," I said.

"I am," he replied, looking back at me in the rearview mirror and adding, with a chuckle, "I myself was quite the runner in my day."

I had always been curious to know why so many great marathon runners are from Ethiopia and Kenya, so I decided to ask him. I expected many answers—genetics, healthy diet, physiology, altitude, instilled discipline—but not the one he gave.

"We did not have radios or television or even newspapers when I was growing up," he replied.

That was a curious answer and one I hadn't heard before, so I asked what he meant by that. "When I was growing up," he said, "we just ran everywhere, always, and as fast as possible, because we had responsibilities."

I still didn't get it. He laughed with good patience and a beautiful contrasting smile before he elaborated: "No one ever told us what the world speed records were. We had no limits imposed on us as children and we did not impose them on ourselves. We just ran everywhere as fast as we could. There were no fences, no stop signs, no finish lines. We had no shoes—our only focus was just getting there quickly and faster than the other child next to us. Up a mountain, no problem. To the next village thirteen kilometers away, no problem. Cold days, no problem. Running for hours at a time, no problem. No one told us to stop and rest, that we could not keep running, or that was too much."

Wow, I thought. *Never expected that.* But those were his words, his reflection upon a time when as children he and his friends just ran and ran and ran unhindered. With no self-imposed limits, no rule-induced time-outs, and no limits from outsiders, they allowed themselves to excel.

We may never know for sure why so many great runners come from that part of the world. I am sure genetics and high-altitude running have much to do with it—but I cannot ignore what he said. There were, as he said, "no finish lines," no limits on time. Surely that is a factor. How could it not be?

We tend to absorb the messages and "rules" of society, institutions, and others that often limit us. I do believe it is possible to let go of those self-restricting expectations. Through your practices, thinking, and behaviors you can rewire your brain, and in so doing change who you are and what you can achieve, and open up yourself to new possibilities.

Take some time to answer these questions honestly:

> ❯ What expectations do others have of me?
> ❯ Do I find these expectations burdensome or motivating?
> ❯ Which ones are in alignment with my own goals and interests?
> ❯ What expectations do I have of myself?

> Are there ways that I might be limiting my own potential?

> What training, information, knowledge, or skills would I need to reach my goals and pursue my interests?

> What, if anything, is holding me back? What could I do to move forward?

Don't let others' expectations tether you intellectually, physically, or emotionally. Don't set limits on your self-apprenticeships and what you seek to learn. Don't restrain yourself in your ideas about what you might achieve. Don't let anyone decide for you what you're capable of—imagine there are no finish lines. Experiment, strive, and find out for yourself.

Can we really change ourselves so profoundly if there are no set limits? Yes, and there is at least one example of not just rewiring the brain, but profoundly changing our physiology and anatomy. Consider the Bajau people of Southeast Asia.

According to researchers, these sea marauders, as they are known, spend up to 60 percent of their day in the water, diving for fish, sea urchins, sea slugs, octopus, and bivalves, without SCUBA tanks. Over the generations, they have so adapted to the necessity to dive deep and for longer periods of time that their spleens have grown 50 percent larger than their nondiving neighbors' in Malaysia (or, for that matter, anyone reading these words), to carry more oxygen-rich red blood cells. This allows them to dive to depths of more than two hundred feet and stay under for thirteen minutes at a time. By contrast, most people can barely hold their breath for forty-five seconds, and even a whale calf has to surface for air at least every three to five minutes.

Scientists theorize that as the Bajau adapted over the centuries to their aquatic needs, what resulted were changes not only in their attitudes in relation to the ocean, but also in their actual physiology. Out of necessity no doubt, but perhaps also because they're free of self-imposed restraints, these aquatic nomads permitted themselves through their fearless relationship with the sea to evolve into super-divers, to the point where their bodies actually changed. This phenomenal capacity is now part of their DNA, permanently hardwired, making them without equal when it comes to diving endurance.

So it bears asking: What could you achieve if you didn't set limits on yourself?

Demonology: Appraising the Flaws That Hold Us Back

Often, I ask my audiences to write down what they believe their weaknesses are, or those things they wish they could improve. Some people seem bewildered about what to write down, while others quickly scribble a litany of flaws that rivals a grocery list. In both cases, I wonder how realistically we see ourselves. Could a person really have so few flaws, or so many? Can we see ourselves as we truly are? And if so, what do we do with that information?

The poet and diplomat James Russell Lovell said, "No one can produce great things who is not thoroughly sincere in dealing with himself." Exceptional individuals are constructively self-critical. They care about being and doing better. This self-analysis, which I call *demonology*, allows them to set a better course for themselves. Perhaps this explains why you're reading this book. No matter what your age and life experience, there's a better world of your own making waiting for you if you're willing to do the following:

> ⟩ Look at yourself realistically.
> ⟩ Ponder how you can change.
> ⟩ Examine how you view yourself and relate to the world around you.
> ⟩ Constructively take steps to constantly rectify or improve your behaviors.

Why go through all this? Because when we begin to change ourselves, we have a positive effect not just on ourselves and our own life satisfaction, but also on others'. That is the foundation of influence.

Self-correction generally happens in one of two ways: either we take the initiative to change through introspection and the exercise of the self-mastery skills discussed in this chapter . . . or we wait for life to teach us a hard lesson. The better (i.e., less painful) choice seems obvious. But think of how many people wait until they have that heart attack before they take exercise and diet seriously. It's astonishing how far people let things go before they confront whatever is holding them back from getting their lives in hand. Sometimes even a crisis doesn't trigger introspection and lasting self-correction.

This is where exceptional individuals differ. They use failure, mistakes, and difficulties to gain insight into themselves and self-correct if necessary, so that they can do things better next time. These painful events can serve as valuable teaching moments. They can shake us into action and a desire to improve.

Deep within your midbrain are two identical structures that to early anatomists looked like seahorses, so they named each structure accordingly from the Latin: the hippocampus. These remarkable structures retain, among other things, everything negative that affects our lives—which is why you only have to learn once not to touch the hot stove.

From our failures, we learn not to repeat the same mistakes if we pay attention to the memories that are stored in the hippocampus. Mistakes and failures serve another purpose, too: they keep us humble—and that keeps us in touch with compassion for our own and others' struggles and travails. Still, it is up to us to learn from our mistakes, faux pas, and shortcomings.

When I meet people who say that they seem to get in trouble all the time, don't last at a job for very long, always date the "wrong kind" of person, and so on, immediately I think: *Here is someone who has had many learning experiences but has never self-corrected.* While certain events can be frustrating, even painful, exceptional individuals don't just learn but self-correct. Over and over. They will self-correct for a lifetime.

Why wait for the next calamity? Head it off: begin that self-awareness now.

All you have to do to start the process is to take the time to stop and think: *Is there something I'm doing that is contributing to what is happening? How can I change for the better?* No one will fix your problems. No one will save you from yourself. You have to do that.

That means taking a look at how and why you do things and isolating those demons that can hold you back.

"Why are you so angry?"

Those were the first words I spoke to the new postal employee behind the counter.

I was at the local post office to pick up mail that had been held for a couple of weeks while I was away for the holidays. I couldn't help noticing while standing in line that Michael, the new postal worker who was serving the customers in front of me, seemed to have nothing but impatience and scorn written on his face as he went about his duties. At times he was even openly hostile, as when he told a customer, "I don't get paid to make your decisions."

I have nothing but disdain for bullies, and I don't mind saying so. If management wasn't going to do something about this, I was. When it was my turn, I skipped the obligatory "Happy New Year" niceties and jumped right in:

"Why are you so angry?"

He glared at me. That was fine. I've been glared at by psychopaths. He was a purse puppy by comparison. I stared back at a point just above his eyes (a technique I found that drives bullies and psychopaths to distraction because they want you to look into their eyes—but that would be a reward, and I don't reward bullies or psychopaths; I look through them). So I looked back blandly with my best *I am waiting for your answer* look. When he didn't respond, I said, "Five dollars' worth of stamps, please." His eyes broke away from me and he slapped a book of stamps on the counter. I ignored the sophomoric gesture, paid for my purchase, thanked him, and left.

A couple of days later, at the side door of the post office, I saw Michael helping to unload a van full of mail, so I walked over. I did it because we were going to have to deal with each other for who knows how long at this post office. I hoped we could be on good terms.

This time, I made eye contact with a smile, leaned against the wall as if I'd known him all my life, and asked again, "Why are you so angry?"

I think he sensed that I wasn't being confrontational. While unloading boxes, he not only apologized, but he opened up. It turned out he had much to be angry about. I won't go into details but in difficult families, often it's not just one thing that's wrong but many things—and they weren't small things.

As Michael spoke, I could tell he was anxious. His chest heaved, he was exhaling with puffed cheeks (cathartic exhales), and his mouth was dry. I asked him if anyone at work knew about what he had just told me. He said no, and since he was out of vacation time and sick days, he couldn't attend to things at home. So, we just talked, and I let him vent.

I don't recall how long I was there; it couldn't have been too long because my beeper didn't go off (yes, we had beepers back then—no mobile phones), and mine went off at least twenty times a day. I told Michael that abnormal situations cause abnormal reactions, and that the day I had encountered him, he had been truly unpleasant. Again, he apologized. I thanked him and told him we all have bad days.

But there was one thing more. I asked him to think about how he wanted to be known. Did he want to be known as a jerk no one wanted to deal with, or as that nice guy at the post office everyone likes to talk to, who gets gifts from his customers on holidays?

Michael stopped what he was doing. I'm not sure what emotions he was feeling, but for a moment he looked like he was about to cry. Then he went right back to work. I asked him to think about what I said because he was starting his career and now was the time to address the question.

As I walked away, he said something I will never forget. He said, "No one ever told us in training to think about how we want to be known."

"They never told me that in the FBI, either," I replied.

Fact is, no organization does. That is the kind of question only the exceptional ask.

How do you want to be known? Few, if any, will ever ask you this question. But it's the only question that matters. Because that is the only thing in life that you can shape.

How do you want to be known? There are many adjectives you might choose: *efficient, precise, resourceful, capable, smart, clever, industrious, creative, kind, joyful*—to name some. I'm sure you aren't choosing words like *indifferent, sarcastic, petty, snotty, caustic, complaining,* or *lazy.*

Who you are has nothing to do with where you went to school, how much you earn, or what level of job you have. Maybe you clean tables at a fast-food restaurant, as I did when I was starting out, or you paint houses (I did that also), or you manage a dozen highly educated individuals (yes to that, too). Your job, whatever it is, is what you do. But you are so much more than what you do. Who are you going to *be*? Thus, the question we must ask of ourselves if we care, if we want to be exceptional as individuals or as leaders: How do I want to be known?

I don't know what Michael did, nor how he did it—I am sure it was a struggle. But in time, that once-dour person I had originally met began to smile when he saw me. He smiled not just at me but at others in line, and when he spoke with the customers, the edge in his voice was gone. He spoke with kindness and patience. I actually began to look forward to talking to him each morning. Turns out we had a few things in common.

Because he treated his customers with kindness, they in turn did the same to him. A year later, when I stepped up to the counter to mail some packages for the holidays, I noticed a gift-wrapped plate of cookies next to Michael's computer monitor. As we greeted each other, he immediately glanced toward the cookies as if to say, *Look what someone gave me for Christmas.*

So what say you? How do you want to be known? Are there things you'd like to work on? Are you impatient, intolerant, restless, ill-prepared, short-tempered, inconsiderate, bossy, crude, a procrastinator, passive-aggressive, prone to playing the martyr, or [you fill in the blank]? You can work on each of those things. After all, they're inside your head, not a commute away. You can resolve to put in the effort and get it done, or you can do nothing and remain the same. You must be willing to look deep and act powerfully to change. It's your choice. No one but you can save you from your demons. "It is only when a man tames his own demons," writes Joseph Campbell in *The Hero with a Thousand Faces*, "that he becomes the king of himself if not of the world."

I can tell you one of my demons: I am impatient. I work on it constantly, especially when it flares up. And here's another that surprises many people: even though I travel the world and speak before hundreds or even thousands at public events, I still find it nerve-racking. I am highly introverted and, in many ways, shy. I don't like big groups. I find small talk difficult and would rather be with just a few friends. While teaching others brings me great satisfaction, being a public speaker is, for me, hard and exhausting work. This was one of my demons, but if I wanted to build a business helping others learn about nonverbal communication and human behavior, I had to do something to address it. I started by speaking to small groups (less than a dozen) over and over, even volunteering to do so. It was really tough at first. But repeated practice showed me that I could do it, even though it made me nervous, and gradually I developed the confidence to speak to larger groups. Don't get me wrong, I still get nervous, and you can often see it in the first few minutes of my presentations, but that's okay. It's one of my demons, but I have strategies for dealing with it. I compensate for my nervousness by preparing meticulously, thoroughly knowing what I will teach and staying current with the latest research, using pedagogical techniques that have served me well such as engaging with members of the audience, and making sure I bring them something new and interesting each time. These strategies give me confidence despite feeling nervous. Then, as the session unfolds and I begin to relish the give-and-take of information with the audience, my nervousness evaporates.

Not sure what your demons are? Think of those times when family, friends, coworkers, or bosses have been candid with you about your missteps or failings. Do some themes emerge? Or reflect on occasions when, for reasons you couldn't quite figure out, relationships cooled, clients quietly departed, or everyone was polite, but you weren't invited back. If things like that keep happening to you, it might be time to self-correct. That can only take place when we take the time to think about how we communicate or engage with others; how well we observe the needs, frailties, or preferences of others and how we respond, and the actions that we take toward others on a daily basis: Are they prosocial and beneficial, or not? These are the very traits that we'll explore in the chapters to come to set you on the journey that exceptional individuals have all taken.

Doing this work has become all the more important, thanks to a change that has taken place over the last twenty years in business practices. Organizations today are far less tolerant of wayward, disorderly, sophomoric, undisciplined, or toxic behavior than in the past. I consult with businesses worldwide, and many tell me that it's much easier now than in the past to identify problem employees, as there are toxic behavior checklists that can point toward whether an employee will be a good fit or will be disruptive or affect the harmony of the workplace. Keeping the undisciplined, disruptive, or toxic person on staff is too big a drag on productivity, morale, and public image—not to mention the potential legal liability. You either have your act together or you will soon be gone. Just look at the news on any given day and see who has been fired for their less-than-professional behavior.

Taking a good look at ourselves isn't just important for the workplace. Our interpersonal relationships can use a checkup, also. Over time in relationships, it's easy to develop bad habits or behaviors that need course correction. Unfortunately, many people erroneously feel that it's up to others to tell them if they're doing something wrong, and if no one complains, it must mean that everything they're doing must be okay. Others know they're not behaving well but are indifferent—they expect or even demand leniency, constant understanding, extended deadlines, second chances, turning of the other cheek, do-overs, yielding to one at the expense of the many, and repeated forgiveness. Still others insist that it is not their fault, that everything that happens is someone else's fault.

The reality is that we can ignore our personal accountability, we can lie to ourselves, we can pretend to be what we are not—but in the end we cannot hide from our effects on others. Our impact on others is the proof of who we really are. There will be consequences for failure to self-correct. Eventually, the message becomes: "Get it together or I'm out of here."

The time is now, not tomorrow, to take a good look at yourself. Do your own demonology assessment. What are your flaws? What is holding you back? Resolve to make self-corrections. Identify your weaknesses. Make a list. Take on each weakness individually, but make it a priority to work on. It may take years. I am still working at it, but I do so because I know it makes a difference. Some days are better than others. And I can say that now there are more good days than bad days. It is a process. But it is one that's worthwhile if we aim to enter into the realm of the exceptional.

We all have demons. What matters is that we continue to confront them. There's nothing wrong with admitting that you have a weakness. Those things that inhibit, frustrate, or stymie us—no matter how clever, successful, or accomplished we may be—need to be addressed and corrected. That's the entry fee to an exceptional life. Remember Leonardo da Vinci's inability to finish commissioned projects—imagine how much more he could have accomplished if he had mastered his demons?

Exceptional individuals are realistic about their imperfections and tackle them head on. Seek out the resources that will help you, be it getting coaching, counseling, mentoring, or help through books and research to gain insight and coping strategies. Whether it's choosing better friends, working on public speaking, getting less angry, or being more organized—whatever you feel weakest at, there are ways to effectively deal with it.

Perhaps you're reluctant to take the risk. What if you fail? Failure is only a calamity if you learn nothing from it. As many successful leaders will tell you, the more personal improvement projects you take on, even if you don't get things completely right, the more positive possibilities will come your way. Sun Tzu said it best: "The more opportunities I seize, the more opportunities multiply before me."

Look at your life, acknowledge your demons, and tackle them, one at a time. Above all, be honest with yourself. There've been moments when I've had to say to myself, *Joe, you're not measuring up—get your act together.* It's not about beating yourself up. It's about facing up to a truth that, once faced, is in your power to deal with. If you want to be exceptional, accept the Demonology Challenge. Tackle the difficult, correct what is amiss, dedicate yourself to becoming better. The immediate payoff? A better you. The unforeseen benefits? Immeasurable.

Self-Discipline: The Scaffold of Achievement

When I taught in the criminology department at the University of Tampa, I got to know Dr. Phil Quinn, who served as both my mentor and my boss at the university. A tenured professor as well as the department chair, he was also a practicing psychologist and a former priest whose experiences and training gave him an illuminating perspective on life.

One day, when we were talking about how it is that people fail to achieve, he said, "In my private practice I see people all the time who feel like their life is out of control. Without exception I have found they managed their life poorly. They lacked the discipline to do the smallest of things on time, and so everything else becomes overwhelming."

Phil had spent years counseling both patients and students to achieve their full potential. In his opinion, consistent failure to do small things, on time, was a reliable indicator of deeper issues, including interpersonal distress. In my experiences in law enforcement and in performance consulting for businesses, I, too, have found that failure to do small things in an orderly, timely manner keeps many from being able to accomplish the bigger things in life.

I thought about Dr. Quinn's statement twenty years later as I listened to an extraordinary individual giving a commencement speech that went viral for its heartfelt simplicity and power. The speaker was US Navy admiral William H. McRaven, who, as commander of the US Navy SEALs that led the raid on Osama bin Laden and later became chancellor of the University of Texas system, is certainly qualified and worthy to give that kind of advice. In his speech, he challenged his audience about what they needed to do if they wanted to be leaders and change the world.

Admiral McRaven said this: "If you want to change the world, start off by making your bed." You can hear students chuckle, but not for long. He goes on to say that you cannot become a Navy SEAL if you don't make your bed perfectly to navy standards every morning, no matter how sleep-deprived, sore, or injured you may be. Every day. No excuses.

As it turns out, fulfilling the smallest of tasks diligently is one of the strongest and most reliable predictors of future success, and that is the essence of the research on conscientiousness. Why would these elite warriors need to make their beds as part of their basic training?

Because when you do small tasks with care, you are valuing yourself and reinforcing a "sense of pride" in how you complete your duties in life. Habitually bringing dedication to the small things we do each and every day creates a positive trend. And a trend, nourished properly, can become destiny.

Command over everyday behaviors allows exceptional people to build the scaffolds of knowledge and emotional stability we've been discussing in this chapter. It enables them to stick with self-apprenticeships while also fulfilling other responsibilities. It helps them keep their lives together even when they're struggling emotionally. It elevates the quality of their presence in the world. Indeed, to "change the world," we must change our own practices first. As Admiral McRaven added: "If you can't do the little things right, you'll never be able to do the big things right."

Discipline and attention to doing the small things set the exceptional apart. They don't cut corners or take shortcuts. It's tempting to think that it's okay to cut corners if no one's looking. But invariably, every time I've thought to do so—even if it's shortening my workout by just five minutes—I'm reminded of long-ago admonitions from my coaches not to cheat myself. Yet there's a higher reason for a life habit of "no shortcuts"—it can serve as a strong deterrent when larger temptations loom.

As I write this, federal prosecutors have announced the indictment of numerous individuals, including TV stars (Felicity Huffman and Lori Loughlin), for allegedly paying bribes to get their children into the best universities. What a lamentable mistake those parents have made in taking that shortcut, robbing their children of the personal growth and satisfaction that comes from diligently doing the many small things necessary to achieve hard-earned success in academics, athletics, and service to others.

Order and Priorities

We practice diligence day by day by getting our life in order. That begins with prioritizing what is important.

Peter F. Drucker, author of the bestselling book *The Effective Executive*, said it best: "Nothing else, perhaps, distinguishes effective executives as much as their tender loving care of time."

Rich or poor, the day comes to us all evenly—with just 1,440 minutes to get everything we need to do completed. What we do with each minute matters over a lifetime. And therein is the difference. Whereas most people think about what they want to do in a day, the exceptional think about time as a valuable commodity, and for them time is measured in minutes.

Exceptional people use time deliberatively. They ask, in effect, "What can and should be done in these precious minutes, so I can accomplish more, achieve my work or personal goals, or have more time for my family?" They have the ability to prioritize what is most important and can pivot as needed to deal with changing circumstances and complexity. When confronted with multiple options, they can quickly do the triage to identify and take on the most important task.

In basic first aid, we conduct triage by remembering ABC—airway (making sure it's clear), breathing (taking place unassisted or assisted), and circulation (heart is beating, irregular, or needs assistance). This is fairly easy to remember, and it can be taught even to children. However, when there are many casualties, where there is catastrophic blood loss or organ damage, it is vastly more difficult to do triage. And yet it is done and it is taught as every first responder and emergency room doctor is taught.

But in life, there is no crisis classroom. We have to teach ourselves how to do the daily triage of the urgent, the significant, the important, the not-significant-but-appealing, and the insignificant. This is a process that can only be learned by doing, through trial and error. When we deliberatively set out to triage what is needed of us each day, we are building a foundation that will serve us well as life grows in complexity. Thinking about what is most important and what we should do in sequential order takes effort, but setting priorities becomes easier the more we do it.

Setting priorities isn't about taking whatever call comes in first, answering the latest email, or making sure your in-box (digital or physical) is empty at the end of the day. It's about taking control of your life through the deliberate choices you make about when, where, and how you'll direct your attention and energy.

In college, I was blessed to have a professor who gave us some advice on setting priorities that would change my life. He told us that before bed, he'd write on a 3 x 5 card, in order, the things he wanted to accomplish the next day. At breakfast he'd review the list, making any necessary changes. Then, marching orders in hand, he'd proceed to master his day. He could also quickly shift or add priorities to his list as the day unfolded.

This wise teacher was Stephen J. Covey, who went on to write the blockbuster bestseller *The Seven Habits of Highly Effective People*. He wasn't world famous in 1972 when I was in college, but he was well known on campus for being a great speaker. He told us that this act alone—thinking about his priorities and writing them down— contributed more than anything else to his success and to the success of many executives he coached.

Then and there, I decided that if making a list each day was good enough for Dr. Covey, it was good enough for me. Ever since, I've carried a card in my pocket listing by priority everything I must do each day. I so believe in this simple method that I have cards printed with my name at the top as a reminder to me that these are my responsibilities, my priorities, my values, and that I must fulfill them. This is a daily contract I must accomplish, like any contract I commit to.

When I give presentations, I'm often asked about what I've come to call my "Daily Action List." I'm happy to show my cards and share how they work. They weren't my idea, but I've certainly benefited from them immeasurably, as have many executives who make them a part of their daily routine.

Why? Because it works and it's so simple. It makes you think about what must be done and in what order. The mere act of thinking about it, I find, allows my subconscious to help me begin the

JOE NAVARRO

hard work of organizing my thoughts and considering how I'll trans-act what I need to do. It has disciplined my mind so I can accomplish more and in the right priority.

There's also something powerful about writing your priorities down in your own hand that gives them greater importance. While I use my smartphone and other devices to keep track of various re-sponsibilities, when it comes to setting key daily priorities, I find the cards more accessible, easier to quickly revise, and more reliable—with that added element of showing my personal commitment in my own hand, almost as if a signature, to what I have set out to do.

I know this simple, low-tech method works because on those days when I can't seem to get anything done, invariably, those are the days when I've decided to "wing it" and not bother writing things down. Life is too complex to not come at each day with a plan; I fail myself and those around me because without that list, I become too easily distracted. It's only when I make that list and prioritize and reprioritize tasks throughout the day that I get things done and achieve my full potential.

And what a pleasure it is to look at the card at the end of the day and see that everything I set out to do has been accomplished. That's my victory lap. As Joseph LeDoux informs us in his book *Synaptic Self*, the brain has a reward mechanism for motivating us when we accomplish a goal. Perhaps that is why at times I've caught myself smiling, knowing I've accomplished everything I set out that day to achieve.

Setting priorities and not losing sight of them leads to self-mastery by giving you control over your life through the deliberate choices you make, day by day, hour by hour, about where you put your energy and effort. Our priorities define who we are. If you prioritize little to nothing, that's a decision you're free to make, but just don't expect the same results.

If you don't set your priorities, others will do it for you. If that idea doesn't appeal, you can start here and now to turn things around by setting your priorities for the rest of your remaining day. Then repeat it again tomorrow and thereafter.

Deliberative Practice: The Power of Myelination

On the third day after arriving at the FBI Academy, we started firearms training. It was 1978. We were a small class, just twenty-one out of eight thousand or so applicants. The first question our firearms instructor asked was, "How many of you have received firearms training before?" Eight of us raised our hands, including me. We'd had firearms training either through a police department or in the military.

I felt pretty good, being one of those eight. *This might put me ahead of the game*, I thought. Maybe we'd even get to skip the training.

How wrong I was.

We had all trained differently, and, as we quickly learned, had acquired terrible habits that made for some very mediocre weapon-handling and shooting.

We were going to learn to shoot the FBI way: quick, dynamic, and effective out to sixty yards with the Smith and Wesson two-and-a-half-inch revolver we'd been issued. We were going to do it safely and smoothly. And we all had to score above a 92 percent to pass the training.

But first, we were going to have to unlearn the wrong ways that had become ingrained in our bodies and brains.

Deliberate or deep dive practice—rehearsing small segments of a process to perfection—is now recognized as the most important component in achieving athletic or artistic greatness. As Rachel Cossar, author of *When You Can't Meet in Person: A Guide to Mastering Virtual Presence*, and a former professional ballet dancer, told me in an interview: "In ballet a detail as minute as how to precisely hold your partner's hand to transition from one movement to the next would be rehearsed hundreds of times, so that it can be performed with rigorous perfection. Something that is insignificant or seemingly inconsequential to the audience is highly significant to the performers for artistic expression or to facilitate technical execution."

Go to a college track, as I have, and you'll see sprinters working on just taking their marks: Crouching down and placing their feet in the adjustable slanted starting blocks. Positioning their hands precisely at the starting line (at the edge—not on), fingers splayed and flexible just so. Feeling the pressure of the soles of their running shoes against the plastic blocks. Sensing and meticulously adjusting the angle of the back—tail high, head low and projecting unnaturally over the starting line; the tension in calves, hamstrings, gluteal muscles; the shoulders poised to unleash the force of the arms in an instant to power through the start.

Over and over they will do this, sweat dripping under the hot Florida sun, before they even get to the point of running. They know that, in a race that could be decided by thousandths of a second, consistency and perfection of movement count. Do it perfectly right each time, and you will, as one runner said to me, "get a good start. And you can't win if you don't get a good start—it just does not happen."

Talk to experts in any field, and they'll tell you that "talent" is something you work at. These men and women may be blessed with talent for running. But perfected practice is how they unlock it.

They are harnessing a capacity every one of us is born with. We are wired for self-improvement. Our brain can do it so effectively that our actions become automatic, bypassing conscious thought, freeing the mind to operate in the moment while the body does what it deeply knows.

Each time those sprinters take that position, they are reinforcing what neuroscientists call *myelination*. Simply put, myelination is the superstrengthening or fortifying of the connections between brain cells (neurons)—and the special communication spaces between them (synapses). The nerve fibers of the brain are basically electrical circuits where impulses flow and neurotransmitters such as acetylcholine and serotonin are released. These are in turn converted into physiological activities such as deeper breathing or rapid heart contractions as needed, or into the more visible physical movements (a perfect start to a race) or even behaviors that reflect our moods.

The more we practice something, the more myelination takes place around the circuits facilitating that process. The more myelination around a circuit, the more robust, focused, and faster the transmitted signal, and the less likely that circuit will be disrupted or corroded over time. Which is why, if we spend enough time riding a bike as a child, we can always get back on and ride, even decades later.

This same process takes place inside the brain when world-renowned classical guitarist Ana Vidović practices on her acoustic guitar. Selecting a small chunk of music, perhaps no more than five notes, she practices the sequence over and over at a very slow speed. With each repetition, her brain in coordination with her fingers builds the myelination necessary to reinforce the brain's capacity to remember the sequence and perform it flawlessly. That audiences are moved to applaud is but one benefit of myelination—but there is even more: it allows the performer to add artistry atop a complex process that has, in a way, become automatic, perfectly executed without requiring a great deal of conscious thought.

Myelination builds the wondrous neurological scaffolding that allows us to develop our skills and express our potential at its highest level. This is why surgeons practice for untold hours how to expertly suture a wound. It is what differentiates the exceptional, allowing them to efficiently execute the difficult or delicate over and over. It is why good teaching, coaching, and parenting, ideally from an early age, are so important for the proper learning and execution of any number of skills.

Myelination only works if we break processes down into manageable chunks that we can, with disciplined repetition, work to perfect. Leonardo da Vinci used to spend hours working on the smallest of brushstrokes to perfect a single swirl of hair on a painting. To this day, his left-handed hair swirls, often done with a single strand of brush hair, are so unique, so perfect, that they are used to authenticate his work.

Unfortunately, bad habits can become as ingrained with practice as good ones—just look at my firearms training. But we can retrain our brain to help ourselves improve in any way that is important to us—for example, to improve our response to stress and difficult situations, to learn better work practices, to cope with fear, or to deal more effectively with others.

One of my Chinese clients in the city of Tianjin had to unite many people from all over China to staff one of his newest hotels. The hospitality industry is now one of the biggest employers in the Chinese economy. Just as in America, assembling staff from different parts of the country brings together a host of regional and cultural differences, right down to how people dress, speak, and gesture.

Many of these differences had to be addressed quickly in order for the hotel to open on time. I decided the easiest way was to harness myelination by picking something small and have them experience it, validate it, and succeed with it, so then they could try it with other things they needed to master.

First, I asked everyone to point to the clock and then to point to me. Then I suggested we try something slightly different. I asked them to open their hand, fingers together or slightly angled, and use the full hand to point—to me, to each other, and to objects nearby rather than using their index finger as most people are prone to do.

What they didn't realize was that as I pointed at them and they pointed at each other in this openhanded way, they smiled.

I explained I had found in my research over the years that when we point to people and objects with our open palm, people seem to appreciate the gesture more than when we merely point with our index finger.

This small bit of information is critical in the hospitality business, which is fundamentally about ensuring that guests have pleasant, positive experiences at all times—and staff is constantly offering assistance and direction to guests. As we'll explore in the chapters to come, understanding the small-but-crucial details that create positive influence is no less important to business executives at all levels.

For the next few minutes, we practiced pretending to point to the elevators, the bathrooms, a chair where a guest could sit, to where the pool was located, to where the gentleman had gone, and to the brochures on the counter. Over and over we rehearsed this simple gesture, and I encouraged them to keep practicing throughout the day, even on breaks as the opportunity arose. By the end of the day, they were all pointing correctly, with their palm open—including jokingly pointing at me in the hallway.

Such a simple gesture, yet it can make others feel good just by how it's executed. How gratifying it was to return a few months later and see everyone, from the doorman to the staff at the front desk to the concierge to the maids, all pointing in this way—turning a small movement into something special. I was even happier to learn that they had used the repeated focused practice method in everything from how to answer the phone to how to open car doors and greet arriving guests to handing out towels by the pool. Proof positive of how with dedicated practice, myelination will help you go from simply completing tasks, which anyone can do, to performing well—which in turn positively influences others.

I wrote earlier of how Agent Moody helped me manage my tendency to be impatient and irritated by the everyday stressors of the job. She didn't just tell me to "relax." She gave me small tasks to practice: take deep breaths; slow down my eating; go for a walk or a run. It took a while, but with practice I was able to adopt these techniques to steady out my emotions, first in dealing with smaller aggravations like interruptions or things taking longer than I thought they should; then in more stressful situations. Emotions are powerful, but even they can be better managed with deliberative practice.

Is there a bad habit you want to stop or a good habit you want to start? Think about how you can break it down into small chunks. Then work on them one at a time, creating new, more robust neural pathways.

For example, let's say every day after work you kick off your shoes, grab a beer, collapse on your couch, and turn on the TV. Three beers and one Netflix documentary later (maybe with your favorite takeout delivered sometime in the middle) and you're ready for bed. You get up the next day and do it pretty much all over again. This is a sedentary life, which most physicians don't recommend. What if you wanted to change? How would that look using this method?

You can overwrite the old encoding in your brain by parsing your habitual behavior into chunks that you can work on and mold a little bit at a time.

You start by thinking about what you'll do after work ahead of time, and you make a plan to change up your after-work routine. What needs to be different?

Perhaps instead of kicking off your shoes in the living room, you cognitively compel yourself to walk to the bedroom, remove your shoes there, and immediately change into workout clothes, including running shoes. This action needs to be planned and executed, but once you've done it, it sets the stage for everything else to happen. What you're doing is shifting your automatic or subconscious patterns into conscious awareness, where you can bring them under your control.

Next, instead of a beer, you drink water or an energy drink. As you hydrate, you focus on appreciating the effects of water on your system, which is most likely dehydrated. This action, too, needs to be brought to the conscious mind to be executed, and at first this may feel uncomfortable—you are breaking a habit after all—but we want to rewire the brain, and that takes effort.

You reward yourself by tuning in to your favorite news service on your smartphone if you're into news, a podcast or audiobook that appeals, or music you like. Then you head out of the house with the intention of kinetic movement, be it walking or light jogging.

Each day thereafter, while you're rewiring your circuits, you think about accomplishing each step of this routine. Slowly you increase your workout distance so that in time your body and mind begin to crave this new physical activity. Through this process, you are gradually reenforcing (myelinating) a new network that becomes self-rewarding. You're burning calories, strengthening muscles, increasing your heart rate through aerobic exercise, your joints are moving and becoming more elastic, you're less sedentary, and you feel good each time. Eventually (the time frame varies with each person), the process goes from being something you have to think about to something you no longer have to think about—your subconscious has taken over. At that point, you have overwritten that old code of conduct with a new, more effective code. That is the power of myelination.

It took a while for my fellow agents in training and me to unlearn outdated techniques that had been reinforced many times through well-intentioned but inferior prior training. At times, we shot worse than those who were being trained correctly for the first time. We had to relearn and remyelinate every movement through focused practice.

We were given red-painted training weapons we could use to practice in our rooms. They didn't even want us pulling the trigger at first, but simply to practice drawing our weapon from the holster.

And so we learned: smoothly unbutton suit jacket, clear jacket out of the way with a single movement of our shooting elbow and arm while blading (turning slightly) the body to make a smaller target, while crouching down slightly and gripping the hilt of the weapon perfectly and symmetrically so that the thenar eminence (the fatty area of the hand under the thumb) of the palm can act as a stabilizing force against the grip of the weapon. Then clear the holster with just enough upward movement, smoothly bringing the rear sights up to eye level precisely fourteen inches from our face, weapon arm slightly bent to absorb the recoil in a straight line as the supporting hand simultaneously joins and firmly grips the shooting hand from the side for greater stability. All this, before the index finger even begins to enter the trigger guard.

At first, just clearing the holster was problematic because the holster was different from any I had ever used before. We practiced each movement separately by the hour, in extreme slow motion; then assembled the pieces; then increased our speed. Eventually, smooth became fast. We could perform the entire sequence in one second or less. No hesitation, no fumbling. There was no alternate way to draw one's weapon—there was only the Bureau way. We could rely on ourselves to do it correctly in the rain, in the snow, in low light, in a car, on command, when arresting someone, when a target popped up out of nowhere, while on the ground—anytime, anywhere. Practice indeed made perfect. Invaluable training, or I should say, retraining, that never let me down in my twenty-five-year career.

Myelination was working its magic, undoing bad habits for us. For the agents who had never fired a weapon before, it created pristine, robust, unobstructed neural pathways, large-bandwidth conduits within their brains to perform this action of paramount importance just right each and every time.

So zero in on a habit you want to change or something you want to perfect. Break it down into small segments you can practice and refine. You'll be putting myelination to work for you. Our brains, we now know, are sufficiently plastic that we can change or perfect our behaviors at any age. That process happens through targeted practice and the miracle of myelination.

Perseverance

What drives our capacity to practice in the way I've described above? Perseverance. It's not enough to sign up for the class, buy the book, take the webinar, or view the video for whatever you're looking to learn or achieve. You have to attend the class, do the assignments, correct the mistakes, read (and reread) the book.

Exceptional people persevere. They may pause to think, to digest the information they've gathered. But they do not lose their way. They may fail many times, but they keep going. Thomas Edison failed thousands—not hundreds, thousands—of times in building the first lightbulb with no guarantee of success—he was, after all, trying to create something that did not exist. But he never gave up. And neither did the Wright brothers—yes, those two bicycle mechanics who, without even a college degree much less an aeronautical engineering background, invented and perfected powered flight. The world is lit and transported because of three men who embodied conscientiousness, self-apprenticeship, but more importantly perseverance.

In the past thirty years, James Dyson, possessing these same traits, restless to improve the world, ever inquisitive, was frustrated by the vacuum cleaners of the 1970s because they progressively lost their suction with repeated use, requiring the annoying purchase of new bags.

And so like those who came before him, he set out to invent what did not exist. He tinkered, tested, refined, and tweaked no less than 5,127 prototypes, which eventually became the first Dyson vacuum cleaner. Dyson devices, from hand dryers to hair dryers to vacuum cleaners, are now found around the world—but that journey was never certain, and it was never easy. Why we have these devices today, and why Sir James Dyson is a billionaire, is because of the one thing that assured he would in the end somehow triumph—he, like Edison and the Wright brothers, had perseverance.

So many of the things we enjoy as a society were discovered, created, improved, or innovated upon by individuals who faced the same challenges as many others, but who persevered.

After conducting thousands of interviews, if there is one attribute that I find that sets the exceptional apart from others, it is their perseverance.

The Rewards of Self-Mastery

Winston Churchill is renowned for leading England during its darkest hour when the British people faced the greatest peril the world had ever encountered to date—Nazi Germany's advance on western Europe. Why he was chosen to lead the government when he had been vilified for decades as a saber rattler and warmonger has to do with something he chose to do at the age of twenty-one. That decision would, years later, leave him the only person in England who could do what was needed to save a nation.

Churchill had had a rigorous education at Harrow and later at the Royal Military Academy at Sandhurst, but on his first overseas posting in India as a subaltern he felt that was not enough. From an early age, he somehow understood he would have an outsized role in national politics. So, while stationed abroad with plenty of time to study and read, and with the help of his mother, who sent him everything she could get her hands on, he began his self-apprenticeship.

He studied ethics, something he had not ventured into previously, and the Greek philosophers (Socrates and Plato were favorites), but also economics. He read voraciously: Edward Gibbon's eight-volume *The History of the Decline and Fall of the Roman Empire*, and Thomas Babington Macaulay's twelve-volume opus magnum on the history of England. By his own account, he would read three to four books at a time to avoid "tedium." He read Adam Smith's

The Wealth of Nations, Charles Darwin's *On the Origin of Species*, *Bartlett's Familiar Quotations*, Samuel Laing's *Modern Science and Modern Thought*, Henry Hallam's *Constitutional History of England*, and so many more. Not the average reading habits of an average person.

He memorized poetry that he would recite decades later on command. It is here that Churchill developed a love for words and a profound grasp of their power. As he noted in his writings, "Of course the Annual Register is valuable only for its facts. A good knowledge of these would arm me with a sharp sword. Macaulay, Gibbon, Plato etc. must train the muscles to wield that sword to the greatest effect." All that knowledge, combined with his love of words, honed Churchill's mind to be exceptional. That exceptional mind would save England.

When war came, the country turned to the only person in all of England who had the credentials, the preparation, the gravitas, the resolve, the strength, and the wisdom—in essence everything that was immediately required of a wartime leader to meet the challenges that a world war demanded.

As Edward R. Murrow, the famous American war correspondent who was in England when Churchill became prime minister noted, "Now the hour had come for him to mobilize the English language, and send it into battle, a spearhead of hope for Britain and the world . . . it sustained. It lifted the hearts of an island of people when they stood alone." It was Churchill's certitude, based on his experience and training, expressed in his remarkable words, that profoundly influenced and gave the English hope. His singular, persuasive voice also convinced President Roosevelt to do something, even if it was just to provision an increasingly desperate country through the "Lend-Lease" program.

Churchill rose to the occasion because of the extensive apprenticeship he had initiated when he was just twenty-one years old and stationed in India. Forty-plus years of service to his country, study, research, writing, and intellectual curiosity built the unequaled scaffolds of knowledge, emotional fortitude, and self-discipline Churchill brought to the table during England's darkest hour. That is what stood as the source of his strength—and that is what made all the difference. Thanks to his hard-earned apprenticeship, he could see a way through the ordeal when many of his colleagues were clamoring to sue for peace with Hitler and Mussolini.

Churchill apprenticed himself to learning for one purpose—to excel in service to his country. When that opportunity would arise, he could not have predicted. But then, isn't that why exceptional individuals prepare themselves? Not for the certainty of a time and a place where their skills will be needed, but because it is the right thing to do.

Self-mastery is both the work and the reward of a life well and wisely lived. I'm on that path. You're on that path also—that is why you are here. As we shape our full potential, we can learn from each other just as I have learned from many. While only you can shape your own future and create that unique scaffolding that reflects your goals and interests, as a fellow traveler and striver on the path to self-mastery, I offer these questions for you to consider within each area we've covered:

Apprenticeship

> Is there something in your life that you would like to know more about or would love to study further?

> Would that require formal training, further reading, online lessons, or mentoring?

> Have you thought about treating yourself to take a lesson, to ask an expert, to try?

> If you haven't done so, make that a goal. Do the research to find help, and then set a date for starting.

> What habits could you cultivate that would help you to educate yourself and expose you more fully to what life has

to offer? Perhaps reading half an hour a day. Researching a topic of interest. Go to a museum rather than the movies; watch a documentary rather than an action film; take a guided educational vacation. Strike up conversations with a new neighbor. Seek incremental changes that would build those habits that educate you, that help you to experience life more fully.

Emotional Balance

> What do you do when you are upset? Is that pattern productive, unproductive, or something in between?

> Have you ever overreacted to a situation and later felt badly about it? If this happens often enough, come up with strategies you think you can use that will work to help you react in a more balanced way.

> If you find yourself frequently frustrated and angry, down and depressed, or gripped by stress and anxiety, have you considered counseling? There's nothing wrong with checking in with a professional to coach us through difficult times.

Conscientiousness

> When it comes to kindness, reliability, honesty, and trustworthiness, do you think you could improve in any one of these?

> What would you need to do to be both better at these and better perceived?

> Starting today, tell yourself, "I will do these things: _____ to be more _____."

And just in case you think you are perfect, ask others where they think you should improve.

Untethered

> Identify some limits or restrictions others have placed on you about your capabilities or potential.
> Resolve to go out and do just a little bit more.

Demonology

> What are your demons? Put another way: What are your weaknesses? Make a list.
> If they bother you or hold you back, what will you do to tackle them? What strategies could you use?
> Revisit your list every now and then. Have things changed?
> How do you want to be known? Answer here and now:_____
_____
_____
_____. Live your life then like you mean it.

Self-Discipline

> In what areas do you lack discipline? (Here again, if you have trouble coming up with ideas, ask someone who knows you well how you could do better in the discipline department.)
> How would you incrementally change that?

> What would be a sustainable goal?

> Would waking fifteen minutes earlier make a difference?
> How about reading two extra pages from a book per day?
> Working out with an exercise buddy? Eating smaller portions?
> Keeping a log of progress toward specific goals? Tidying up
> your bed, your room, your kitchen one drawer at a time? Start
> small.

Order and Priorities

> Of all the things you have to do each day, what should be a
> higher priority?

> Start your own Daily Action List and put your name boldly at
> the top. This is your commitment to yourself.

> On your Daily Action List for today, write what you will
> resolve to accomplish today.

> Follow through with your Daily Action List for a week, a
> month, a year, and see if this alone doesn't change how much
> you get done each day.

Practice (Myelination)

> Identify something you want to perform better. Is it giving
> a presentation? Parallel parking? Your jump shot, lifting
> technique, or swimming stroke? Set up a practice routine by
> slowing down the process, parsing it into small steps, and
> practicing each step, not jumping to the next one, until that
> step is done perfectly. In time, speed it up.

> If you dread public speaking, practice walking up to the stage
> confidently. Make eye contact, stop and get your bearings, let

the audience get used to you, and begin with a simple, "Good morning." Then stop and do it all over again, until your pacing and your bearing grow in confidence. I heard the great Dame Helen Mirren once say that walking onto the stage or into a scene is an actor's most difficult challenge. Work at it.

Perseverance

> Have you stopped doing something you wanted to do, such as writing in a journal, working out, staying in touch with friends, keeping up with current events, volunteering, improving your work or family relationships, saving more money? Whatever it is, dedicate yourself to do it, even if it's just fifteen minutes a day, or taking a tiny step forward in the process.

> Perseverance is not about big moves and then losing momentum. It's about steadily sticking it out for the long term. As someone once said, the largest seagoing vessel in the world can make a complete circle if you but move the rudder just one degree.

> It's okay to take a break, but don't allow yourself to be distracted. Get back to it.

Albert Einstein, who knew a thing or two, said, "Try not to become a man of success but a man of value." Self-mastery doesn't come from somehow managing to get things right and succeeding in the moment. That's luck, not self-mastery. Self-mastery comes from days, weeks, months, even years of work, thought, study, and habit. It comes from persisting even when we don't get it right. It comes from making our metaphorical bed in every way that matters. Placing our feet in the blocks every morning. Holding our breath and diving deep even when we aren't sure we can.

Developing the habits of self-mastery is one of the most profound and rewarding ways you can value yourself. You are never too old to learn self-mastery. As you gain mastery over yourself, you gain mastery over so many other aspects of your life—from your mind to your body to your most noble intentions.

Taking steps toward self-mastery amid the ups and downs of life isn't always easy, but that makes the striving and victory all the more precious. In fact, the beauty of self-mastery is that it is not handed to you. It is earned day by day, and once earned, it cannot be taken away. It's a quest that can profoundly change you for the better. And when you embark on that quest, something even more remarkable happens.

Self-mastery garners the trust, cooperation, and admiration of others—it is the most powerful tool a businessperson can count on repeatedly with the greatest return on investment. No one says, "I want to be like the most average person I can find." We seek out those who are exceptional so that we can emulate them. We seek out those who have mastery over themselves because they inspire us to better our own lives. Now, *that* is power. That is what we mean by being exceptional. It all begins with self-mastery.

CHAPTER 2

Observation

SEEING WHAT MATTERS

—————

By increasing our ability to observe the needs, preferences, intentions, and desires of others, as well as their fears and concerns, we are better prepared to be able to decode people and situations with speed and accuracy, gaining the clarity to do what is best, what is right, and what is effective.

"You see but you do not observe."
—Sherlock Holmes, "A Scandal in Bohemia"

The Cessna 150 had just reached twenty-five hundred feet, which I was monitoring on the altimeter while enjoying the view outside the cockpit windows, when my flight instructor, Bob Lloyd, hit me over the head with his clipboard.

"Where are we in relation to the airport?" he barked.

I started to look for the airport. The clipboard descended on my head again.

"What's our heading?"

My gaze jerked to the instrument panel, desperately seeking the heading indicator. Again, the clipboard.

"Your engine just quit," Bob announced, pulling the carburetor heat on the Cessna 150, intentionally throttling to idle—in essence making us a heavy and not-very-efficient glider. "Where can you do an emergency landing right now? *Right now!*"

Bob repeatedly pushed left and right on the rudders, yanking the plane side to side, while turning up the volume on the Opa-locka airport tower frequency, filling the tiny, yawing cockpit with staccato callouts to landing aircraft.

As I tried to get my bearings in this noisy, vertigo-inducing environment, Bob handed me the microphone and said, "Declare an emergency. What are you going to tell ATC [air traffic control]?"

The microphone might as well have been a brick because by then I was useless. I was sweating, my head was spinning, my stomach was queasy, my chest muscles felt tight, my heart was pounding against the shoulder harness. I couldn't form the simple words of the international emergency call sign that millions know: "Mayday, Mayday, Mayday!" I couldn't even call out the aircraft number—and it was glued to the panel in front of me.

As a good flight instructor should, Bob Lloyd had created *complexity*: a trainload of anxiety-producing events that tax (and teach) the ability to observe, think, and take action under stress. He was testing my ability to, as pilots say, "aviate, navigate, communicate."

"You want to be a pilot, you better know where you are at all times, where you're headed, what can hurt you up here, and where you can land at any moment," Bob thundered over the noise of the Lycoming engine as he took over the controls and added full throttle. "You need situational awareness at all times!"

Twice more he said it, each time more emphatically as he turned down the radio volume: "Situational awareness! Situational awareness!!! *Know* where you are. *Know* your surroundings."

When I first heard those words from Bob Lloyd, I was not yet a junior in high school. I never forgot them. They were an admonition and a challenge, a mantra and a metaphor: to always be aware, to know what is around us in every situation, but especially in those that matter. I didn't realize it then, but it was while sweating and trying not to throw up in that cockpit that I first learned that merely looking was not having awareness. To have awareness, you must *observe*. And to succeed in life, be it as a parent, in a relationship, in a skilled occupation, or as a leader, you must be able to acutely observe. In this chapter we'll break observation down into its component parts, explore how it contributes to exceptional performance, and provide exercises to help you increase your powers of observation and use this inborn capacity to maximal effect.

Observation: Turning Information into Insight

Looking is something we all do. It's how we get by. We look to see if we can cross the street safely . . . whether we should take an umbrella . . . which supermarket line is moving the fastest . . . what our neighbor is doing. All day long we look.

Looking is a passive experience that's useful, but may or may not provide complete information. Observing, on the other hand, is active. It requires effort—but the results are more enlightening and useful.

When you are observing, you're decoding the world around you on a multisensory level in real time. When you observe, all your senses are in play—visually of course, but you're also listening for sounds and words; you're smelling the air; your skin is talking to you about wind and temperature; the millions of neurons in your gut are sending signals to your brain about your moment-to-moment wholebody awareness of your environment—in an exquisite yet fluid mix of impressions that deeply inform. These impressions interlock at a conscious and subconscious level like pieces of a 3-D puzzle, giving you a nuanced grasp of situations. As you pass people on the street, you notice their hands: some are hidden from view, some are carrying things, some are held close to the body, some swing with the stride. You see who looks tired, preoccupied with their phone, alert, or tense. You note who's in a hurry to make deliveries and who's passing the time. You see what people are wearing, and this tells you a little about them: the carpenter's overalls, the pinstripes of Wall Street, what team and sport they favor, how much they're influenced by trends, how indifferent they are to social norms.

At a restaurant, you notice the table where the teens are focused on their phones while the parents converse with the waiter. You can tell which server is stressed and who's hustling to keep up with demanding tables.

At the supermarket, you examine the chicken wrapped in plastic and think it looks a little "off," so you smell it and decide that this is not for you.

You don't just see your neighbor get into her car to head to work. You notice *how* she got into her car. Was she walking more slowly? Did her frame look a little bowed today?

These are the differences between looking and observing.

The world is constantly transmitting information. The truly astute—the exceptional—are attuned to it.

You may be thinking, *How can I do this when I'm already on information overload?*

There is a way. It just requires a little more effort initially to build observational habits and develop that skill set—which you can start to do using the information and exercises in this chapter. In time, I promise, it gets easier.

The world is full of people with no situational awareness. Watch people getting off airplanes or escalators. They just stop—perhaps to wait for someone or to check their devices for messages or directions—forcing others to scramble around them to make their connections or avoid a pileup on the moving stairs.

YouTube has thousands of videos of distracted people running into glass doors, parking meters, bears—or other equally astonishing mishaps. We laugh at them and at ourselves, if it happens to us. But lack of awareness has serious consequences. So many traffic accidents are caused by people texting while driving that the police are seizing smartphones as evidence of inattentive driving.

What's behind this mindlessness? A fast-paced society? Overwhelming amounts of information? Our neurological need for novelty, once largely fed by changes in our environment, now fed by constant digital stimulus? Perhaps these and more.

It seems counterintuitive, but observation, not just looking, is a powerful antidote to information overload because it forces you to cut out the blinking, distracting, overwhelming white noise of life so that you can focus on the information that can best inform. By focusing on the critical rather than on the loudest or brightest, you can conduct your analysis much faster and more accurately. This is the essence of Daniel Kahneman's extraordinary book *Thinking, Fast and Slow*. By observing, we hone the skill of knowing what to look for that will inform us best and most efficiently. Consequently, once you learn how to properly observe, there's less overload because a quick scan provides the information you need—if you know what to look for.

Observation is also a safeguard against being blindsided when situations suddenly become complex—as happened to me in the Cessna cockpit. It allows you to remain calm under pressure. It ensures that you can detect and attend to what is most important.

Finally, observation helps you to take more appropriate and productive action by permitting you to better attend to the needs of others while attending to things important to you.

Whether you're a parent, a teacher, a manager, or a busy executive, if you're ill-prepared for observation when circumstances compel you to do so, then you're like that young pilot in training: at a disadvantage when things go south—when complexity sets in. The consequences can range from inconvenience or embarrassment to neglecting our duties or putting ourselves, others, or organizations in jeopardy. We cannot properly lead ourselves or others; we cannot understand change; we cannot discern the needs, wants, desires, aspirations, intentions, preferences, concerns, or fears of others if we do not observe. Ellen DeGeneres came under attack in 2020 for failing to notice what her TV show guests, such as Brad Garrett, claimed to notice, which was that there was a toxic work environment on her show. DeGeneres was forced to publicly apologize, and it is a reminder to business executives of what can happen when we don't make an effort to observe.

The good news is that we're born observers. We just lose touch with this skill as we grow up and the demands of life clamor for our attention. The science is overwhelming that we can change our brain by being more observant. Our brain is not only up to the challenge, it's built for it through neuroplasticity.

Neuroplasticity is the now well-recognized phenomenon that the brain has the capacity to make new neural connections and change the interweaving of pathways and circuits, giving us the ability not just to learn new things, but to learn more quickly. The more we use our brains and the more we expose them to novel experiences, the more efficient they become as we reinforce or rewire synaptic connections and create new ones. In essence, the more we observe and decode the world around us, the easier it becomes.

Indeed, as the famed Spanish neurologist Santiago Ramón y Caja, one of the first to explore neuroplasticity, said, "Any man could, if he were so inclined, be the sculptor of his own brain."

We can proactively activate and enhance those connections, building the infrastructure to observe faster and more comprehensively, so essential and key to the success and influence of exceptional individuals. And that's not all. Being able to observe enriches our lives and brings greater value to the workplace and to our relationships. Look at any profession and you'll find that the better observers are usually more successful because their powers of observation allow them to see things others miss—that is what differentiates them.

Reclaiming a Natural Ability

From the moment we emerge from the womb and meet the gaze of a fellow human being, we are observing. The most prominent feature on a baby's face is the eyes. When those large orbs fix on the parent's face, they're collecting information, feeding that fist-sized area of the brain called the *visual cortex*. Each moment the baby is awake, movements are tracked; neural connections are made. Gradually the baby learns to detect the smallest facial nuance. Within months, babies can differentiate between individuals, imitate behaviors such as arching the eyebrows, and even sense the mood of others around them as famed researcher Ellen Galinsky describes in her book *Mind in the Making: The Seven Essential Life Skills Every Child Needs.*

From these beginnings, the foundation for acquiring a lifetime's worth of visual information is laid and will grow, so long as we are active and curious. New synaptic connections are made and reinforced, while over time "neural pruning" will take place. In other words, if we don't use our brains, if we're not exposed to a variety of different things, for the sake of economy, the brain's neural connections begin to disappear through lack of use. The more we work the brain, the greater the number of neural connections; the less we work the brain, the more connections virtually disappear.

While information arrives in abundance through the eyes, they aren't the only source of input. With little control over our bodies at first, our main waking occupation as infants is to exercise our senses, which explains why babies put everything in their arguably secondary sensory organ: their mouth, where even toes enchant. As we come to know our parent's face, we begin to associate that face with emotions, with a voice and its tone, and with smell. Even in the womb, by the third trimester, a fetus becomes accustomed to the "prosody" of the mother's voice—its rhythm, melody, cadence, and accent. Babies learn this so well that when they are born, their crying mimics the lilt of the mother's native voice. In other words, a German baby will cry with a different lilt than a French baby, because while still in the womb, the baby is already making those synaptic connections it will need to more readily fit in and survive.

The drive to survive and thrive is where the other sensory sources of information come into play. The olfactory bulb, which is very ancient in our brains, detects the unique odors of the mother's skin.

The nape of the neck, the areolas of the breast, and the nipple each produce distinct smells that the baby associates with comfort and feeding, while the baby's mouth, full of nerves, registers the warmth of the mother's skin and the taste of her milk. The tiny fingers and hands—grasping, pushing, pulling—collect tactile input that in time becomes a touch on a parent's cheek or a probing finger into a birthday cake.

This process of acute observation, synaptic connection, and neural invigoration through repetition continues as we grow. The toddler may follow a butterfly around the yard or chase an ever-elusive squirrel. A discarded box may provide endless pleasure in observing its perfect corners, precise edges, and how it is held together.

By the time you're in school, you've observed those around you countless times and have figured out who is friendly and whom to avoid. It is through observation that we begin to understand who our all-important nurturing community is—first within our family, and then as we venture out in the world and acquire friends.

We observe keenly when we learn and practice anything new, engage in a hobby, or play a sport. And when we gaze on the face of a lover or a baby, we subconsciously transition from looking to observing. We note the lovely nuances of the facial features: the *simpatico* eyes with their interest-widened pupils, the folds, coloration, even the pores of the skin—because what we're really doing in observing is taking in information about this treasured being that will help us understand when our beloved is sick, troubled, upset, or simply needs our attention. Thus, observing prepares us for that weightier responsibility of the exceptional, which is to have empathy and to care.

Our hunter-gatherer ancestors acutely observed their environment. They knew where they were at any moment; where there was water; where not to walk or cross; where medicinal plants were located; and where game could be found along with edible wild berries, nuts, grains, and honey. They knew where danger lurked, always on the alert for species-specific hiding places, fresh scat on a trail, irregular movements, paw prints, or the warning calls of nearby animals. At night they could navigate by the stars or by the vegetation that brushed their skin. Their nostrils were ever alert to the musky smells, scent markings, or urine of animals, which provided information the eyes could not see but which could lead or warn them as they traversed terrain that to us would be inhospitable.

Deep in the Amazon rain forest there are still people who live this way, relatively untouched by the modern world, marvelously attuned to their habitat. For them, observation is a matter of survival. Yet, if you were to ask them, they'd tell you making these observations is not difficult, once you know what to look for. They have in a way, as Santiago Ramón y Caja said, sculpted their brains to attend to their very specific needs.

Look at the cave paintings found all over Europe, some dating beyond forty-four thousand years (BCE) (the Lascaux and Chauvet caves in France and the Altamira and the Cantabria caves in Spain). The animals are drawn with superb attention to detail. These early artists were able to do so because they lived among these animals, studied their movements, their musculature, and their patterns of life. With reverence they saw, heard, touched, tasted, smelled, and literally lived in the skins of these animals. That intimacy enabled them to depict the animals' vitality and beauty with assurance and grace. Their skill came not from an art school, but rather from that school of life that allows us to draw upon what is deeply embedded in the mind through acute, sustained observation.

Observation allowed humans to understand time. The Mayans' careful observations of the movement of the stars and the planets allowed them to develop a calendar more accurate than the one you and I use today.

Observation is almost unfailingly behind advances in science and in medicine. In many parts of the world (China, India, and Africa), going back to the 1400s, cowherds and farmers noted that milkmaids who had contracted cowpox did not later catch the much more deadly smallpox, which at times killed more than 35 percent of those infected.

Through curiosity, observation, and validation, they figured out that they could inoculate themselves against the deadly smallpox by scratching their skin with the less-lethal cowpox. We think of vaccines as a modern medical practice, yet astute societies were doing it long before Christopher Columbus arrived in the New World.

Observation still ignites our greatest opportunities for advancement, creativity, innovation, insight, and influence. Observing, questioning, seeking, testing, and decoding the world around us—that is how we have always not just survived, but thrived.

With practice, we can reclaim this native power.

The Limbic System and Awareness

Where do observation and situational awareness originate? In the eyes, you might say. Or in the five senses. I propose a different answer.

I've spoken and written elsewhere of the great work of Paul Ekman, Joseph LeDoux, David Givens, and Gavin de Becker (all noted in the Bibliography and References section) in pointing out that our emotions and responses to the world are often governed by our exquisitely responsive limbic system—which reacts rather than thinks—and that this lightning-fast system is the key to our survival.

The structures composing the limbic system, including the thalamus, the hypothalamus, the hippocampus, and the amygdala, are part of our mammalian brain. They take in information through our senses but especially through smell and sight. They react to our environment: elevating our heartbeat when we are under duress, triggering sweat glands so we remain cool, or keeping us still when danger lurks nearby. This happens without any thinking on our part. It is reactive—which makes the limbic system efficient and often very authentic in what it reveals about us.

The limbic system is why we inch toward the cliff edge rather than bounding over to look down. Our limbic brain simply forbids it. It's why we freeze at a sudden loud noise, lest our movement trigger the chase/trip/bite instinct of predators, particularly large felines from millennia ago. Limbic reactions are so hardwired in our paleo-circuits that children who are born blind display limbic responses even though they've never seen these behaviors performed. Our needs, feelings, emotions, thoughts, and intentions are processed by the limbic brain and expressed in our body language. These reactions are immediate, dependable, time-tested, and universal.

The limbic system also helps us to communicate to each other in silence. The survival efficacy of this cannot be overstated. Early hominins and even *Homo sapiens*, our species, survived by avoiding movement and noise when predators were nearby. When one in the group saw a lioness, his freeze reaction and look of fear were enough to warn everyone else without his having to vocalize and blow their cover. This system became so resilient and useful to our species that even though we developed the ability to speak long ago, our primary means of communication remains nonverbal. Indeed, we still pick our mates, demonstrate our emotions, show our love, and many other things based primarily on nonverbals.

Our limbic responses, especially those related to comfort and discomfort, like and dislike, confidence or lack of confidence, and more, are usually reflected nonverbally—immediately, and very accurately. When we're trying to be quiet and someone makes a noise, we furrow our forehead and squint our eyes to communicate our disapproval. It's an instantaneous display that accurately reflects and communicates our sentiments.

When I entered the FBI, I'd been studying nonverbals for about a decade. For an investigator, being able to see humans displaying nonverbally in real time that they were contented or displeased, at ease or agitated, confident or otherwise, was like having a gallery window into the mind of the individual under investigation. I could see which questions they liked, and which caused them stress. A simple question such as "Where were you last night?," which for most people is easy to answer and shouldn't cause too much stress, would at times unleash a torrent of facial distortions (jaw shifting, downward lip-pulling) in those who perhaps had something to hide or who for some reason were distressed by the question. Observing these reactions gave me as an investigator even more reason to seek additional details or at least an explanation for why I was seeing these signs of psychological discomfort. Their nonverbals spoke to me even before hearing their verbal answers: the tongue hard pressed against the cheek, the tight compression of the lips, the hard swallow followed by the lowered chin—all suggested that the question I just asked was somehow problematic. For an investigator this was gold. It was similar to noticing the suddenly discolored spot on the ceiling after a rainstorm—following that clue may eventually lead you to the drip in the attic and then to the cracked tile on the roof.

But these insights also apply to people in general, in every walk of life. And because these comfort and discomfort displays are universal, crossing cultures, they offer the observant ample insight into others. In business this is invaluable. A very successful wedding dress retailer in London told me that she attributed her business success to her ability to read her customers. The exuberance of the bride-to-be for a certain dress sometimes didn't match what the parents and adult siblings revealed through their nonverbals. Finding that magical dress that would make everyone happy was often a journey in the study of body language as it contrasted with the words that were spoken. Being able to discern what they really felt about each dress helped her to navigate a field where personal aesthetics, trending fashions, family traditions, and budgetary constraints often collided.

The universal language of nonverbals to reveal what is in the mind is invaluable in innumerable ways. A baby who dislikes a certain food will purse or pucker her lips in Britain and in Borneo. When we get bad news, our lips compress in a version of that rejecting pucker. When the flight leaves without us, we rub our neck or forehead similar to a parent's soothing strokes to calm an infant. When we're asked to work over yet another weekend, the orbits of our eyes narrow and the corner of our mouth pinches, demonstrating our dislike.

Conversely, babies everywhere express delight with dilated pupils at seeing their mothers. When we see someone we really like, our eyebrows arch (defying gravity), our facial muscles relax, and our arms become more pliable, even extended, demonstrating affinity. In the presence of someone we love, we'll mirror their behavior (isopraxis) and tilt our heads, exposing the vulnerable neck. Blood flows to our lips, making them full and warm, as our pupils dilate to take in even more of this pleasing person and situation.

In all these comfort and discomfort displays, we're transmitting how we feel or what we're thinking—with a precision that our limbic brain has perfected over millions of years. Our gestures are silent, but they are powerful.

So, while we may have put our observational powers and situational awareness on mute somewhere along the way of life, make no mistake: the world is speaking loud and clear to our limbic system if we choose to listen.

That's why, when your staffer says, "Sure, I can work this weekend," but while saying it they pinch their eyes shut with their fingers and bow their head slightly, you can be certain there are unspoken issues there. What are they? Could be anything from *This is an unexpected surprise that screws up my weekend plans* to *I'm tired of being asked to work when others get to enjoy their weekend.* You may not know for sure, but you do know that your remark caused discomfort—especially the very accurate discomfort display of eyeblocking.

What you do with the nonverbal tells you observe is up to you. We'll discuss this more in the coming chapters. But what's immediately important is to notice a person's authentic limbic discomfort response, especially when it is absent in their words. Later in this chapter, I'll share twelve nonverbal behaviors that are extremely accurate at revealing strong psychological discomfort. They can give you a tremendous advantage in understanding others and may improve your ability to identify issues or problem areas.

Situational Awareness: Observation Meets Experience

As I leave my house to walk my dog, I smell the air. Dry and brisk. In Florida, this means a cold front is moving in.

I cross the street, glancing about for oncoming traffic and to see who else is around, spotting runners in the distance. Passing the first house on my left, I see lights on inside. Looks like someone got up earlier than usual.

I pass an old Volvo parked not in front of a house but between two houses. Hmm—odd. Everyone on our street parks in their driveway. Leaves and debris are accumulating around the tires. The windshield's dirty. There's quite a bit of rubbish in the front and back seats. The car appears to be abandoned. I wonder why it's here?

Farther along, I notice someone sitting in a car with the engine idling. In the reflected light of her phone, I see it's a woman. She looks at the front door of the nearby house, then back to her phone. She eyes me, looks away. School-age children live in that house. Perhaps she's waiting to give them a ride. A cat stops walking and sinks low to the ground as I near; fortunately, my dog doesn't see her.

This is a daily walk taken with situational awareness. Situational awareness might be described as having three components:

1. Awareness of our environment: sights, sensations, smells, sounds, et cetera

2. Awareness of how individuals are behaving in those environments

3. Awareness of our knowledge base (life experiences, professional training, schooling, self-apprenticeships)

The first two come to us via observation. The third relies on our natural neuroplasticity that draws on our past to comprehend our present and anticipate the future—all in the time it takes to spot a dusty car in the road. These operate in dynamic fusion in real time. But to do so, we must give ourselves the opportunity to make those connections and not ignore them.

In my morning walk, I'm allowing the environment to talk to me. Everything that at that moment matters, I notice and decode. The weather, my safety (where to cross; the presence and activities of other pedestrians), where to walk my dog with the least amount of traffic, what's happening on the street, what my neighbors are doing habitually or differently. It is all important to me. My police training and living in the area for many years allow me to notice details and irregularities others might not see, like the Volvo parked on the street and the buildup of leaves around the tires, possibly indicating that this vehicle has been abandoned. My situational awareness comes from my real-time observations coupled with my knowledge base. I am culling the noise and focusing on specifics.

Exceptional individuals take in life's information in a purposeful, intentional way. It's not a burden. Not extra work. This information is there to be observed and deciphered. Then they take one further step: they compare what they observe to what they know. From that further process, they can make more informed assessments and better decisions.

What if circumstances don't allow you to observe? Then you do the next best thing. Here's what a well-established clothing brand executive in New York whispered to me while taking me to the loading dock: "To be successful, I need to know where I want to take this business, but I also need to know what my employees know. These folks"—he pointed to them on the loading dock—"they know things I need to know, from delivery issues to unreliable truckers to when cops are ticketing double-parked trucks. They are my eyes and ears, and I count on them to fill me in where I can't be." One way or another, the exceptional find a way to observe, and that in turn can lead to success.

Toward an Exceptional Life

Perhaps you've never considered that observation could give meaning to such a small slice of life as a morning walk. Or perhaps you thought that only trained observers could observe on this level.

It's true we've outsourced observation to many besides ourselves. We want the dentist to observe the gumline that seems to be receding before it becomes a problem. We want the police officer to notice the vehicle parked behind that business at 2:00 A.M. that normally isn't there. We want the teacher to notice that Felicity moves her book to arm's length to read, suggesting she's having eye problems. Or we outsource our observation to automation: I ask Alexa or Siri to tell me the weather instead of looking outside. To lighten our workload, we've done ourselves a disservice—we are less observant and more reluctant to do so.

This is what differentiates the average individual from the exceptional one. The exceptional deem it critically important to have that greater awareness of themselves, others, and their surroundings. They stand out because they're willing to look, investigate, dig deeper, test, and validate, and in doing so more precisely learn about themselves, others, and the world.

In business, the art of observation is an absolute requirement and offers a competitive edge that goes beyond numbers and current stock price.

At one time, Nokia dominated the mobile phone industry. Dominated! Until they didn't. As Stephen Elop, Nokia's CEO, said in 2013 at a press conference announcing the sale of Nokia's mobile phone branch to Microsoft: "We didn't do anything wrong, but somehow, we lost." Six years earlier, half the cell phones in the world were made by Nokia. But within just six years, the value of Nokia dropped 90 percent.

How could something like that happen?

Someone should have been tapping them on the head with a clipboard, saying, "Look around." It's not that Nokia executives didn't know Apple phones existed. It's that they failed to observe what was happening around the world. We were transitioning from one human interface to another—from pushing a button or manually scrolling to one that was faster and more elegant: merely touching a screen.

Nokia made other well-documented mistakes, to be sure (e.g., reluctance to abandon established suppliers; fixation on the hardware rather than the software). But failure to read the potential implications of the real-life phenomenon going on outside corporate headquarters—that people preferred touching the screen and not pressing buttons—was a major misstep.

Exceptional people actively seek the truth. Anyone who accepts responsibility for leading others—as a manager or corporate executive in a company, or as a leader in a community, nation, school, sports team, medical team, or in a household—has that greater responsibility. And then to test, to validate, that truth. We do that through observation.

If that statement sounds challenging, just think about the price that's paid when leaders don't face reality, don't seek the truth, or avoid it. Often it can be ruinous for a company. Often, too, it's paid by us who place our trust in those leaders—the stakeholders and shareholders, employees, students, athletes, patients, friends, or family.

We want those who work with us and expect those who lead us— whose decisions affect our safety and well-being—to be exemplary practitioners of situational awareness. Think about it: Would you get on a commercial jet if the pilot had the situational awareness skills of my teenage self in that Cessna? Of course not. You trust that the pilot is trained in situational awareness over countless hours of drilling in simulation and actual flight, including emergency training. For our peace of mind, we want and expect that pilot to be highly qualified. This is why the story of Captain Chesley B. "Sully" Sullenberger landing his crippled US Airways Flight 1549, an Airbus A320, on the Hudson River and saving all 155 lives aboard is so compelling; why we repeat it, marvel at it, feel reassured and inspired by it. It's a striking example of virtuosic situational awareness—and we find people with this capacity supremely comforting, thanks to their preparation, skills, and ability to observe.

How do exceptional individuals accomplish this? They take the information they absorb and do something transformative with it. They have what I call enlightened awareness.

Enlightened Awareness: The Path to Exceptional Understanding

We sit in her modest home in Caruaru, a town in the state of Pernambuco, Brazil. She is self-effacing, gracious, her elderly skin papery soft, the veins visible on the back of her delicate hands. She's famous for her exquisite embroidery—*reticella*, what the French call *point coupé*—an exacting process for making lace or embroidery that requires individual threads to be pulled out of fine linen. It is meticulous work requiring precision and patience. Her embroidered baptismal gowns are sought by people from all over Brazil. When you look at her work, you realize this person has been touched by angels. For Dona Severina has been blind since childhood.

Her fingers are so sensitive that with a needle in hand she can count threads, separate them from the other threads in the woven cloth, and pull them out completely or just enough to make a design. You'd be forgiven if you asked for a magnifying glass, as I found it difficult to see how she pulls those delicate threads and makes minute, almost surgical, knots. She creates these masterpieces using touch alone.

"My fingers are my eyes," she said, with a smile, no doubt familiar with my stunned reaction.

When Dona Severina learned that my wife and I came all the way from the United States to see her, she welcomed us into her home. We discovered that she's exceptional in far more than her needlework. She brought sixteen children into the world, of which twelve survived, and cared for them without help for most of her adult life. We could sense her love for the two grown daughters who still live with her and help out. When one daughter rises from her chair, just from the sound of her walk and where she was sitting, Dona Severina calls her by name to check on the café. She tells us to sit back and relax. Somehow, she senses that we're leaning forward on her well-worn sofa.

When the coffee arrives, she hears the small spoon I use to stir in brown cane sugar vibrate against the demitasse and quietly says to her youngest daughter, "*Minha filha traz um guardanapo para ele,*" and with that a hand-embroidered napkin arrives so I can place the spoon more securely on the saucer. Dona Severina senses the world around her with such exquisite ease that I am humbled by her abilities.

I've met and worked with many trained observers. But this unassuming woman, living a life of caring and purpose against so many odds, triumphing by masterfully honing her personal gifts, was one of the most observant and situationally astute people I've ever met. It was during that brief encounter in 1984 that I understood there is yet one higher level than mere awareness. Dona Severina possesses enlightened awareness. When observation and situational awareness are coupled with curiosity and caring, the result is enlightened awareness—the realm of the truly exceptional.

Enlightened awareness is the ability to observe and decode the world around us in context, with minimal bias, through the use of all our available senses, so that through our experiences, learning, and accrued knowledge, we can draw powerful inferences that give us immediate insight, meaning, clues, or even courses of action to take, for the benefit of ourselves and others.

This isn't some sort of new age alchemy. It is tried and proven methodology. It is Sully Sullenberger keenly observing his options, distilling decades of aviation experience into minutes of life-or-death decision-making while struggling to control an A320 jetliner that's falling out of the sky, with 155 lives literally in his hands. It is world-renowned primatologist Jane Goodall, spending thousands of hours benignly observing primates in a malaria-infested jungle, transforming how we view our closest cousins and thus ourselves. It is Thomas Edison, who left school at age six, yet went on to receive over a thousand patents for his inventions in electric lighting, power distribution, phonographs and sound recordings, mining, cement production, motion pictures, and telegraphy, to name a few, through tireless and repeated observation, testing, and validating. It is Marie Curie, who, with her husband, Pierre, discovered radium and polonium and their radioactive properties, and the ability of x-rays to see through the skin, leading to research into using those rays to fight tumors and cancer. It is two brothers in Ohio named Orville and Wilbur, who repaired bicycles for a living but who got to wondering how birds fly, which led, through years of risky and painstaking learning, to inventing the first fully maneuverable powered airplane that would liberate humans from the earth. And it is an elderly artisan in Brazil, discerning what for most would be an inconsequential sound, a spoon vibrating against porcelain, and instantly knowing what is needed.

We are the beneficiaries of those with enlightened awareness. But they'd tell you that they, too, benefited. How could they not? And that's the point. Enlightened awareness isn't a burden, but a gift we give ourselves—and the world benefits also. Which perhaps explains why former First Lady and social activist Eleanor Roosevelt said, "I think, at a child's birth, if a mother could ask a fairy godmother to endow it with the most useful gift, that gift would be curiosity."

Enlightened awareness allows you to take in everything known and experienced, the old and the new, and through your dedicated and sustained interest, void of prejudice or bias, deepen your understanding. Not perfectly at first, but better and more easily with practice.

In a nutshell, it works like this:

> You resist the temptation to quickly assign patterns and explanations. This is not the time to try to be the smartest kid in the class and shoot your hand up with the answer. Instead, you pause and let what's coming forward speak to you.

> Freed of preconceived ideas, you ask neutral questions about what you observe:

- What am I observing?
- What might it mean?
- How does context play into all this?
- Are there antecedents to take into account?
- How could it be important and useful?
- How does this correlate with what I already know?
- Should I seek more information or knowledge?
- Can this be improved?
- Does something need attention?
- Is everyone comfortable?
- Will a response be needed?

To conduct or especially to grow a business requires asking many questions that go far and wide; and for the exceptional, the more questions the better. Constant questioning, constant curiosity, constant validation are at the heart of successful enterprises.

What if Nokia had sought that greater understanding—that enlightened awareness? What if, without bias toward their own product, they had sought what was trending or whether there might be a more favorable way to interact with their phones? What if they had asked: Is there a better way?

No leader or entrepreneur can exercise influence, take advantage of opportunities and trends, or overcome potential obstacles and hazards if they can't go beyond observing and enter the realm of enlightened awareness.

Enlightened awareness can take many forms. Often in my FBI career I had to look past what was said, question what we knew, reexamine old information, and explore new avenues to determine the truth. In one espionage case, a woman who had worked as a typist for the US Army in Europe and who had a Secret Clearance came under suspicion, as many of the missing documents came from her unit. During our first interviews, she told a somewhat believable story. And since the evidence was in Soviet hands, it was impossible for us to corroborate or disprove what she was telling us.

We could believe what we were being told, or we could examine other aspects we hadn't yet focused on.

When it comes to espionage, few people have both the necessary access and are so flawed of character that they're willing and able to betray their country. So we asked a different question: Who in this investigation had the opportunity, personality, past history, and the willingness to break laws?

We began, systematically, to pursue this line of inquiry. Who had access to those classified documents? Who knew which documents would be most valuable? Who had freedom to travel and carry the documents out? Who needed money for drugs and alcohol or a free-wheeling lifestyle? Who had a history of bending rules, not measuring up, or repeatedly committing minor infractions? Who was skilled at lying and had traits of psychopathy—uncaring, lacking remorse, willing to put others at risk?

In the end, only one person fit that description. Only one person was that cold and calculating that she was willing to sell out her country for money. So we persisted, and in time, her story began to fall apart, until finally she admitted to the crime. Indeed, through her own admissions, she painted a picture of a person lacking morals, judgment, and respect for the law. Her initial story had made superficial sense, but enlightened awareness told us that to commit espionage repeatedly, you have to have certain traits. She had them all: reckless lifestyle, drug abuse, habitually bending rules, lying, cheating, and more. Taking what we knew from experience and expanding on it enabled us to ask the right questions and pursue a course that eventually uncovered the truth.

Enlightened awareness can happen anytime you choose to turn on the beam of your attention. We all go to meetings. They're routine, often dreaded. Frequently the person leading the meeting arrives, does a quick head count to make sure everyone's present, and then jumps into their agenda.

So much information gets missed with this approach.

When I attend a meeting, I make it my business to discern what's going on. This may start outside the room as we gather before going in. What's everyone doing? Are they having private, serious conversations or jovially talking together about something? Does someone look stressed or worried? As we walk in, who enters the room first? Who's in a hurry and wants to get this over with? Who's giving their phone priority over connecting with others?

In the room, there's more information: Who's standing or sitting with whom? Who's busy emailing, or rubbing his brow while pondering a text message? Are there telltale signs that there might be issues, discord, or anxiety—such as compressed lips, arms or hands restrained, people avoiding eye contact (and with whom?), people sitting side by side but with their shoulders turned away from each other? Is someone eagerly looking to be recognized so that they can speak first? Are there unresolved issues from the previous meeting?

Even virtual meetings can yield much information if we look at people's gestures and expressions—from the restless to the distracted to those displaying the lip compressions or front-of-neck massages (rubbing or pulling the skin of the neck or under the chin) that speak of tension or concerns, or jaw shifting signaling growing displeasure. I would argue that virtual meetings require us to be even better observers because consciously and subconsciously our brains are working overtime to understand each little window of information visible on-screen. Not only are we trying to decipher each other, but our brains are also seeking to decipher why Phil's so close to the camera, why that painting is hanging crooked in the background, why Len's wearing the same T-shirt three days in a row, and why Zoe has a poster of Barry Manilow on her door. Our subconscious is being compelled to do extra work, assessing multiple venues or images (living room, office, kitchen, et cetera) in addition to monitoring the words and gestures of all the participants. No wonder people tell me they're exhausted after a virtual meeting.

In any meeting I'm running, if I observe that there seem to be issues, I now have choices for action and opportunities for learning and insight, where before I had none. I can choose to solicit feedback during the meeting to see if some who are showing discomfort displays will put any concerns on the table. If there's unwillingness to do that, I can either invite them to air their concerns right then, or let things ride and then meet individually with people to try and learn what's going on. Deciding which way to play this is where enlightened observation comes in, as this call has to be made in the moment based on that greater contextual awareness that comes with practice of our observational skills, coupled with our knowledge of the situation and the individuals involved. We don't want to make more reserved people uncomfortable who might feel put on the spot if asked to air their concerns in front of others. Interpersonal politics can also come into it, where others ridicule or ostracize the person who airs differences or disagrees. Yet we want to provide the opportunity for others to be heard or validated—and sometimes it's important for the group to see and experience this process. There's no single answer, as the dynamics of every situation are as unique as the new day that dawns. But the more you use your observational skills to pick up on these dynamics, the more your acumen and success in real-time assessment will increase and be on tap for you when you need it, allowing you to bring all your knowledge, skill, and awareness of context to bear to achieve a goal.

In addition to discomfort displays (for a list of common ones, see Observing for Nonverbals, page 103) and reluctance to talk, observing what someone talks about first provides insight into their priorities or sentiments. Also telling is the person who habitually makes excuses for subpar performance. As one clinician in tony Coral Gables told me, "I knew there were problems with the office manager when I started hearing excuses for not having the financial information I requested immediately available." Eventually this oral surgeon realized that the office manager was embezzling money, and the reason she didn't have the information was because she needed time to figure out a plausible lie. Something as innocuous as a delay in answering a question on multiple occasions was the first clue to this physician that something was amiss.

Enlightened awareness allows me to perceive what's going on— not with perfect certainty, but with greater insight than if I plowed ahead with my goals and agendas. It's this kind of inattention that contributes to disharmony and reinforces the belief, sometimes correctly held, that management doesn't care or doesn't *get it*.

Often, if a problem ends up at HR, it's because management wasn't paying attention. A regional representative for a large photocopier servicing center told me how a previous manager had failed to notice that sending two particular service representatives on road trips together invariably caused problems because there was so much personal friction. Once the new manager took a closer look and realized this was not a match made in heaven, all that was needed was a simple fix: pair each one up with someone else. Tension in the office went way down, as did customer complaints. These two service reps knew their stuff, but they just didn't get along and never would. The solution, based on the new manager's experience, was not to compel a change in their attitude, but to come up with a viable and sustainable solution. Three years on, the arrangement was still working just fine.

Alvin Toffler said of the future: "The illiterate of the 21st-century will not be those who cannot read and write, but those who cannot learn, unlearn, and relearn." The better we observe, the faster we learn. The more complex the environment, the more critical learning is. What is life today if not complexity? On any given day, so much goes on at school, in our growing strained cities, in our digitally interconnected global space. Whether it's seeing what customers want, navigating a crisis, or realizing that changes are necessary to meet the needs, wants, and desires of society, we must constantly observe and decode what's happening around us so that we can stay competitive, ready to pivot on a moment's notice.

When I was growing up, the local news and perhaps what was happening in the financial markets in New York mattered the most if not exclusively. Those days have long passed. With my consulting work, and because of the time difference, what is going on in Sydney, Beijing, Athens, Rome, Berlin, Amsterdam, London, and Quebec often takes precedence over local events. There are new demands being placed on us to understand what is beyond us—requiring the expansive-yet-focused and unbiased view that is the cornerstone of enlightened awareness.

This sounds lofty, perhaps even intimidating, I know. But enlightened awareness begins with embracing something every one of us possesses and exercises from the time we're born—something, as you'll see, that is also an essential trait for becoming exceptional.

Curiosity: The Gateway to Enlightened Awareness

How do those big eggs come out of a chicken? That's the question that puzzled five-year-old Jane Goodall. As she tells it, she went into the coop and waited for hours to see it happen (without telling her mother, who began to think she'd better call the police to report a missing child). That quest for information spurred other questions, and then more. Her curiosity was and remains boundless.

Endless curiosity took Goodall from her backyard to the London Zoo to the British Museum and eventually to Africa in her early twenties, where renowned anthropologist Louis Leakey was so impressed by her curiosity and observational skills that he hired her on the spot, even though she didn't have a college degree.

Jane Goodall's curiosity led her to discover that apes make tools, have emotions and petty jealousies, and can be vicious as well as loving, loyal, and caring; and they can mourn their dead for days. She altered our understanding of primates through her curiosity and in the process she changed how we do research and how humans view themselves.

Goodall's example is inspirational because of the example she sets for all of us. Curiosity has a value all its own. Benjamin Franklin had boundless curiosity also. It led him to discover that lightning was electricity. From that observation, he invented the lightning rod to carry electricity to the ground, away from wooden structures that at times would set whole neighborhoods on fire because no one knew how to control the wrath of lightning—until Franklin's curiosity allowed him to unlock one of the mysteries of the universe. Franklin freely bequeathed his invention to the world to make it a safer place. When years later he arrived in France as America's first ambassador, this gift to humanity made him a "rock star" of his time—all because of his curiosity.

Incidentally, while sailing from Boston to France as America's first ambassador, Franklin was curious about why the US rivers froze at those northern latitudes, but the ocean currents were relatively warm. By dipping a thermometer in the water every hour, he discovered that the warm water was coming up from the south. Franklin's curiosity led him to make the first scientific observation of what we call the Gulf Stream—that circular rotation of water that starts in the Caribbean, travels up the east coast of the United States, then circles clockwise toward the British Isles. One man's curiosity helped to explain not just fish migration, but also the violent and deadly storms that so often arise in the North Atlantic.

In my own life I count my curiosity as a blessing. I would not be writing about body language nor would I have been an effective FBI agent but for my curiosity. My childhood curiosity about why when people lined up to enter the movie theater, they all seemed to keep the same distance from one another was prompted by wondering why birds line up equidistantly on a power line, which in turn led me to explore how violations of personal space can cause problems between people. My childhood curiosity about all things nonverbal led to my study of nonverbal communication in college and over the next forty-five years, and eventually to lecturing and writing books on the subject.

Fortunately, my parents encouraged my curiosity and I never strayed far from it, though at times sports, after-school work, and social events took up quite a bit of my time. It happens to all of us. Curiosity is something we all have at a young age. Indeed, it drives much of our very early learning—though many of us gradually lose touch with that drive over time, distracted by ever more demanding responsibilities, or even a formal education, oddly enough, or when others actively discourage us from pursuing our curiosity.

But our deep-rooted curiosity can be reinvigorated. Indeed, research shows that curiosity has the same effect on our brains as the expectation of a money prize, a juicy steak if you're a meat eater, or a favored drug. Dopamine is released by the brain to make us feel good when we anticipate a reward, or curiously enough, when we exercise curiosity. Nature intended for us to receive rewards for being curious.

Curiosity launches a beautiful feedback loop for learning. Curiosity leads us to ask questions. Questions lead to exploration. Exploration leads to discovery, or novelty. Novelty adds to our knowledge base and leads to more curiosity and questions. The cycle continues. Understanding and insight build, again scaffoldlike, in the brain, allowing us to scale ever greater heights of inquiry as the years pass.

Curiosity can be part of our daily activities, even in difficult times. In 1941, in the middle of World War II, when most people were preoccupied with other things, Albert de Mestral, a civil engineer, noticed during a hike that burrs attached to his socks and to his dog's fur with such tenacity they were difficult to remove. What de Mestral observed millions of people had seen throughout the ages and you may have experienced after a walk in the woods. But he was curious.

De Mestral placed a burr under a microscope and saw that it had microscopic hooklike features that would attach to anything looped or hairlike. Applying his engineering knowledge base to this observation, he resolved to reproduce this marvel of nature. Over eight years, through countless experiments in looming techniques to get the right combination of materials, he invented the "loop and hook" fastener we now call Velcro, which quickly and securely fastens everything from toddlers' shoes to the weightless tool kit on an astronaut hurtling through space.

One man, with no prompting from anyone, out for a walk with his dog, with just a little curiosity, invents something we all use. Imagine if we all showed such curiosity. Millions had looked; only he observed. Exercising curiosity led him to the level of enlightened awareness: to look further, explore, decode, and understand. The result: innovation. You cannot innovate if you cannot observe.

Sadly, curiosity is not taught in business school, but it should be. It can unveil hidden and unimagined opportunities. The exceptional explore because they embrace curiosity. Goodall, Franklin, de Mestral, Edison, Pasteur, Curie, Galileo, and so many more achieved greatness not because they were smarter than others, but because of curiosity.

Giving free rein to our curiosity feels wonderful. But you can also put your curiosity to work for you. As an FBI agent, I had to be prepared to interview people from all over the world—that's the nature of counterintelligence work. You never know who will walk in the door. It might be someone from the Philippines who has been approached by a Chinese national to work at a research facility in the US, or a Russian defector seeking sanctuary. So, early in my career, I decided to develop my communication skills by exercising benign curiosity—curiosity without preconceived ideas, bias, or prejudice—to learn about others. I've been doing it ever since.

I sought to understand others. I wanted them to open up to me. People will do that if you accord them benign curiosity. If they feel they are being interrogated, assessed, or judged or are made to feel inferior, they clam up. As an agent, that was the last thing I wanted.

Often using food as a way to foster comfort and rapport, I gained the confidence of others by listening and being genuinely curious about where they came from and what their lives were like. To work on the Native American reservations in Arizona, for example, I had to do a deep dive to learn about their culture and to be able to empathize and communicate effectively. None of my reading and certainly nothing from television or movies educated me as much as breaking bread with the Havasupai Indians and getting to know their culture and ways. Sitting with Palestinian refugees in Jordan opened my eyes to their perspective of what they call *al naqba* (the catastrophe)—the mass exodus of Arab Palestinians when the state of Israel was created. Listening to the lamentations of an Armenian athlete who lost his family during the Armenian Genocide between 1915 and 1917 at the hands of the Ottoman Turks drove home the horror of what humans can do to other humans. Through my listening they grew to accept me, and the information they offered in return filled reams.

In many of the cases, I could not fix their historical grievances or issues: there was little I could do about the high alcoholism rate on Native American reservations, or about a pending conviction for homicide, but I could comprehend their perspectives, even if imperfectly, because I had taken the time to listen, to benignly inquire how they see things. Then and now, it is not my job to convince anyone of anything. It *is* my job as a thinking, feeling human being to practice benign curiosity so that I can better understand. In my work, even from the most suspicious or ardently antagonistic individuals, I was always able to elicit something of value by exercising benign curiosity. I have spent hours talking about an arrestee's life before even broaching the crime they were accused of committing. Benign curiosity, a friendly approach that seeks only to understand, more often than not helped people feel comfortable to open up.

Daily interactions—even a cab ride—can be a learning lab, thanks to benign curiosity. I often start by pleasantly asking, "How is your day so far?" Depending on how they answer, I might ask, "How long have you been on duty?" If they're willing to talk, I'm always interested to learn how they got into the business. If it seems right, sometimes I ask about their family or where their family is from, as I share my background as a refugee to the US. Interestingly, no one has ever refused to answer my questions.

They talk about the foods they miss from their hometown or native country, the things they value, such as their children's education, or their grandparents. It is always enlightening, and I always feel better for it. Perhaps it's the dopamine dump of learning something new.

You may ask: Why is this important? I will never see this person again. Maybe not. But if you're asking this question, you're missing the point. When you take an interest in others, they in turn take an interest in you. They will extend courtesies and privileges you may not otherwise receive. I've been shown treasured family photographs; been offered candy from Lebanon (really good) and prayers for my sore back to get better; been driven to wonderful out-of-the-way local restaurants I would never have discovered; been invited to dinners, café gatherings, recitals, and more, all because of my interest in others. Without fail, whenever we've been able to talk at length, I made a friend. And one more thing: I am honing a powerful skill—benign curiosity coupled with conversation—a dual process we'll explore in Chapters 3 and 5—which has always served me well when I needed it the most.

Dale Carnegie in 1936 published *How to Win Friends and Influence People*. Nine decades on, some think his ideas may be outdated. But there's wisdom in what Carnegie said. If you want to be interesting, become interested in others. As my friend and fellow author Robin Dreeke emphasizes in his book *It's Not All About Me*, make it about them and not you, and you will soon win them over.

Through benign curiosity, you learn what no college class teaches you: how to engage, how to fit in, interact, deal with controversy, overcome fears or suspicions, inspire trust, establish rapport quickly, and how to take a back seat and just listen and learn. General Norman Schwarzkopf Jr. once told a group of us FBI agents he had learned this from his father who had been stationed in Iran in the 1940s. "The more you talk to people from different groups and tribes, the easier it becomes to communicate," he emphasized, especially with people you'll meet in the future. This is a lesson for all businesspeople in our interconnected world. What we do now, by just taking the time to talk to others, can prepare us for whatever we may encounter in the future.

To be exceptional, let curiosity into your life, and let it flourish. Give yourself time to be curious. Not just in one area, but in many areas—any area that interests you, and some you aren't sure will interest you, but you decide to check out just to see what they're about.

All it takes is a few simple steps of inquiry, even while out on a walk, as I did recently. I hold my niece Aja's hand as we step onto the wooden platform over the lake. We're looking for that snapping turtle to come up again for air. We activate the timer on my watch, and we wait. We are practicing patience in observation as well as the scientific method. Finally, after forty-seven seconds, up pops its head. The water hardly ripples. We marvel at how silently it moves. Must be for survival reasons, we speculate, or to help it feed. That leads us later to look up how long a turtle can hold its breath underwater.

This leads to other curiosities: how an alligator sinks gently and silently in water without causing ripples (perfect for predation), or on another walk how a hummingbird the size of my thumb can hover and fly effortlessly backward in its quest for nectar. How is that even possible? Back we go to books and photographs online. Thus, the marvelous feedback loop of curiosity fulfills that aspect of humanity that has always motivated us to look further, travel on, explore, and imagine. We had a learning "adventure" Aja tells her family, excited by her newfound knowledge.

Will this information solve any of the world's problems? No. And that's not why we do these things. We have, for a few moments, allowed ourselves to observe, to question, to speculate, to expand our minds—one at age six; the other at age sixty-six. It is the sheer joy of wonder that drives our behavior. But in allowing ourselves to wonder and ponder, we are building that precious neurological scaffolding that will support a lifetime of learning, of observing for the subtlest nuance, for changes and novelty that will serve us well into the future.

Observing for Nonverbals

Years ago, I was conducting behavioral training at the Ritz Carlton hotel, a beautiful facility with grand vistas of Sarasota Bay on the west coast of Florida. The manager and I were in the lobby discussing best practices before the class started when he politely excused himself. A couple had stepped off the elevator, and he could see they wanted something as they looked about, lips compressed, seemingly unsatisfied. Others perhaps saw what we saw, but he responded first.

Just seeing that nonverbal was enough for him to take immediate action. He guided the couple to the bell captain, who then escorted them down the hall.

"That was quick," I said, impressed, when he returned. Then he said something that exceptional leaders abide by: "If I see someone has a need and I wait while they seek me out, I have failed. Our staff is trained to seek anyone out who needs assistance and not wait until they come to us. We go to them."

Think about that standard of care for a moment. Yes, it's the hospitality business, so you might expect attentive service. But recall hotels you've been to that fail that standard. Probably most of them.

Observing nonverbals opens a world of information that can help you be more capable, influential, and effective. When you see someone's foot suddenly turn toward the door while still in conversation, it's useful to know that they're indicating they need or want to leave, even before they say so. When you approach a group talking together and note that their feet don't move at all and they continue to face each other despite your approach, you can surmise fairly accurately that they don't want to be interrupted. Having this level of greater awareness will serve you well.

While there are many books on body language (see the Bibliography and References section), including my own, here are twelve behaviors that I think you'll find immediately useful in any setting, be it at work, among friends, or at home. Of the hundreds of behaviors I discuss in *The Dictionary of Body Language*, these are consequential because they are particularly accurate in letting us know that something's not right, there are concerns, or there's an issue. The exceptional dig deeper when it comes to understanding others, and nothing achieves that quicker than the messages we get from the body that come to us, without exaggeration, at the speed of light. Messages that reveal in real time clues to others' thoughts, doubts, wishes, or apprehension. So here are twelve behaviors that will help you begin to achieve that greater awareness the exceptional seek, at home or in business:

1. **Eyebrow Narrowing/Knitting.** The area between the eyes and just above the nose is called the *glabella*. When the glabella becomes narrow or furrowed, usually there's an issue, concern, or dislike. This universal sign may happen very quickly and can be difficult to detect, but it's an accurate reflection of sentiments. Some people knit their brow when they hear something troubling or are trying to make sense of what they're being told. The sentiment is communicated with the >< emoji.

2. **Eyelid Touching**—Momentary eyelid touching can be a form of eye-blocking coupled with tension relief. Often when people say something they shouldn't have, people nearby will touch or scratch their closed eyelid—this is a good indicator that something improper was uttered. You see this often with politicians when one misspeaks and the other catches it. The longer the fingers touch the eyelids, the greater the stress being felt. Touching of the eyelids actually helps us to self-soothe and release stress.

3. **Covering of Eyes**—Sudden covering of the eyes with a hand or fingers is a blocking/pacifying behavior associated with

a negative event, such as receiving bad news or threatening information. It also indicates negative emotions, worry, or lack of confidence. You may see it in people who've been caught doing something wrong. Interestingly, congenitally blind children, too, will cover their eyes rather than their ears when they hear something they dislike. Clearly this behavior is well established in our ancient circuits to both block incoming information (visual), but the touching or closing of the eyes also serves to pacify or soothe us.

4. **Nose Wrinkling ("bunny nose").** The signal or cue for disgust usually involves the nose wrinkling upward, while the skin contracts along with the underlying muscle (the nasalis), which is very sensitive to negative emotions. Often this gesture causes the corners of the eyes near the nose to narrow. Starting at roughly three months and sometimes even earlier, babies wrinkle their noses when they smell things they don't like. This disgust cue remains with us all our lives. When we smell or even just see something we don't like, our nasalis muscle contracts involuntarily, revealing our true sentiments.

5. **Lip Compression.** Throughout the day, as we encounter negative events or uncomfortable thoughts or concerns, our lips will press together tightly, accurately transmitting, even if only for an instant, our concerns. This is a quick cue that something's wrong. Lip compression can be very subtle, or dramatic to the point of the lips being compressed so tightly that they disappear.

6. **Pursed Lips.** We purse our lips (compressed tightly toward the front of the mouth) when we disagree with something or when we are thinking of an alternative. When audiences disagree with what's being said or know it's wrong, you often see this behavior. The more dramatic the movement of the pursed lips outward or to the side, the stronger the emotion, which is usually negative or alternative (see Pursed Lip Pull, below).

7. **Pursed Lip Pull.** In this nonverbal the pursed lips are dramatically pulled to the side of the face, significantly

altering how the person looks. Usually this happens quickly and may be held for a few seconds. This is a very emphatic gesture that says, *I have real issues here; I don't like what I was asked, what I just heard, or where this is going.* This nonverbal is highly accurate in telegraphing that there are serious issues. The more dramatic the gesture or the longer it's held, the greater the discomfort or stress.

8. **Jaw Shifting.** Jaw displacement or repetitive jaw shifting from side to side is an effective pacifier. In some people, however, it can simply be a compulsive behavior, so note when and how often it occurs and look for other confirming discomfort displays. Most people do this infrequently, so when you do see it, it's accurate in communicating that something is bothering this person. They have doubts, are unconvinced, or are incredulous.

9. **Covering of Suprasternal Notch.** Touching or covering of the "neck dimple" or suprasternal notch (the indented area of the neck below the Adam's apple and just above the upper chest) indicates concern, issues, worries, insecurities, or fear. Men tend to grab their neck or throat robustly or cover this area with their full hand as they adjust their tie or their collar. Women touch this area more frequently than men and tend to do so more lightly, with their fingertips. Either way, covering the weakest point of the body signifies that something's at issue. Covering our neck when we feel threatened most likely evolved as a result of the countless encounters our species had witnessing acts of predation by large felines that usually go for the neck.

10. **Straight Interlaced Fingers ("teepee hands").** When stress, anxiety, or fear are high, people will self-pacify by interlacing their fingers and rubbing them slowly against each other. The friction relieves tension by stimulating nerves. This is one of the best indicators that a person is severely stressed. We actually "reserve" this behavior for when things are bad; the rest of the time we wring our hands or rub them together.

11. **Ventilating Behaviors.** When someone asks us to do something or asks a question and we have to ventilate to answer—by lifting our clothing, pulling on our collar, adjusting our socks, et cetera—we're communicating that something's bothering us. Our skin temperature can change in less than a fourth of a second. We ventilate to cool off without consciously thinking about it, which often reveals that something's amiss or disconcerting.

12. **Ankle Quiver.** Some people repetitively twist or quiver their ankle (side to side) in a show of restlessness, animosity, irritation, or anxiety. It's usually seen when the person is standing, which can make the whole body shake—it's quite noticeable to others, while most people doing it are oblivious.

As you begin to practice observing for nonverbals, keep these points in mind:

> **Nonverbals reveal much, but they don't reveal everything.** We may never know what causes a behavior, but we can observe it happening and we can note what preceded it. This gives us an opportunity to further observe, to ask, and if necessary, as the Ritz Carlton manager did, to intervene.

> **When in doubt, believe the body.** I have learned in my forty-plus years of experience that if there's a conflict between what is said verbally and what's transmitted nonverbally, believe the body. It's almost always the more candid communicator. Why? Because before we had spoken language, we had body language. This has been our primary means of communication for millennia. So, when we cringe at being asked to work late and then override that by saying, "Happy to do it," that negative reaction is far more accurate than those subsequent words of compliance.

> **Boil it down to the comfort/discomfort equation.** It can seem confusing when you first start observing nonverbals. You

may see multiple nonverbals and not be sure what to make of them. Try to clear your mind of assumptions and just note what you're seeing. Then ask yourself: *Am I seeing comfort or discomfort?* Concentrate only on that at first. Simply assessing for comfort and discomfort can take you far, because in essence we are very binary in how we communicate.

Once you get a feel for that, work on mastering and validating one or two behaviors—for instance, neck touching and lip pulling—so that when you see them you don't have to think about them. You immediately know something isn't right or the person is thinking of something else.

Bottom line: Whether in business, at home, or in relationships, one observational skill you can put to use immediately and see equally immediate real-time results is to simply always assess for comfort and discomfort. That's the key to reading body language.

As you improve at assessing for comfort and discomfort, you can go further, trying to gauge what others might be thinking, feeling, or intending, or what a given situation might mean. Here are just a few of the insights we may have on any given day, simply from observing nonverbals:

Danger—Is that person following me again?

Legitimacy—Yes, I see he's in his UPS uniform and the UPS truck is outside.

Insecurities—Harold looks worried; he's wringing his hands.

Hierarchy—Look who's sitting next to the boss today.

Concerns—Those pursed lips are telling me we're not going to make the deadline.

Fears—Sure are lot of students biting their nails before the exam.

Accessibility—Good luck trying to get a meeting with her; her office door is always closed.

Respect—She rolls her eyes whenever anyone disagrees with her.

Desires—Look at how those two look at each other; they are so into each other.

Preening—He keeps fiddling with his watch and tugging at his shirt sleeve . . . he sure cares about how he looks.

Grooming—He is so concerned about his hair being just right.

Pensiveness—I wouldn't go in there right now; he's stroking his chin; that means he's probably working on next week's schedule.

Worry—She is constantly touching her neck; she must really need to ace this test.

Imagine growing your knowledge base far beyond this short list through your ability to observe. You can! People say knowledge is power. What is knowledge, if not the accumulation of observations, pooled to form a deep reservoir of understanding?

That is precisely what exceptional people know how to develop and then draw upon in real time. They do it through enlightened awareness born of observation.

Exercises to Strengthen Your Powers of Observation

Ever drive to an unfamiliar location or are driving around endlessly looking for parking, and you find yourself feeling stressed, perhaps even exhausted? You might not have realized that your exhaustion is from having to observe, not just look, and be situationally aware for a sustained period when most of us aren't accustomed to doing it for more than a few minutes.

Even with training, it can be taxing to walk into new situations and try to take everything in. I remember my first week in the Manhattan office of the FBI. I was twenty-five and newly arrived from

Yuma, Arizona, where a heavy traffic day was four cars waiting at a red light. This densely packed city of seven million was overwhelming my ability to observe.

Fortunately, an older agent took me around and helped me transition from looking and experiencing sensory overload to observing.

One day, we walked up to East Fifty-First Street, where he showed me how to spot pickpockets. They worked in groups, dressed dissimilarly. They'd suddenly stop on the sidewalk, forcing people to bump into them. In that confused instant, someone from behind would steal whatever was accessible from a handbag or a back pocket. The subway pickpockets worked alone, focused on men in suits reading papers. They would slowly back into them as if distracted. Then, when the subway car doors opened, in the rush of people getting out, they'd use one finger to push the wallet up from the victim's trouser pocket, while the other fingers lifted the wallet out.

Once I knew what to look for, it was hard to miss what previously would easily have slipped under the radar. Eventually, building on those experiences, I learned to observe how spies behaved. That took my observation and situational awareness skills to a whole new level. Nothing like working counterespionage to train you to look for the smallest of details, such as a suspect walking on the inside of the sidewalk against buildings to hide in the open; or the increased need to look at his watch because he must be at precisely the right place and time, otherwise the fleeting transaction is off; or the slightly more erect walk as an overactive limbic brain through the sympathetic system keeps vigilance in flight-or-flight mode.

Learning how to observe is one thing; practicing and maintaining your observation skills is something else. Observation is a perishable skill that needs to be developed and practiced. As one trauma room surgeon revealed to me, "When they bring in a car-crash victim with severe internal trauma, I have only minutes to avert a death. How quickly I do my job is based on my skill at observing the signs and finding my way through the thoracic cavity. When I came back from maternity leave, I felt sluggish my first day back in the ER—in a few months my skills had become rusty." The same thing can happen in business. When we are out of practice, or distracted, we lose our observational skill.

Situational awareness is exhausting if you aren't used to it or force yourself to do it for extended periods without preparation. But if you do it every day, it becomes easy to build observational strength and stamina as you would a muscle.

Some of these exercises may not be familiar to you and may strike you as odd, but they're worth your time and effort. Some might feel easier than others—just as some activities come more easily to you than others. All will become easier with practice. With some patience and dedication, there's no reason why you can't significantly sharpen your skills as an observer.

So, get up, have some fun, and learn a few tricks or hacks for expanding your observational skills.

Exercise: Identifying Your Visual Range

> **Stand outside or in a large room, eyes forward.** Pick an object or a spot in the distance or on a wall in front of you and focus on that. Take some quiet breaths and try to relax your facial muscles and the muscles around your eyes. At all times keep your focus on the object or spot you've selected.

> **Now lift your arms out to each side to form a T shape, arms level with your shoulders.** You may feel your eyes twitching left and right to see what's out to the sides. That's normal at first, but concentrate on looking at the spot you chose in front.

> **Keeping your eyes straight ahead but relaxed, slowly bring your hands forward, gently wiggling your fingers as you do so.**

> **Stop moving your hands and fingers as soon as you can comfortably see them while still looking ahead at that preselected spot.** That is your *peripheral vision*. Everything from where you see your hands to directly in front of you is

your *visual range*. You'll be surprised how far to the side your eyes can see even while focused on something in front.

Your peripheral vision will at first lack detail, but it will detect movement. That alone can be quite effective: peripheral vision can discern, at a four-way stop, which vehicle got there first or who is moving faster.

You'll be able to identify things in the center of your visual range more accurately than things out to the sides. This is natural in the sense of seeing things cognitively—but be aware that your subconscious is also processing information, though you may not be aware of it.

Repeat this exercise once or twice a day for a week so you develop the confidence that you'll be able to spot things out of the corner of your eye. This is how I trained myself to look at someone in front of me while talking to them but also see what everyone else is doing at the very edge of my visual range. This also helps you to scan a room more quickly and to not make it obvious when you are trying to observe something or someone.

Exercise: Scanning

> Once again, relax your facial muscles as you look straight ahead at a distant object, with arms extended in a T shape.

> Now, have someone flash a picture or a card with a word or a few words written on it near the edge of your visual range. You'll be tempted to look directly. Resist, relax, and keep your eyes straight ahead.

> As you continue to focus forward, have the person begin to move the object slowly toward the front of your body in stages. When the image or word is perfectly clear to you, tell them to stop. When and where that happens will depend on whether it's a picture, a word, or series of words.

You'll notice that the more relaxed your eyes and body are, the more the object or words eventually begin to reveal themselves. Objects near the edge of your visual range will never be crystal clear, but this exercise begins to prepare you to observe a greater area without having to look at it directly.

This exercise shows you how narrow our acute visual range is, compared to our overall range of vision. Most of what we observe in life is coming in out of focus—and that's okay. Our brain can still discern much, even if it's fuzzy. We walk, drive, and go about our lives every day with many things a little blurry—our subconscious busily sorts things out. It allows us to glance and look—in essence, to function. But to really observe, one must focus.

How do we do that, especially if we're looking at a large area such as the outdoors, where there's a great deal to focus on? We scan.

Scanning for Information

Scanning is key to faster, more comprehensive observation when there's much to look at—be it a pilot looking to find a small craft in a vast ocean or a speaker addressing a hundred attendees. It allows you to take in more information at a glance than trying to focus on one thing at a time, as we're prone to do.

If you did the previous exercise, you realize that there's much we can take in on the margin of our visual range and that our eyes will pick up on behaviors, in the case of an audience, or on a speck of debris in an ocean, if we scan—and faster than with overly focused looking—which is important for situational awareness.

The key to scanning is to keep the eyes moving. Depending on where you are, that may also require that you move your head to cover a larger area. If you're talking to a group, you may think this means focusing on each face in the audience one at a time, but that is not scanning. Scanning requires you to keep the eyes moving—whether back and forth, left to right, up and down—everyone does it differently.

As you scan, your subconscious brain will register the facial features and general body language of the audience. Your brain has this capacity.

After you've scanned the room—let's say it's a small audience—a few times, you can relax a little more and slow down so the muscles of the eyes are not overworked and you don't look odd. As you scan back and forth more slowly, you're taking in even more information, which your brain can now contrast with what you saw earlier.

Try practicing scanning in different settings, such as when walking down hallways as you see people coming toward you, or when you're waiting for an appointment or meeting and watching others pass by. Especially at first, you may find you have to scan several times to pick up details you missed initially. Rest assured your eyes are picking up a lot of information before you consciously realize it.

You can even practice stationary scanning of another person. Suppose you're talking to a business colleague in close proximity. You can scan without moving your eyes. As you talk, without breaking eye contact, ask yourself questions like: What color shoes are they wearing? Are they moving their feet? What are the hands doing? Are they fidgeting? What kind of watch are they wearing? Is there a pen in the pocket and if so what kind? If the woman is wearing a scarf, what is the design? If you're doing this right and your eyes are relaxed, you shouldn't have to look down at the person's feet to see their shoes or directly at their wrist to see the watch. You are using your mental focus to target (scan) specific areas the eyes see in front and in the periphery, without moving the eyes. Try it out with business colleagues and you'll find over time that you can converse while also gathering ever more visual details as you chat. That sudden pulling of the collar (a ventilating behavior) when a political topic comes up will cue you that there are issues there to be avoided. When someone in a group shifts their jaw in response to a question, you'll have an opportunity to assess whether there's more there to be explored. When in the middle of a conversation your colleague orients her foot toward the exit, you'll know that she's signaling she needs to leave, and you can begin to wrap things up.

As you practice scanning, don't fixate on any one object (unless of course you must). Give yourself the latitude to take it all in. You'll soon be surprised at how much information you can absorb in two or three quick scans of your environment. If you're scanning while walking outside, if something moves or is coming your way, even in your peripheral vision, you'll be able to better spot it as you're forcing your eyes, radarlike, to cover a wider peripheral area.

It's easy and fun to practice scanning in daily life. In a restaurant or anywhere people are gathered, do a quick scan and guess how many people are present.

In the beginning you may be way off—maybe there are only twelve people when you thought there were twenty. But with practice, your brain will learn to do this calculation by seeing, not counting. No, you're not guessing. You're letting your subconscious do the heavy lifting of doing the actual calculation.

Eventually with one quick scan, you'll be able to see precisely how many people there are without having to count each one individually. Try it. As your brain begins to adapt to this new way of looking at the world, your eyes in conjunction with your brain will pick up even greater detail.

Scanning People

I'm asked all the time: How do you do it? How do you know what everyone is doing in a circle of colleagues? It's easy, once you learn to scan and not stare. You can practice scanning for facial features, movements, foot behaviors, and any other nonverbal behaviors of consequence.

One of the benefits of scanning is that it's a way to observe people without being intrusive. If I look at you too often or for too long, it will affect how you feel about me and thus how you behave. If people think you're staring at them, they'll naturally become suspicious and tense. So we avoid intrusive observation by not looking at people directly, but rather by scanning: we glance *by* them by keeping our eyes moving rather than focusing for too long.

Try this technique first with family members or people you are close to. If it's done correctly, they shouldn't notice anything different about you. If they do, then something needs to be corrected because it should be a natural look on your part as you smoothly scan from person to person.

Or you can practice it this way. Have someone find an interesting ten to fifteen seconds of a movie you haven't seen and play it for you at twice the speed. I like short scenes where people are contemplating an issue, where bad news is received, or when someone learns a truth that has long been concealed. Explain what you think you saw and what was going on in the sped-up clip. Now check to see how much you got right. You can make this a game and take turns, each of you practicing your scanning skills using film clips to see who sees the most accurately.

Do this enough times with different scenes and different movies, and you'll find that you stop focusing on faces and start scanning. As you develop this skill, in time you'll be able to read the faces as well as what else is happening in the scene, and to articulate your observations with greater clarity.

Exercise: The Color Order Game

Try this exercise the next time you drive into a parking lot:

> Scan left and scan right and notice the vehicle colors without focusing on each car.
> After you've parked, ask yourself: What were the colors of the first three cars on the left and the first three cars on the right, and in what order did they appear?

At first you may have difficulty with this. But with practice, your accuracy will increase. Eventually you can build up to remembering the colors of the first six or seven cars on each side, having only scanned them once. But keep practicing if you want to keep your edge.

Exercise: Observing Without Seeing

> **Sit outside, making sure your arms are exposed, and close your eyes.**

> **Now, simply listen.** You might feel tense or find it hard to settle at first. That will pass. You're missing visual stimuli—that's because your enormous visual cortex, about the size of your fist, is demanding to be fed. You can override that. Take a deep breath and exhale.

> **Listen to your own breathing.** Spend some time just with this awareness.

> **When you feel more relaxed, keeping your eyes closed, shift your attention from the sound of your breathing to the sounds of the world around you.** See if you can name all the sounds you hear, and where they're coming from. Do some noises seem to emanate from one place? Are some coming toward you or moving away from you? Soon you'll be putting the need to look aside and will be able to identify sounds and pinpoint their location. Exhale again. Keep those eyes closed.

> **Now, bring your attention to the movement of the hairs on your face, neck, head, and arms.** The smallest and thinnest of hairs on your body will be stimulated as the wind blows, the temperature changes, vehicles pass, or people move about you. See if you can sense the difference between each—the long, steady brush of the wind versus the sudden pressure from a passing truck, for instance. In time, you'll sense when someone walks near you or even enters a room, if you allow yourself the pleasure of observing with your eyes closed.

Yes, you can observe with your eyes closed. You have sensors in the form of nerves all over your body. These nerve endings sense moisture, heat, noises, odors, pressure, air movement, vibrations—all sorts of things. This was impressed upon me one memorable day when I found myself in an elevator during an earthquake. My senses were overwhelmed; vibrations competed with sounds, my clothes shook on my body, stimulating nerve endings in a way I'd never experienced before, and the earth's tremors came up through my feet, making my feet tremble even as the elevator descended quickly and the rush of air through small openings around the door further added to the moment. So much information was coming in that I had to freeze in place to figure out what was happening as all my sensors seemed to go off at once in ways that were completely unfamiliar. Perhaps there was a time in your life when you experienced a similar sensory overload.

As with the other exercises, you can take sensory observation practice on the road. If you're waiting for someone in a restaurant, resist the urge to check your phone. Lower your eyelids and just listen. What sounds do you hear? Where are they coming from? What about in the doctor's office? Sitting on a bench in the museum? Or in familiar places where we tend to tune out: Your workplace? Your bedroom, just after you wake up? Your backyard?

And when was the last time you exercised your nose? When you enter a vehicle, what do you smell? An elevator? A hotel room? How about when you enter a food store, a clothing store, a hardware store, a gas station, a pharmacy? What are the scents and odors, strong and subtle? Can you smell when a weather front is moving in? You'd be surprised what you can pick up if you pay attention.

The moment you begin to do these observation exercises and games, you start to strengthen those synapses that help you observe and collect information. As you develop your scanning ability for environments, activity, and nonverbals, you'll begin to be able to assess the multiple inputs you're receiving at any given moment. On the street, for instance: What time is it (without looking at your watch or your phone)? Where is the sun in relation to you? Who else is near you? How many cars are there?

In the office, you'll be able to quickly scan the faces of everyone arriving for a meeting: Who's smiling and cheerful? Who looks troubled, tired, or is avoiding eye contact? It's not for you to make judgments about them but merely to observe the information they're transmitting. The principles of benign curiosity should apply. We are assessing for available information that suggests, but in itself shouldn't be viewed as conclusive (in Chapter 5, I'll share a model for reaching clearer conclusions as we interact with others). Let every person you see speak to you nonverbally as you scan quickly. In time, you'll be able to decode their nonverbals faster and faster.

The more you exercise your observation skills, the more proficient you'll become. But to get (and stay) there, you have to practice. Otherwise, just like shooting baskets or playing the piano, your skills diminish.

So test yourself and keep practicing. Turn it into a game. Open up worlds of understanding in the world you encounter every day: master the wonderful skill of observation.

Observing to Care

I'd like to leave you with this thought: being exceptional isn't just about exercising your powers of observation for maximum effectiveness. It's about *how* you exercise these powers.

How we view the world and observe others matters. We can do it gently and kindly, or with cold indifference. Jane Goodall didn't look on primates with clinical superiority, as many scientists before her had. She looked with care, appreciation, concern, and an enlightened awareness of their unique traits. As a result, she saw with penetrating detail: the exquisite bond between a chimpanzee mother and child; the permissiveness they grant their offspring to play, fall, and express their personalities; the dalliances and naughtiness of the older apes as they establish relationships; their toolmaking abilities, which shocked scientists, that apes pass on to their offspring as if in a classroom; their grieving and mourning for their loved ones; the jealousies and aggression that at times can be frightening, as well as their warmth and need for gentle hugs and kisses, which they grant judiciously to maintain their social order.

No scientist had looked upon primates in this way until Jane Goodall. Perhaps most interesting of all: the apes themselves recognized her benign and empathetic interest and permitted her to get closer than anyone had before. Goodall's caring observation fostered the trust that allowed her to gather even more information because she could observe from such an intimate vantage point.

From the second we are born, that trust process begins: someone is there, not merely watching but observing with care to understand us. Notice parents as they behold their newborn. They are not just admiring; they are acutely focused. Every nuance of that brand-new human is being noticed and remembered: the little hands that grasp and twitch; the lips that distort when there is discomfort; the tiny veins threading through those tissue-thin eyelids; the soft cooing noises. Those observations will be repeated thousands of times in the coming days and months. They will help the parents know when the baby is hungry or cold, what the baby prefers (to be held close after finishing his feeding or gentle swaying before nap time). While the parents are doing this, the baby is examining the parents, building his own neural network of knowledge, reading them, assessing them—and, with consistent caring from his parents, coming to trust them. In time that little baby will communicate and connect with his parents by crying, whimpering, making faces, smiling, giggling, and reaching to be picked up.

We are primed to care for each other. But to do so we must be able to observe others' needs, wants, desires, and preferences. And we must *want* to do so.

We've all dealt with people who are clueless as to others' needs.

They hear you coughing, but they don't offer you water. You're on the phone and say loud enough for everyone to hear, "I need to write this down," and no one offers paper or pen. You're entering the store while pushing a stroller or carrying a lot of packages, and no one helps you with the door. Someone comes into your workspace and starts talking to you, seemingly oblivious to the fact that you're clearly immersed in a complicated task.

Perhaps that's why, when we encounter someone who demonstrably cares—who makes our lives easier, who closely observes what we're all about, who "gets" us—they win us over. The one attribute these caring individuals have in common is their ability to observe and decode what's happening and thus understand what's needed in the moment. It is situational awareness with the intent to care.

How much more rewarding, interesting, and quite simply happier the well-observed life is. It makes sense: being aware of and attending to the needs and the feelings of others is bound to enhance relationships.

How nice it is when a husband, seeing that his wife, working from home, hasn't moved from her desk in three hours and hearing her sigh several times as she struggles to meet a deadline, brings her favorite beverage. Or when someone lets you go ahead of them in line so you can make your purchases before your child, who is fussing, starts crying. Or when your boss, noticing you were quieter than usual in the meeting, stops by to ask how things are going.

When I meet with corporate leaders, the conversation quickly turns to the human factor. It doesn't matter the industry; we're all in the people business. The biggest eater of time, especially for leaders, is the human factor: interacting with others and attending to their needs, issues, or concerns. To be human is to care. In order to care, we must be aware. That means we must be able to observe and understand.

People ask me what I observe for. Everything that matters, I reply.

What matters? Anything relating to peoples' needs, wants, desires, fears, or intentions. Anything in a situation that's different, novel, or unusual. Anything that can cause psychological discomfort or can contribute to making someone more comfortable or at ease.

You don't have to be Benjamin Franklin, Thomas Edison, the Wright brothers, or Marie Curie to be a master observer. You just need to be able to see what matters and draw inferences from what you see.

Observation, while transportable, is a perishable skill that needs to be nurtured and grown—that challenge is within our reach and within our power. And you can begin right here, right now. It's useful in everything you do, from visiting a new city to starting a new relationship to conducting business. When practiced daily, it becomes part of who you are. You become that person we so admire for being interesting and interested. Your influence grows as you become more benignly curious, more observant, more aware.

Do you want to be exceptional? Then do what exceptional individuals do each day. Observe the world with kindness, curiosity, and genuine interest, and it will reward you in kind. It will assist you in your thinking, prepare you for what to say, and suggest actions you can take to help others or to improve your own life as it unfolds before you.

Jane Goodall summarized it best: "Only if we understand, will we care. Only if we care, will we help. . . ." It is that simple. If you truly want to be exceptional, it begins with this powerful and necessary skill set that opens the path to understanding and leads to insight and caring: the ability to observe.

CHAPTER 3

Communication

FROM INFORMATIVE TO TRANSFORMATIVE

———

By embracing both verbal and nonverbal skills, we can express ideas more efficiently and intentionally, appealing to the heart and mind and establishing bonds that build trust, loyalty, and social harmony.

> Communication is the most important skill in life.
> —Stephen R. Covey, *The 7 Habits of Highly Effective People*

Every Friday, young FBI agents in training—and field agents like me, back at the FBI Academy in Quantico, Virginia, for in-service training—got our morning run in before classes started at 8:15 A.M. Sometimes we ran in small informal groups—other times alone.

Either way, no sooner were we pounding along on "Hoover Road" (named after FBI director J. Edgar Hoover), than we'd sense someone coming up behind us. This individual would catch up with us, say, "Good morning," and then proceed to join us for the remainder of the run.

That morning salutation wasn't from another Academy attendee or one of the instructors. It came from Louis Freeh, the director of the FBI—my boss and the man in charge of more than thirty thousand people.

You could have mistaken him for an agent with his youthful looks, short hair, and quick stride. Why was he there, seventy-five miles from Washington, every Friday? True, he'd be attending the graduation of new agents in training later that morning. True, he disliked Washington and its politics and loved getting away. But the real reason, as he told a group of us, was that he wanted to know what was on our minds. He didn't want to hear it from unit chiefs, section chiefs, or assistant directors from Headquarters.

Director Freeh refused to let anyone from HQ run with him. He knew that the best way to get clear, unfiltered information was to be "in the trenches" with the troops.

And we didn't hesitate to tell him: how New York agents were having to quit the Bureau because they could no longer afford to live there; how long it was taking some agents to be appointed to their OP (office of preference)—which every agent yearns for, especially if they have children approaching high school age—and how that was causing divorces to skyrocket; how spouses were no longer willing to put up with the constant moving—not least because many were now earning more than the agents.

He got an earful, too, about Special Agents in Charge with closed-door policies, stupid Headquarters rules like only being allowed to land a Bureau aircraft from the left seat and not the right (it really makes no difference, if you're a qualified pilot), and how the bulky surveillance equipment the Bureau was buying was virtually useless because suspects could easily detect it under our clothes.

These were the everyday complaints of agents, which never would have reached his ears through the higher echelon. We didn't expect every complaint to be resolved. What mattered was that he took the time to listen to us. He was with us, unfiltered. No director had done that before or since. That's what inspired our loyalty.

Communication is the resin that holds society together. It is essential for developing and nurturing relationships. It allows us to engage meaningfully with others, whether planning the day with a loved one, assisting a child who's struggling, or working with a business associate eleven time zones away. We communicate constantly—information, instructions, requirements, ideas, insights, and discoveries; but also our needs, preferences, emotions, or desires: "Two tickets, please." "I'd like to return this for a larger size." "I need this report for the Monday staff meeting." "What if we try it this way?" "I just realized something." "This isn't what I expected." "It's urgent." "You look happy." "I miss you."

Yet often we take communication for granted until it fails or is lacking: when a hurt child calls out and no one answers; when someone gives us the silent treatment; when the directions are impossible to understand; when there are no signs to help us navigate; when governments fail to inform us of the seriousness of an epidemic.

We're a deeply communicative species, so when communication is absent or poorly executed, we can quickly go from being perplexed to disappointed to frustrated and angry. But because communication is second nature to us, we sometimes think we've communicated clearly and are dismayed to discover we haven't. As George Bernard Shaw said: "The single biggest problem in communication is the illusion that it has taken place."

This chapter is about the kind of communication that goes beyond the purely factual and functional. It's about the transformational kind of communication, practiced by exceptional individuals, that elevates the quality of our relationships. That allows us to collaborate and cooperate and brings out the best from all involved. That inspires—even changes—lives. How they do that might be different from situation to situation, adjusted to the circumstances and the emotions of the moment. That's why, instead of complicated strategies or scripts that are hard to remember or adapt to your needs, I've provided guidelines in this chapter for communication and rapport-building that you can apply flexibly, in whatever setting you're in.

In particular, we'll explore three powerful, proven traits that exceptional communicators convey in their interactions with others, in situations ranging from the routine to the uncommon:

1. **Caring:** An abiding empathy based on our common humanity.

2. **Validation:** The ability to express that empathy by acknowledging others' experiences, perceptions, and emotions.

3. **Rectitude:** Living a life that inspires others by example, communicating trustworthiness, reliability, and dedication to what is moral and ethical.

We Are Always Communicating

From the time we are in the womb kicking, letting the world know we're there, we're communicating. Human beings are living transmitters of information. Merely by being, we are communicating— everything from our heart rate to our skin temperature to our expressive eyes showing our desires and even our fears—and that's before we open our mouths or unleash our digital devices. Indeed, we are *never* in a state where we're not transmitting information. Even in our sleep, we reveal things about ourselves (during REM sleep, for example). If you are breathing, you're communicating.

We are the most communicative species on Earth. Yet despite our unequaled ability to express ourselves, any therapist or manager will tell you that communication is the number one problem in interpersonal relationships and in business.

Most of us genuinely want to communicate constructively and accurately but sometimes, despite our best efforts, we screw things up.

Examples abound of the communication flubs we've made, from the mistaken interpretation of a message to inadvertently copying someone on an email who, embarrassingly, shouldn't have seen it.

Then there are the screw-ups that make headlines, such as when the Mars Orbiter spacecraft went off course in 1999 because the Lockheed Martin engineering team in Denver used English units of measurements (inches) while the NASA engineers in Pasadena, California, used the more conventional and scientific metric system (millimeters). That failure to communicate cost NASA, and thus you and me, the taxpayers, $125 million dollars.

Closer to Earth, in March 2019, a British Airways airplane scheduled to fly from London City Airport to Düsseldorf, Germany, accidentally flew to Edinburgh, Scotland, a fairly noticeable five-hundred-plus miles away from its intended destination. According to airline authorities, there had been a "miscommunication" because someone filed the wrong flight plan.

These we can wonder at and sometimes laugh at, until we're the ones affected or afflicted.

Never is mastery of communication more important than in a crisis. Imagine you're the CEO of a multinational company and eleven of your workers are killed in one day. Eleven lives destroyed, their families devastated, because of something that happened at the business you run. You're the person in charge, the one everyone looks to in this tragedy. Now imagine allowing days to pass before you go to comfort the family of those eleven souls. Then when you do get there, because of all the hassles of dealing with this catastrophe, you say, "I'd like my life back." What have you just communicated?

You might say this story strains credibility. But that's exactly what happened in 2010 when BP CEO Tony Hayward took his time in getting to Louisiana and then uttered those words: *I'd like my life back.* Just five words that indelibly framed the response to the horrific *Deepwater Horizon* oil spill—the worst of its kind in US history, which took the lives of eleven platform workers, spewed over two hundred million gallons of oil into the Gulf of Mexico, and damaged sea life so profoundly that recovery might take decades—in terms of the bother it created for him personally. This failure to communicate quickly, effectively, and empathetically eventually cost Hayward his job, tarnished BP's reputation, and will no doubt be studied for decades to come by business schools everywhere.

Fortunately, most of us won't experience such a catastrophic and expensive failure to communicate. Unfortunately, because we're human, these things do and will occur. And whether the consequences are minimal or colossal, failures to communicate are failures, nonetheless.

I have spent decades studying the communication patterns of exceptional people. Their skill lies not in how perfectly they communicate, but in their ability to move and motivate us. They actively strive to communicate verbally and nonverbally with honesty, clarity, and conviction—what we often call speaking from the heart. They're keenly aware that their words and actions have consequences and seek ways to give comfort, assuage concerns, fortify relationships, or inspire. Their messages resonate because of their ability to communicate the one crucial message that matters—that makes all productive communication possible: that they care.

Caring

I think back on my memory, so vivid, of Director Freeh running alongside us. Getting an earful. He never acted as if it was a burden. Why? Because he cared. That's what exceptional leaders do.

We tend to think that caring is something a person either knows how to do or doesn't. But similar to observing, communicating caring is something we can improve, if we understand its components.

What, exactly, was Director Freeh doing to communicate that he cared? What can *we* do?

If you say that he showed he cared by listening, you'd only be scratching the surface. Let's examine the totality of his actions to better understand how the exceptional listen.

Dedicating Time

First and foremost, Director Freeh gave his time. More than money, time is our most precious commodity. A finite amount is allotted to each of us. How we use it shows what we value.

By dedicating time in his unbelievably busy schedule to be with us, Director Freeh was showing us that he valued us—that he cared. What's more: it was that precious commodity I lecture about called "face time." Face time gives us an opportunity to impart and receive information with greater nuance—the more face time we have with each other, the better we communicate, and the greater our chances of success together. No wonder we have come to rely on videoconferencing platforms like WhatsApp and Zoom—they give us that golden opportunity for face time.

We treasure alone time with important people in our lives. By getting up at 4:30 A.M. and driving down from the DC area to hit the track at Quantico when he knew the agents would be out running, that's what Director Freeh gave us.

Crafting Opportunity and Proximity

Director Freeh created an opportunity to communicate his interest in what we had to say. He didn't ask us to email our concerns. He didn't send an online survey. He didn't convene a meeting and invite us to ask "any questions you may have." He observed our habits and behaviors and took pains to place himself where candid communication could happen. We in counterintelligence similarly crafted opportunities to run into hostile intelligence officers (spies) so that we could chance an opportunity to talk with them. By watching their meal habits or interest in sports, we could create opportunities to "accidentally" run into them at a bar or restaurant, or even play tennis with them as a pickup partner. Certainly in business, exceptional individuals craft opportunities to glean unfiltered information from the source, as close to the front of action as possible, while also supporting relationship building.

Director Freeh overcame space and distance to craft these opportunities to be with us. That demonstrated how much he cared. He traveled to meet us on our turf, where we felt comfortable and more likely to speak candidly. We weren't summoned to HQ. No one-on-ones in his office. No ledger to record who came in to talk. He made sure no one got in the way. This was off the books, personal, and proximal: running side by side made us feel we were together, part of a powerful organization. Where other directors had created barriers (formality, forms, chain of command, appointments), he removed them. He was "with us" in every sense of the phrase.

This isn't that different from a wise parent knowing a teenager isn't likely to open up about a sensitive subject if the parent summons the teen to the family room for a "talk" or invades the inner sanctum of his bedroom. There's more likely to be a real give-and-take in the conversation if things happen in neutral territory, or while doing something the child likes—shooting baskets, suggesting a drive to a store to check out a sale, or going out for something they like to eat. Does it take more effort? Yes. But when you care—and when what you're trying to understand is important—isn't it worth it?

Asking Questions

Director Freeh didn't arrive with answers. He came with questions. The kind that make you want to open up, such as: "What office are you in from?" "How are things out there?" "When were you last transferred?" "How is your wife dealing with the stress of moving?" Probably he had learned this skill as an assistant US attorney in the famed Southern District of New York office of the Department of Justice. But more importantly, he was a family man. In his own life, moving around had been difficult and his wife did not hesitate to let him know when his job was interfering with their life. He understood that his agents were more effective when their families were happy. And so he asked those carefully chosen questions about the things that mattered the most to us.

When was the last time your boss stopped by to ask how you are, how your family is doing, or if you have any ideas for improving things? Communicating caring by taking genuine interest in others is not as common as we might think. And no, a suggestion box doesn't cut it, nor do mass emails. How exquisite it is to the ear, and to the mind, to be personally asked for an opinion, a thought, a suggestion, or just a little bit more about oneself. When was the last time that happened to you, or you did that for someone else? I ask because that's what exceptional individuals do.

Did talking to Director Freeh directly help? In some cases, yes. In other cases, there was nothing he could do, as Congress, for instance, could never seem to pass a budget that was adequate or on time. But what was important for us was not that everything got worked out. What was important was that in listening to us, unfiltered, with such care and caring, he was doing something that many fail to do: validate our concerns.

Validation

As I pass the children's play area en route to the pool at the YMCA where I swim, I'm always struck by how many children are doing things for the benefit of their parents or caregivers sitting nearby. Unfortunately, most of the adults can't be bothered to acknowledge that Andrea just did a perfect cartwheel or Noah his first pull-up, because they're preoccupied with some transient, probably insignificant, event on their phone. Or worse, the adult says, "good job," without looking up and in a monotone, just confirming what the child already knows: that the adult doesn't really care. At times like this, children tend to either give up or escalate to more brazen attempts to get attention.

These parents and caregivers are failing to validate. We've all done it at times. But do it often enough, and don't be surprised if later there are lingering issues, even emotional wounding. Do it at work enough times as a manager and don't be surprised if your employees jump ship at the first opportunity. Humans seek to be legitimately recognized, as it contributes to their self-esteem.

I know what it's like to be busy, to multitask, to be hyperfocused—present yet not there. But I also know, from talking to many people, that recognition and validation are important to us. I've heard story after story of someone who worked hard and was rarely if ever recognized, or the child who constantly had to compete for undivided attention; decades on, the pain lingers.

Being physically present is not enough to demonstrate that we care. Showing up is doing the minimum. That's part of the job description—whether of parenthood or employment. It's to be expected. To be exceptional, we must demonstrate we care by being empathetic through the volitional act of validation.

Validation is the act of listening, witnessing, acknowledging, observing, or accepting what someone has performed or communicated by words or actions. It requires interacting in such a way that the recipient is made to feel recognized, understood, consoled, or aware that they are valued, and that at least one person—you, the listener and participant—cares.

Validation can take many forms. Sometimes what we validate is demonstrative, such as a child displaying a bruise or an arm in a cast and we comment on how much that must hurt and inquire as to how it happened. The kind of everyday validation we do when we care. Sometimes it's giving our complete and undivided attention to someone telling us something that is worrying them or something significant that happened. Other times it's about recognizing others for the work they've done, their ideas, or their loyal commitment to the organization. Every culture that I am familiar with has some form of formal validation, even when it is a dance around a campfire extolling the hero of the hunt.

Validation is also about actively communicating as we observe, to demonstrate that we are listening, understanding, and giving value to what others are saying. And this is crucial—it's about trying to understand things from their perspective—what we call empathy. Validation is taking that greater interest in what someone has done, experienced, or has to say. That is how we affirm the worth of others. Study after study has shown that in business, people want to be valued, they want to be respected, that more often than not, what motivates individuals is not money, but recognition and validation.

Validation isn't always easy. Even among caring couples, there's a tendency at times to shunt a full explanation, to be distracted as something is being said, to say (or think), *I already know where this is headed* or even *I don't want to hear it yet again*. In business, too, there are many distractions, priorities, and issues that often get in the way of validation. Unfortunately, failure to validate is not an option when it comes to the exceptional. Often workers don't quit because of the organization, but because the person who is in charge never takes the time to validate the concerns of others.

Maybe what we're hearing is difficult to process, unpleasant, perhaps even painful, but to be exceptional, you must be willing to listen. Because failure to validate invalidates, and to invalidate is to devalue.

As an FBI agent, I've listened to countless victims over the years tell me how devalued they felt because no one, not even a family member, would validate what they were saying. When a boy reported that the clergyman in the car put his hands on the inside of the boy's leg, the parents refused to accept what happened. They failed to validate. Forty-nine years later, that boy, now a grown and accomplished man, still remembers that physical violation, but remembers even more the indelible pain of having parents who didn't believe him and refused to pursue it further. It hurts even more years later because of the failure to validate.

Not only can individuals fail to validate others, but groups, institutions, and governments can, too. When a government cannot admit that it caused suffering or in some cases was responsible for murders or even for genocide, this is not simply a failure to recognize a historical event. It is a failure to value human lives by failing to validate their suffering. It leaves an open festering wound that will not heal, especially when it is compounded by a failure to apologize for misdeeds or injurious incompetence. There is perhaps no faster way to marginalize people than by demonstrating indifference to their plight. Isn't that what the Black Lives Matter movement is all about?

Elie Wiesel wrote: "The opposite of love is not hate, it's indifference." As a Jew who had survived a Nazi concentration camp, he knew full well what it was like to be cast aside as human waste, and how it felt when governments and people, then and even thereafter, failed to acknowledge or validate the suffering endured by six million Jews.

Validation is more than just listening. Anyone can do that and simply walk away. We validate by giving others the full measure of our attention. By giving them the time and the space, even finding the right location, to fully express themselves and what they have experienced. We cannot fully empathize until we take these active steps to communicate validation. As Stephen Covey said, "The deepest desire of the human spirit is to be acknowledged." Validation is acknowledgment, in the present, in the now.

When Larry Nassar, the medical doctor for US Women's Gymnastics, was convicted of sexual abuse, for many of the victims, this was finally the moment they had been waiting for, to have their agony, anguish, and trauma validated in court. To finally be acknowledged. What a triumph that was after decades of suffering. Finally, someone was listening, and there were going to be consequences. The same thing happened after decades of abuse by priests in the Catholic Church. Finally, those young boys, many of them now men, received the validation and acknowledgment they long sought and needed to help end their torment from decades earlier.

Former Hollywood producer Harvey Weinstein was convicted in 2020 of sexually abusing women. His victims finally received recognition for their suffering, and that acknowledgment started the #MeToo movement. If we look closely at the essence of this fast-growing movement, it is about finally validating and acknowledging the fact that men in power were using that power to sexually abuse women and that society was looking the other way. Looking away—by a person, a group, a profession, or a country—is failure to validate. That pent-up anger, that suppressed tension from knowing that something terrible took place and no one was willing to listen, is what we are experiencing now, and deservedly so.

Validation can open up and elevate the conversation around many of our most pressing and sensitive issues. It can be cathartic and therapeutic, healing hearts and minds. It can also, on a transactional level, recognize the hard work, caring, or contributions of others, fostering a positive, collaborative environment. But it requires that those in leadership positions, whether in institutions, businesses, communities, schools, or in the home, take the time and make the effort to do it. Yes, we want our best friend to validate us. But that alone isn't enough. It's often when those in higher authority validate us that we feel redeemed.

Validation and acknowledgment shouldn't just be reserved for traumatic or major events. A job well done and loyal dedication to a task merit our validation. Sometimes it's the everyday stuff people deal with—the kid being teased on the playground, or the person superbusy at work—that needs validation. That's what makes for exceptional individuals: they observe and notice, and they muster the inner resources to lend credence, show respect, and provide recognition of others.

Make Yourself Accessible: The First Step in Validation

Validation takes effort. It requires a willingness to engage, to create an environment where forthright communication can happen. Sometimes the opportunity arises in the moment, or when someone unexpectedly but needful knocks on your door. And sometimes, as Director Freeh did, you have to craft the opportunity.

There's a long-running TV show on CBS called *Undercover Boss* (Studio Lambert) in which, each week, a company owner or CEO goes undercover and works in disguise at an entry-level position in their own organization. Each episode is a testament to three valuable rewards of being present and observing at the ground level: (1) it provides knowledge you wouldn't get any other way, (2) it offers a powerful opportunity for CEOs to appreciate, acknowledge, and validate the concerns and needs of employees, and (3) it lets the employees know that someone in high authority cares deeply about them.

Invariably, every owner or CEO comes away better for their efforts, more connected to their employees, grateful for the experience, and able to see things more clearly. And we, the viewers, celebrate the "big reveal," when the employees discover whom they've been working alongside. We celebrate because we wish in a way that our circumstances would be validated by our bosses or those in authority—but it's all too rare. It's rare because validation and acknowledgment are within the realm of the exceptional.

George Logothetis is chairman and CEO of the Libra Group, a global conglomerate dealing in renewable energy, aviation, shipping, real estate, hotels and hospitality, and other diversified fields. I've known George for two decades and have watched him blossom as a man, a father, a global entrepreneur, and a humanitarian. What struck me early on about him—and how we came to know each other—was his overwhelming desire and ability to communicate effectively, to bring out the best in people and to get them to open up. George travels worldwide to visit the Group's offices and subsidiaries. "I visit all these offices not because I have to," he says, "but because to me it is important that I personally listen to what people within our group have to say. To look people in the eye, hear from them, ensure everyone has a voice."

Think about that for a moment. He could just as easily say on a video call, "Hi everyone, great to see you—email me any concerns or comments." But no. His wife, Nitzia, a remarkable executive, psychotherapist, and humanitarian who created and runs the Seleni Institute, a world-renowned mental health institute in New York, agrees: "George needs to visit these far-flung places because that is his way, and there is no other way."

He'll talk to everyone, from the new hire or the intern to the lobby guard and the seasoned multilingual executive with an MBA. And from those conversations, he can have the confidence of knowing that all is well, or what needs to be addressed. Everyone is given a voice, empowered, heard.

This is what it means to communicate caring. To validate. In return, George receives valuable information that at times, as he recently told me, has made "outsized positive impacts" to the success of the group. This kind of personal, interactive, hands-on style of communication has immediate as well as long-term consequence, and that is why Nitzia herself also is a proponent. "Because," as she emphasized, "the pulse of the organization on any given day is in the person-to-person, face-to-face arena," not in an email.

No organization today can afford to ignore the input of anyone at any level with knowledge to share. The industrial-era days—rigid vertical hierarchy, bosses who didn't have to listen to subordinates who had flooded into cities from farms and felt lucky to find a job—are long gone. Now, the person running the IT (information technology) department knows more about the system that keeps the organization afloat than the CEO does.

Leaders can have a vision for a company, but if they aren't listening, they are, as one German manufacturer told me, "hobbling themselves." Those who implement that vision have frontline information about what's working, what's not working, and where problems, trends, or opportunities are happening. The executives I work with tell me that more often than not, it's one-on-one conversation with their valued people at all levels that keeps them informed of issues and events that affect the company.

A CEO I've worked with for years said it best: "Joe, I can get the answer to any question I have from the internet or a consultant. But I have to talk to my folks in the fulfillment department to find out what slows things down from the time we take an order to when the items ship. No computer knows what these folks know."

You can become irrelevant fast if you don't have a trusting, close relationship with those who matter most: the people with their finger on the pulse. The leader who doesn't go out into the field, as Director Freeh did on those morning runs, will lose touch with the life force of the organization.

At its root, complacency is lack of caring as expressed in the unwillingness to listen to others and consider their opinions, to validate their knowledge and ingenuity.

There's a greater cost, too. When others conclude that we don't care, they eventually do the same. Don't expect people to tell you the truth about what's really going on if you don't have an established pattern of open communication. Trust begins and ends with communication. There is no other way.

Validation can be challenging. But it's essential for establishing trust and healthy relationships at home and at work. There is, however, another tool, a silent tool, that exceptional individuals use to communicate caring and set the stage for transformative results.

Rectitude

Have you ever been with someone who made you feel good, just being in their presence? Someone you wanted to emulate, who you felt was made of better stuff, who inspired you simply by who they were? I have, and they've come from all walks of life. Decent people, kind people, people you can trust, who somehow seem to uplift others with little effort. For them it's not work. It's how they live their life.

If you've met someone like this, did you ever consider that what you're witnessing—what they're communicating—is rectitude? Rectitude is not some old-fashioned concept. Rectitude is doing the right thing. It's moral, upright, ethical, and honorable behavior. We may have called it something else from time to time and through the ages, but it is rectitude that we treasure. It's what we've always sought in those stalwarts we can rely on. Why do we punish and despise corrupt officials, coaches, politicians, or corporate leaders? Because they lack rectitude—we placed our trust in them and they let us down. Those with rectitude never let us down.

Rectitude is about how you comport yourself day in and day out—how you demonstrably show the world that you are accountable; that you live a purposed life; that you will not lower yourself, seek to take shortcuts, cheat, lie, or do things that undermine others deliberately; that those things that are immoral, unethical, or illegal are anathema to you. Rectitude is the expression of self-mastery (see Chapter 1) in daily life. It is what we communicate through our behavior—not just when we're having a good day or when it's convenient, but as a life choice.

Rectitude is not attitude. How many times have I heard this refrain from HR personnel and CEOs: "We hired for skill but fired for attitude"? While a positive attitude is important, rectitude is decisively more than that.

Rectitude is about traits that communicate that this person is reliable and trustworthy, that they will not alter the books, take from the till, sneak out with what doesn't belong to them, cheat others, take a little more for themselves, bend the rules, take shortcuts, or cut corners. Through their demeanor and actions, they communicate that we can count on them, trustingly seek them out, and have faith that they will not let us down. I know people who can't say that about their own family members, and many who can't say that about those they work with. That's why, in business, where too often it's dog-eat-dog, a person with rectitude is one to treasure.

Those who live a life of rectitude know that living an ethical life is not only the right thing to do, but it is also powerfully influential. Be it for reasons of religion, upholding standards their family and mentors passed on to them, or for their own reputation, they have purposed their life to one of rectitude and in so doing they positively influence others. It matters not their motive; it matters only that they consistently live and act this way. That's what makes them so re-markable and influential.

I wouldn't be discussing rectitude if it weren't for the fact that there are so many people who let us down, who don't live a life of rectitude that allows us to say: *I trust you with the keys to the build-ing, to take care of my children, to administer my mother's medicine when I'm not home, to carry out complicated negotiations without supervision.* While many people hold positions of trust, that doesn't mean that they can be trusted. Look at how many sexual abuse or financial scandals have been perpetrated by people in positions of trust who in point of fact couldn't be trusted because they lacked rectitude.

We are what we do each and every day, whether someone sees us or not. Exceptional individuals lead an exemplary life by communi-cating rectitude verbally and nonverbally, day in and day out—not just when the cameras are on, the office door is open, and the bal-ance sheet is looking pretty good—but behind closed doors, when no one is looking, after hours, and most especially under duress. That they do not waver is a hallmark of their rectitude.

Rectitude begins as a state of mind—a philosophy, if you will. But it can only exist when actively communicated through words and deeds. If you communicate rectitude as a daily practice and habit, then when a crisis hits and you need to rally the troops, or you need to trade on your reputation to call in favors, you will be responded to, believed, or heeded, precisely because of your established repu-tation of rectitude. *THAT* is influence. As Albert Schweitzer said, "Example is not the main thing in influencing others. It is the only thing." And it is so powerful.

How do you transmit that you have rectitude? By demonstrating through what you say and do that you are going to uphold the high-est standards, that rules and laws are not plastic, that boundaries exist and should be respected, that all individuals have and deserve your respect and that you stand for something. That your charac-ter, your reputation, is more important to you than any worldly thing someone might offer. That you don't push the moral or legal envelope, nor even the appearance of it—because that is not who you are.

In short: you communicate rectitude by living life as if always under examination, as if you're setting an example—because you are.

My father oozed rectitude. Even when he ran his own small hardware store in Miami, he stood in line just like the other customers to pay for a bag of eight galvanized nails that he needed to mend a fence. He could have just taken them. No one would have noticed, and it was his store, anyway—but he lived honesty as a daily habit. He didn't have to lecture me on integrity; his whole life was an example of it. Countless times throughout my life people came up to me unprompted to say, "Your father is such a good man, an honest man." His rectitude was exemplary to those known and unknown to him. Here was a humble man who didn't swear, who didn't speak ill of others, who would do anything for his family so long as it was proper. What an example he was.

How influential is the power of rectitude? I'm reminded of what Nelson Mandela endured in prison where he was forced into hard labor. In his book *Long Walk to Freedom: The Autobiography of Nelson Mandela*, he tells of the time when the prison came under the command of someone notorious for being harsh. He made life hell for the prisoners, working them to exhaustion or denying them bedding or blankets to stave off the cold. But Mandela had something going for him that couldn't be taken away. He had rectitude. He had the firm belief that what he stood for was right and that those who imprisoned him were on the wrong side of history. Nelson Mandela would not buckle under pressure even when it meant his wife could not come to see him, warm clothing would be taken from him, and food would be rationed to try to make him yield. When food was limited, he made sure the other prisoners ate first. When there weren't enough blankets, he made sure the neediest stayed warm even if it meant he suffered. Every attempt of his guards to compromise him, he thwarted. He simply would not give up what he and the other political prisoners stood for. He was resolute, a stalwart; he was the epitome of rectitude even if you did not agree with his politics.

Mandela's rectitude was more powerful than anything thrown at him or his fellow political prisoners. His example became legendary. Within the prison, the guards knew that here was a special human being—no matter how inhumanely he was treated, he remained humane toward his captors. By the time Mandela was released after serving thirty-two years, those who sought to oppress him, who incarcerated him, who denied him his liberties, had become his ardent supporters. His purity of purpose, his belief in equality for all, was enshrined in his character, a character that would not yield, and through his transformative example of rectitude, he won over even his enemies—the very people who incarcerated him.

Most of us will never confront what Mandela faced, so let's look at some ways to communicate rectitude.

Speaking Out, With and Without Words

Exceptional individuals speak out for what's right, and they don't wait for the perfect place or time to do it. Martin Luther King Jr. spoke out with unforgettable eloquence as he stood before the Lincoln Memorial, but he also did it on the streets of southern towns where white police officers wielded their batons while unmuzzled German shepherds were unleashed to maul black citizens, merely because they sought equality. He spoke out in frightful circumstances, never knowing when he would be arrested, beaten, shot, or firebombed, or if he would be one more black person lynched in the night by racist thugs.

As he said, "There comes a time when one must take a position that is neither safe, nor popular, but he must take it because conscience tells him it is right." And so he did—with dignity and respect even for those who did not respect him.

Dr. King, who had studied Mahatma Gandhi and his struggle for Indian independence through nonviolence, understood that messaging was not only about words, but also about the optics of how we comport ourselves—what we now call our nonverbal presence.

He didn't cower in the shadows, nor act in hatred under cover of darkness like the hooded Klansmen who hated him. He was at the front of the line, setting the example, openly communicating his belief in the equality of mankind through nonviolent demonstrations. He too had a kind and gentle spirit.

Wherever he went, Dr. King was immaculately dressed, as if going to deliver a Sunday sermon—and, in a way, he was. No matter how hot and humid it was, no matter that police water cannons awaited him and his followers, no matter how many dogs strained at the leash to tear at clothing and flesh, knowing he would be spat on by crowds of angry whites, pelted with garbage, he was there; ever dignified, poised, showing no fear, his shirts pressed, shoes clean and polished, his words well-prepared, communicating with unflagging dignity and certainty that racism was a "hate-filled cancer" in America, and, like it or not, America needed to hear it.

He gave no cause to be disrespected because he respected even those seeking to, without exaggeration, destroy him. The stirring images of him walking among those who sought to harm him, leading the march, demonstrating absolute dedication to truth in the face of power, would be transmitted around the world. They are a case study in the galvanizing power of nonverbals and a lesson in the importance of speaking out when a cause demands it.

Exceptional leaders, the truly worthy, don't wait for the perfect moment to speak. They speak out when it is most needed. How they communicate that message is very individual. But in the end, it's a choice they make to be seen, heard, noticed.

This is our duty: To speak up when it matters. To defend against the bullies, tyrants, and social predators of this world who seek to do harm, or the organs of state that would do so. When a businessperson says, "I will not tolerate bullying or sexual harassment of any kind," it sends a powerful message. These leaders are telling their employees they care while simultaneously putting would-be violators on notice. And when someone is being bullied, it is the by-stander who speaks up and says "knock it off" whom we value, not those who stood by and did nothing.

Greta Thunberg, a young girl, diagnosed with Asperger's syndrome (a mild form of autism), hasn't held back from speaking her mind to world leaders about the dangers of climate change. The vitriol of even heads of state has not curbed her. Like all exceptional individuals, she instinctively and wisely knows that the moment to speak out about climate change is now. She knows there will be a point when there's no turning back, and immediate action must be taken. So she speaks now. Not when she graduates from college, or at some future time.

Now's the time to speak out because if we don't, who will speak out for us? If you want to change or improve the world around you, speak up. If you want to be exceptional, speak up now, in the moment, when it is needed the most.

Shunning Lies

Lies have no home in the vocabulary of the exceptional. When an individual, an industry, or a government presents untruths, they must be challenged by those who seek to be exceptional, particularly if they're also raising other barriers to communication: sowing mistrust and attacking those who would tell the truth.

Consider the cigarette industry, which for decades not only lied about the dangers of smoking, but produced bogus research to encourage smoking despite knowing it caused cancer. Or Lance Armstrong, now discredited and stripped of his seven Tour de France wins, who not only cheated and lied by claiming he wasn't taking chemicals to enhance his prowess, but then attacked those who called him out on his lies. That was not shameful. Shameful is forgetting to get your kid a birthday gift. Attacking and threatening those who tell the truth—that is criminal.

Those who communicate lies, who lie repeatedly, who distort the truth to sow discord while attacking their critics deserve our most ardent opprobrium. When industries lie, when governments lie, when presidents lie—whatever their motives, be it protecting profits or shareholders, personal reasons, or political agendas—they create an environment that ultimately destabilizes society. We become cynical and lose confidence in our own institutions. After all, as Albert Einstein said, "Whoever is careless with the truth in small matters cannot be trusted with important matters." Thus, an environment where rectitude is endangered is an environment that endangers humanity.

Our responsibility in the face of lies is to call them out and not repeat them. This is so important to our social fabric that in 2002, *Time Magazine*, for the first time, recognized three women as Person of the Year because they witnessed the consequences when people in power lie—and they did not stay silent.

> › **Coleen Rowley, an attorney for the FBI, called out her superiors at FBI Headquarters** for ignoring early signs of a plan to attack the United States on 9/11 and later stating there were no such signs. She spoke out to let the world know that agents in the field had tried to do their job and that we had connected the dots, even though people at Headquarters were reluctant to act.

> › **Cynthia Cooper single-handedly dug up $3.8 billion in accounting irregularities** (we call those lies) at WorldCom, exposing massive fraud being committed by the senior executives at a publicly held company—brazen corruption at a level that astounds. Her efforts shed light on a fraudulent scheme that would have done even greater damage to shareholders.

> › **Sherron Watkins warned her bosses at Enron that the company was in danger of financial collapse.** And so it was—because the senior executives were committing fraud and then lying about it to their own employees, telling falsehoods about Enron's worth and stability to get them to invest in a company that was basically underwater, insolvent, and beyond redemption. She was right.

In choosing to speak truth to power, these conscientious whistle-blowers demonstrated that they were exceptional individuals. They never forgot that the essence of ethics, indeed its very definition, is to do that which befits others—be it a nation, employees, stakeholders, or the average citizen. That means caring enough to communicate the truth, even if it means incurring the wrath of those more powerful than they. They could have easily kept their mouths closed and said nothing. But that's not the way of the exceptional. When you have rectitude, you rise to the occasion because this is who you are each day—including on that day when it becomes necessary to speak truth to power.

Communicating to Inspire

Most of us won't have our moral character tested on the world stage, endure challenges such as those faced by Nelson Mandela or Dr. King, or be confronted with the decision of whether to become a whistleblower. But we all do have the power to inspire others through communication, even if we often underestimate ourselves.

I'm fortunate to hear from people from all over the world through my lectures, videos, blog posts, books, and interviews. I've received thousands of messages about how something I wrote or said helped to change a life, offered insight, or encouraged someone to learn more. I feel honored to have helped others in this way. But when I'm struggling to write a sentence, fighting to find the right words as I write a book, all I'm thinking about is my responsibility to communicate my knowledge as best I can. Only when I receive these messages do I realize that we really have no idea just how far our communications can travel, nor the impact they can have on others.

Inspiring others through communication often isn't about lofty rhetoric or heroic life choices. It can be as simple as recognizing someone by name each morning and saying hello. About encouraging someone to stay the course, study harder, read more, write down their thoughts, speak out, try out, pursue something different, change their lives or behavior, or strive to do something better.

Something as simple as saying, "You made the right decision—well done" can inspire someone who's down or second-guessing themselves. Affirming, "You should be proud, you worked so hard" can make someone's day.

We never know the effect our communications will have on others. Years ago, working in the FBI Tampa office, I got a call one day from the FBI switchboard in Washington, DC. Such calls aren't that common, and I wondered who was trying to track me down. I was told the call was from an agent going through new agents' training at the FBI Academy in Quantico, and she needed to speak to me right away.

On the line was a voice totally unfamiliar to me. She said, "Agent Navarro, this is Kylie—you won't remember me." (I didn't.) "I was in your daughter's eighth grade class." I still couldn't picture her. "I just wanted you to know that I will be graduating tomorrow as a new agent, and I wanted to thank you for inspiring me to become an agent."

I cannot begin to describe how happy that made me. Over a twenty-five-year career, I'd given scores of presentations in schools wherever I was stationed. I never imagined someone would hear that presentation and say, "I want to do what he does." What had I said that had moved this young woman to dedicate the next twenty-five years of her life? Or was it something in how I carried myself? This is the beautiful mystery of our beneficial influence on others. All of us remember someone who communicated with such impact. And all of us have the power to communicate it to others.

Perhaps your visit to your child's school will inspire someone to become a firefighter, an engineer, a doctor, a veterinarian, an artist, a singer, a researcher, an athlete, an electrician, a librarian, or a better human being.

In my travels, I meet untold numbers of people who, after hours, are coaching soccer, teaching mountaineering skills, giving guitar lessons, involved in youth athletic programs, showing students how to code, and more. Others are mentors on the job, sharing information and teaching coworkers. When the COVID-19 pandemic exploded in the US, people taught one another how to conduct meetings online, revise and restructure educational curriculums, navigate new systems and rapidly changing services, and innumerable other important measures that had to be put into immediate action. Others shared songs, prayers, poetry, artwork, comic relief, and did whatever they could to lift up others in an overwhelming situation most of us had never faced in our lives.

These individuals sought to inspire, even if by degrees, so that others might have a peaceful moment while calamity struck all around.

Exceptional individuals teach, share, educate, guide, mentor, and encourage not because there's a reward in it for them, but because it's the right thing to do. Nothing says "I care" more loudly than when we communicate our sentiments through our actions. As we emerge from this pandemic, we'll remember those small acts people did to make our lives just a little bit better, even if it was just a hearty smile.

You never know what life has in store, but know this: how you live your life can inspire others. How you do that is up to you. Who will be that person who says, "You are someone special I want to emulate"? You never know.

At my leadership presentations I ask, "Where on your computer screen or your desk is the *Help Folder*?" I go on to explain that, no, I don't mean the folder where you put things you need help with. I mean the folder where you keep track of what you have resolved to do—and what you're doing—to help others. That folder should be prominent in either electronic or paper form. It should list those things that you're working on or plan to work on to help others. Maybe it's sending a letter of encouragement to someone going through a tough time (a friend of mine mailed a card with a short handwritten note every week to a neighbor who was hospitalized for long-term medical treatment). Maybe it's tutoring a student online, mentoring a professional new to your business, helping a colleague avoid a pitfall, or assisting someone who's having challenges beyond the scope of what they can cope with—whether it's picking up some groceries for a housebound neighbor along with your own, or helping a handicapped person to rearrange furniture. When your personal help folder is hefty, it speaks volumes about you and your character.

You want to improve this world? You want to be exceptional? Start now, today, communicating that you care by living a life of rectitude. You don't need anyone's permission or authorization. And for the most part it's free. Influence others through your comportment and I promise you, your life, and those around you will change for the better.

Through my study of human behavior and my work in coaching executives over the years, I've learned a great deal about what makes exceptional communicators so good at the things we've discussed above. Below are some tips that can make anyone a more effective communicator—not only in simple transactional situations, but especially when collaboration, cooperation, negotiation, and sensitivity are called for. When you couple these priorities with the principles above, you will significantly improve your influence.

The Primacy of Emotions

The first rule of exceptional communicators is this: deal with emotions first—all else follows.

Emotions Come First

This is hard for many people to accept. We want to proceed logically. It's sometimes uncomfortable to allow emotions to dominate communications first. But we must attend to emotions before logic can gain traction. It makes sense, if you understand the human mind and the survival role of emotions.

Have you ever had an argument with someone and when it was over, after you've calmed down, you think of all the clever lines you should have said? We all have. You didn't think of them during the argument because of "limbic" or "emotional hijacking." When we're upset, emotional, angry, startled, displeased—in fact, anytime there's strong psychological discomfort—our emotional brain (the limbic system), for survival reasons, takes primacy. It hijacks our neural pathways; we think less so we can deal with the more pressing needs that might require us to distance ourselves through flight (running, climbing) or if necessary, to fight in order to survive. This neuro-electrochemical cascade goes to work instantly, overriding other circuits or anything that could slow or inhibit the brain's response to a perceived threat. That's the only way we could have survived as a species. It's also why those clever lines escape us in the heat of the moment, why we forget our PIN when we're in a hurry and flustered, or stammer when the boss asks a pointed question we're not prepared to answer.

We understand the primacy of emotions naturally in many situations. When a child comes in crying from an incident with a friend, we reflexively attend to the child with an embrace and comforting words—often before asking for the full story of what happened. But somehow, when it's adults we are dealing with, we lose our way. Perhaps we assume that we outgrow our need for comfort. So, when we see an employee visibly struggling with something emotionally, that strikes us as different from the struggling child. It isn't. Whether child or adult, emotional needs must be tended to first. Teachers say of students: "Mad or sad, cannot add." It applies to adults, too. When we're emotional or stressed, we're inhibited from thinking or performing at our best.

Here's another way to think about this. Nonverbal displays of distress are really no different than if I came to you and said, "I am having a tough time." We evolved to communicate emotions nonverbally, so those around us could engage us quickly without having to vocalize. Most people in business, I have found, will display that something is bothering them long before they are forthcoming and say something. Don't ignore what you're seeing, just because it's not expressed in words. If it's in the mind, is distressing, and is percolating to the surface through behaviors, then it's up to us to address what's going on just as we would if someone said, "I have a bone to pick with you."

During the COVID-19 pandemic, you may have noticed how many video or phone conversations, even with strangers, began with, "How are things where you are?" Or "Hope your loved ones are okay?" We naturally extend these invitations to talk, even if just for a minute, about the stress another person is undergoing because we can visually see it in their faces or hear the tension in the tight, quivery, or slightly breathless sound of their voice.

Occasions arise all the time where emotions need space before thought can take place. Exceptional communicators know this.

A colleague shared this story:

"One morning at work, I was, in essence, professionally threatened on the phone by a superior I didn't report to, because I hadn't attended to a situation as promptly as he thought I should have. I was a senior manager, a longtime employee and respected performer of many years, and it was a total shock to be spoken to this way. I hung up the phone and was literally kind of staring numbly and dumbly at my desk, and then not quite knowing what else to do, starting to somehow get going with the rest of my day—when my boss called me (this didn't often happen) and asked me to come to his office. Oh, great, I thought, What else can go wrong this morning?

"I trudge to his office, go in, we greet each other, I sit down. Silence. We just sit there for a number of seconds. Then he says something like, 'So, how are things going?' I'm like, 'Uh, fine.' (Thinking: What the heck is this? The boss doesn't call you into his office to chat. Where's this headed?) A little more silence. Then he asked if something had happened that morning. Whereupon, I'm ashamed to say it, I burst into tears.

"I didn't tell him everything that was said, but it turned out

I didn't have to. The other exec had called my boss (I won-
dered later if he thought I'd report him, or maybe he felt badly
about what he said) and said something about our conversa-
tion. My boss and I discussed what to do next, my boss let
me know by his calm demeanor that this wasn't something he
was worried about as regards me or our relationship, I went
back to my office and implemented the plan, and we never
discussed it again.

"I really appreciated that he cared enough to proactively ad-
dress how I might be feeling, and not wait to see if it was going
to become his problem because I'd report it to him. Maybe he
knew me well enough to know I'd just suck it up and move
on. Either way, he wouldn't have had to let on that he knew
anything about it. But he chose to check on me."

There. It's that simple. You don't go directly into work matters
or business transactions until you deal with the person's emotions.

Before words can soothe us on a logical level, they must first soothe
us on an emotional level. Humans aren't faucets. We can't turn our
emotions off at will—remember, limbic hijacking is an electro-
chemical cascade that has a natural arc before we are back to nor-
mal. Which is why, if we're struggling, we prefer to hear a calming
voice: "Can I help you?," "Are you OK?," "Want to save this for another time?," "Would you like to say what's on your mind?," or "Don't
worry, you got this," instead of: "Sorry, but you just have to suck it up.
We're all in the same boat, so get with it," "You need to chill, buddy,"
"Get your act together before the boss sees you," or worse, "Please
don't snivel in my office." I've heard them all.

What are these latter responses if not a lack of caring, validation, or empathy? Negation of our emotions often makes us more
upset—it leaves us unfulfilled. A person whose feelings have been
invalidated in this way doesn't soon forget. Perhaps you remember
times when it's happened to you.

So observe your colleagues and customers for the discomfort

displays we discussed in Chapter 2 that say, "I am not in a good mood." Those tightly compressed lips, that furrowed glabella between the squinting eyes, the tight or shifting jaw. It could be for any number of reasons—maybe they were late to your meeting, having been stuck in traffic, and annoyed at additional delays in the lobby of handing over ID, having a photo taken, and waiting while their name was checked off a guest list. The exceptional communicator sees discomfort displays and inquires as to what's wrong. We do that by asking, "How was your trip in?" Which gives them the chance to exhale and get the story out, "I'm sorry I'm late. There was an accident on the highway that tied up traffic. Then there were visitors ahead of me in the lobby." And that's our cue to reflect and validate their experience: "Sorry you had such a tough commute. I've been stuck on that highway, too. The lobby rigamarole can be a real pain." And then seek to ameliorate: "Please, have a seat. Would you like some water?"

Sometimes all someone needs is space to vent for a moment: "Yes, I'm pissed because I couldn't find any parking nearby and I'm soaked." Validate that first: "Ugh, I'd feel just the same. Here, let me take your coat. Would you like to freshen up? The restroom is down this hall to your left." Then get down to business.

Bottom line: When someone's having difficulties, emotions are inevitably involved. Get them to open up about what's bothering them. Don't ignore or dismiss whatever may have transpired, however small. Validate their sentiments, because what they experienced today may also be cumulative—perhaps there have been a series of incidents in your interactions that have led to this moment where the emotions are on display. Listen to what they have to say and elicit what emotions are affecting them, whatever they are—maybe they're flummoxed, upset, angry, disappointed, tired, sad, hurt, worried, frustrated, longing, irritated, and so on. Business can wait. First, get the emotions straight.

If you provide an opening and they don't take you up on it, don't push. Passing annoyances will fade and some people can be reserved or stoic. But if someone continues to display discomfort, there may be something significant that you should revisit when the time feels right. Seeing them more at ease in the chair, head tilted or nodding in approval as they listen, their hands becoming more relaxed and open, a smile returning to their face, or perhaps beginning to mirror your behavior—are some nonverbals that can let you know now may be the best time.

Dealing with emotions first also establishes or reinforces social rapport. When you communicate caring and attentiveness, the other person perceives that you're genuinely interested in their well-being, not just in carrying out a transaction. That paves the way to trust and improved communication. If you doubt that emotional validation has this level of power, just recall Tony Hayward's now-famous gaffe at the scene of the BP oil spill disaster that took the lives and livelihoods of so many: "I'd like my life back." Is there any going back from such a statement? Often not.

Rapport-Building: The Power of Being at One

Why are some people an absolute joy to be around? You know the ones: they leave you smiling, feeling energized, reassured, understood, and cared for. What are they doing that others aren't?

They are reinforcing and nurturing rapport through their attentiveness. We flock to such people and want to spend time with them: they make us feel good in their presence.

We tend to think of rapport-building as something we only do once—perhaps when we first meet and get to know someone. Not so. Rapport-building is something exceptional individuals do whenever they interact with others. That's how they help us to feel comfortable and special.

I know parents who do daily rapport-building with their teenage children. They know they have to nourish the relationship through adaptive rapport-building that may vary from day to day depending on their child's moods and needs, but that always says, *I'm here, and I care.* Some days that may require giving the teen space, asking their opinion on something, validating an issue, discussing needs versus desires, or any number of things that say, *You are valued, your thoughts are valued, but above all you are important to me.*

Couples, if they're wise, also have to do occasional rapport-building, as circumstances, work, finances, and responsibilities can drive a wedge between them. In some families, rapport-building is reinforced through scheduled dinners with no electronic devices so that harmony can return through communication. In homes where everyone eats at different times, scheduled events and outings help to reaffirm bonds.

Let's be honest: distractions (busy schedules, electronic devices) abound, and we've all gotten sucked in. It happens. But if you want to build the rapport that leads to empathy, understanding, and validation in communication, nothing should be allowed to distract. A senior executive of a financial institution I deal with makes it a point to very visibly turn off her smartphone in front of others when there are serious or private issues to be discussed. In time everyone who works for her has followed suit. They're appreciative of her willingness to place emphasis on the here and now, on them individually or collectively, with no distractions. Many business executives tell me that this is a simple yet powerful gesture that says, *You are important to me; you have my undivided attention.*

At work, you'd be surprised how often we have to do rapport-building because even though we may rely on each other's help, we haven't had the proper amount of time to get to know each other, we see each other too infrequently, or we work on different floors. Other times there's fence-mending to be done. Incidents that cause tension or suspicion may require having to reach out and do rapport-building to restore trust and to ensure and nourish long-term relations. "It is silly to wait for the executive retreat to build rapport—I insist we do it as often as we can," says an executive with a nationwide home appliance service network. He doesn't wait until the perfect time, or a company getaway (which they do hold every year to build rapport)—he does it with every phone call or interaction in the hallway every day. Why? Because rapport-building isn't something you ration—it needs to be exercised whenever you can.

Rapport-building always starts at an emotional level. The implicit message is: *What you are experiencing right now is important to me. So that you know I am one with you in thought and sentiment, I will try to ascertain where you are emotionally.*

There have been times in meetings with colleagues when I've had to say, "Look, I know you're upset, I can tell you're upset—here is your opportunity to tell me your thoughts." And I've gotten an earful. But we needed to go through that process because we were both going to continue to work together, and I would rather have them vent in my presence than vent behind my back. Invariably, things always went better when we could talk it out.

Being at one with someone may seem like a strange phrase to use and yet, in a way, it describes rapport-building at its best.

Being at one with others entails bringing together all the capacities we've discussed so far. When you've repeatedly practiced observing others, exercising benign curiosity, and mastering the art of nonverbal communication, you can establish this higher communicative level of understanding and rapport.

As someone charged with getting criminals to cooperate or getting foreign spies to defect, it was something I had to do every day. When you're with those individuals, you're taking in all their ideas, thoughts, concerns, and fears. You are, in that moment, seeing things not as "you" and "me," but "we." As you ponder what they must ponder, you are at one with them, and they sense it. When they hesitate out of fear, you understand; you can empathize. When they make a decision whether to cooperate or not, you validate the difficulty of that decision no matter how it turns out. And though it might turn out that at the end of the day one of you goes to jail and the other home, you had that rapport that allowed you to accomplish your task, and in that moment, you were at one in understanding, even if there is disappointment in the outcome. That can only be accomplished through the power of rapport-building and being at one with another person.

Through verbal and nonverbal communication, shared concerns and desires, and mutual understanding of dangers and consequences, you can reach an understanding from each other's perspective. Here is one such conversation with someone who was going to be prosecuted for manslaughter on the Colorado Indian Tribes Reservation in Parker, Arizona:

"But if I confess, I will go to prison."

"True, but the reason I'm in front of you is because we already have enough evidence to take you to trial."

"I might not get convicted?"

"True, but then luck as you know doesn't always go our way."

"Maybe."

"No maybe. I am here in your house. I would say that is bad luck." [Chuckles] "Dennis, what do you think my job is?"

"To arrest criminals."

"No, my job is to collect facts, and then I turn that over to a prosecutor."

"And?"

"And that prosecutor is going to ask me, 'Was your job made easier or harder by the accused?' What should I say to him about you, Dennis? Did you make my job easier or harder?"

"Well, I'm not going to sign a confession."

"That's fine, but do you see the dilemma I'm in? What do I tell the prosecutor about you? You see, I want to say, 'Yes, Dennis screwed up, but he recognized his mistake and he admitted his mistake.' That's what I want to say." [Silence] "Dennis, in this town, I am probably the only person not upset with you. Everyone else from the mayor to the tribal leaders to your neighbors, they are upset. But I am not. You know that. I am sitting here next to you and I am not upset. We are talking,

but right now it is one-sided. You want all of this to go away?
But it can't go away. It won't go away. So, we have to drive
through this together, and I am here just for that purpose. So,
tell me, how do we do this? Help me to navigate this, please."
[Longer silence.]

Now the nonverbals kick in. I look at Dennis with my head canted
slightly. My facial expressions are neutral. I am patient as if waiting
for someone to finish their coffee before parting ways. We look at
each other in silence. His instinct is to stay quiet: he does not want
to go to jail. I've let him know that I understand his reluctance. But
I've helped him to see what I am up against: my job is to keep society
safe. My efforts aren't personal; I hold no animosity, and we do have
a solid case. I have laid that out, while also taking in his point of
view, and he is beginning to consider what I am saying.

In the end, he pushes away from the table, crosses his arms, gives
a deep exhale, and says:

"You write it. I don't know how to do it."
"I understand. I will write it, but it has to be your words,
Dennis."
"OK."

In that interchange, which took about two hours overall, I grew to
appreciate Dennis's reluctance, but I also made sure he understood
where I was coming from—I understood that he wanted to avoid going to jail but at the same time I had a job to do. In the end, we shook
hands and he placed his wrists together in front so I could handcuff
him. We were at one with each other.

In business, rapport-building can take many forms, from stepping up to help out a coworker who's swamped to backing a colleague's statement in a meeting to being cooperative while working
on a task together. Having a friendly manner, strong skills, and a

good reputation are pluses, but nothing is more powerful than being trustworthy. Whether you're collaborating or contesting, as I was with the suspect above, being trustworthy is that one characteristic that can open the way to succeed and establish rapport. It can even happen when parties are adversaries. You need just enough trust, to begin with, to start an interaction. Once you've begun, then rapport-building can help each party take gradual steps toward each other. Adversaries who can stick with this process long enough to actually bridge differences both reinforce and grow their trust in each other.

When we call someone in our network to ask their opinion about a prospective boss or client, much of what we seek to know has to do with whether we can trust them and work well with them—that is, have rapport. When attorneys call other attorneys and executives call former colleagues to get the "dirt" on someone they'll be dealing with, they may ask a lot of questions—"Can I trust this guy?" "How is she to deal with?" "Is she willing to compromise?" "How far can we push?" "Is he good to work with, or a total asshole?"—but they all boil down to two things: What is rapport going to look like, and is the person trustworthy?

Establishing that vital rapport necessary for being at one with others is something we have to work at. It's not always easy. Are you going to run into people who are just plain toxic: difficult to work with and totally untrustworthy? Yes, and there's no secret formula for dealing with them, because they choose to be that way. You may never be able to establish rapport. That's fine. You do what you can to move things forward without compromising yourself, keep good records of your interactions, and watch your back. But know there will be better days and better people, too—people who will be worthy of your trust and whom you'll be proud to count as colleague, community member, or friend. When you find them, your trustworthiness and your rapport-building skills will put you in harmony, able to quickly connect and enjoy what you can achieve together.

Being Present

I once interviewed a former Soviet intelligence officer (what most people call a spy) who turned out to be a wonderful man in his own way: personable, erudite—my sworn enemy, but charming, nonetheless. I asked him, "I noticed in the file that you traveled to Vienna to meet with your recruited source [who turned out to be an American military officer spying for him]. In doing so, you exposed yourself needlessly. Why? You didn't have to." He replied, "I needed to see firsthand. I needed to look in his eyes; I needed to hear it directly from him. No report, no matter how well-written, and no film [there was no video at that time], can convey what I can see up close. You must be able to smell your friends to appreciate them."

I will never forget those words: "You must be able to smell your friends to appreciate them." What a metaphor for being present, for having hands on, for establishing personal rapport. They wanted a long-term relationship with the recruited American, and being in the presence of this recruit was worth it to him; even though it meant risking being identified—the worst thing that can happen to someone in the intelligence arena.

To establish rapport, to communicate caring, to really understand others, we must be present. To be empathetic in large part has to do with being there, seeing, feeling, assiduously observing, being part of the experience. That's what Director Freeh was communicating when he made it a point to run with us. His presence among us told us far louder than words: *I care.*

It takes time to be present. You may have to travel and physically be there with others. Schedule video calls. Get up early or stay up late to connect with someone in another time zone. Being on "their" time is your commitment to being present and bespeaks of the effort you're making to be at one. This is what George Logothetis is communicating when he travels the globe to personally visit staff at Libra Group's offices.

Ten Ways to Speak with More Than Words

Words matter. But when it comes to demonstrating that we genuinely care, it's our nonverbal communication that carries most of the load. If you have a way with words, by all means use it. But from the smile we find so welcoming from the time we are infants to the tone of voice that transmits our joy in seeing someone, to the exquisitely sensitive response we have, nerve by nerve, when someone simply rubs our back or holds our hand when we are scared, sad, or sick—caring begins and ends nonverbally. Below are ten examples of nonverbals that make indelible positive impressions. At the very least, they may warm a cool or skeptical reception. At most, they'll steer you smoothly onto the road of rapport-building.

1. **Small gestures mean much.** The gestures we use to welcome others, the gracious manners that make them feel special and comfortable, all fall under the umbrella of nonverbal communication.

    That small signal you give—perhaps just a wave of the hand or flashing the eyes by quickly raising your eyebrows at someone you know across the street—lets them know you care. Your arms can make others feel included, too; your outstretched hand toward a person who approaches while you're talking with someone says, *Come, join us; be part of what we're sharing.*

    Even our feet convey inclusivity. Usually when we talk to others, everyone's toes are directly facing each other. Though we may turn at the hips to greet others, it's when the feet angle out that we make others feel really welcome to join us.

    Exceptional individuals literally go out of their way to make others feel comfortable and let them know that they care. Taking a moment to walk over to greet someone or to say hello to a group can mean so much, especially if you are a manager, senior executive, or CEO.

2. **Be prompt.** Make sure you communicate in a timely manner. This is so important in business. We demonstrate that we value others when we attend to them and communicate quickly. This is part of rapport-building and validation: if it's important for them, it's important for us. No one, and I mean no one, likes to wait long for a response. Some people procrastinate on saying no. Rest assured, a timely no is far better than a slow one, or no response at all. Bad news, too, shouldn't be delayed, once you clearly understand what needs to be communicated.

3. **Let them vent.** If emotions are high and there's tension, one of the best ways to diffuse things is to let them vent. Remember the primacy of emotions—that before we can soothe with words, we must soothe emotions—and that people are positively influenced by validation. Just last week at the airport, I saw a traveler miss his connection. He was pissed, and he let the gate agent know it. Experience tells us that when someone is in the grip of limbic hijacking, letting them vent helps.

   If you're present when that happens, or if you're the target of the vitriol:

   - Try to create more space between yourself and the other person. Back away slightly. Angle your body so you're not face-to-face head on.

   - Focusing on the person's face rather than looking into their eyes may help to reduce anger.

   - Saying "calm down" rarely works, but lowering your voice and speaking in a calm manner does.

   - Take a deep breath. We gravitate toward those whom we perceive as being under control. This deep breath and long exhale, I have found in my research, sends a subconscious message to cue the other person toward the path to beginning to calm down.

   - Maintain boundaries. You are caring, but you're not a human chew toy. When venting passes the point of what's reasonable, then it's time to bring the conversation to a logical conclusion, though it may not be perfect, or to distance yourself. As I noted in my book *Dangerous Personalities*, you have no social obligation, ever, to be victimized.

4. **Consider seating.** Communication research (including the study of primates) reveals that we are more comfortable when people sit at slight angles to us rather than directly opposite us. In the FBI I avoided sitting directly across from anyone I was interviewing and for the most part I succeeded. Sitting or standing at angles assures us of greater face time as well as greater social comfort. In business, the research is ample: you get more done sitting at angles—so if it's an important meeting, consider finding the right place and optimal seating to conduct the meeting.

5. **Mind your head.** Tilting your head as others speak increases the amount of time people will engage us and helps others to the feel that you're receptive and open-minded.

6. **Mirror behaviors.** Mirroring, also known as body echoing or isopraxis, is a shortcut to the subconscious. It has been shown repeatedly that synchrony is harmony. In other words, when we're conversing with others, our bodies will echo or mirror each other when there's a high degree of concurrence in thought or feelings. This translates into psychological comfort. We see this with mother and baby, between good friends or colleagues immersed in productive conversation, or between lovers at a café staring at each other in perfect synchrony.

    We encourage others to communicate more freely and openly when we mirror their behaviors. I'm not talking about cartoonishly copying every move, but following the general pattern and rhythm of their movements: when they lean back, we in short order lean back; if they order a drink, we also order a drink. Think of a conversation as being a guest in someone's psychic space: you're relaxed and attentive, following the house rules with warmth and responsiveness, as you would if you were at the home of someone you know.

When we mirror others properly, it's so seamless and harmonious as to be unnoticeable. When conducting long debriefings in my FBI career, I found mirroring invaluable in getting others to cooperate.

You can mirror activity, too, as Director Freeh did in running in synchrony with us. It could be getting a tray of lunch in the company cafeteria and asking a table of your employees if you could join them . . . standing in the buffet line along with everyone else . . . bringing your brown bag lunch to the working meeting . . . boarding the bus to the church retreat instead of driving on your own . . . working out with the team . . . walking the factory floor and asking how things are going.

7.   **Mirror language.** Mirroring words is also powerful. If you're talking with me and I use the words *problem*, *family*, *character* and you respond using words like *issue*, *wife and kids*, *personality*, we're not really in synchrony. Subconsciously, I'll perceive that the importance and weight I personally attach to the words *problem*, *family*, *character* are not being valued or properly understood. Yes, we're talking, but we're not communicating effectively—certainly not as one. To communicate effectively, we must show we understand each other by recognizing the value other people place on certain words. When they talk about *church*, or *grandkids*, or their *baby* (pet dog), those words have a special weight and significance; when we also give value to those words by using them, we are helping to establish more sympathetic channels of communication. When we tap into those precise words others use, as the famed therapist Carl Rogers found more than sixty years ago, we tap into a level of the mind that finds this synchrony appealing and influential.

I practiced verbal mirroring constantly in the FBI. One day I'd be just this side of the border of San Luis, in the state of Sonora, Mexico; the next I was on the Upper East Side of

Manhattan debriefing a Soviet defector or an East German refugee, or down in Miami where the cocaine wars brought us into contact with Jamaicans, Colombians, Cubans, or Puerto Ricans. In each case, we had to adjust, whether we were talking to informants, witnesses, victims, their families, their neighbors, the suspects, or anyone of informational interest. It wasn't just a language issue; it was a word value issue, and we used that to our advantage to build rapport.

If a New Yorker from Queens tells you so-and-so "is a stand-up guy," that has special meaning. To respond "So you trust him?" doesn't begin to capture the weight of what was meant. You are at that moment not in harmony. I remember the first time I heard a Tampa native say, "He's a Yankee." Now, there was a loaded word. It was clear she wasn't referring to the baseball team.

Mirroring doesn't mean we must use all the words other people use—some are disgusting and dehumanizing. So there are times when we won't be in harmony. Still, we must recognize the weight others have given to certain words. And in this case, Yankee was code for anyone from up north or a recent arrival, or a legacy term alluding to "carpetbaggers" who arrived from the North after the Civil War.

8. **Listen for primacy and recency.** Listen not only for what is said, but also in what order (primacy), and how often (recency) certain words and topics are mentioned. This can be invaluable in discerning what's troubling someone, pointing toward what their priorities may be or what issues are on their mind. If a topic or even a word is often repeated, pay attention. Repetition can shed light on unresolved or underlying issues, even pathologies.

9. **Take notes.** When conversations matter, especially in business, take notes. Richard Branson, one of the world's most enterprising people, doesn't just listen; he talks to everyone who works for him, wherever he finds them—and then he goes one step further in his quest for clarity: he takes notes. To me it demonstrates that he cares so much about what his

employees have to say that he will write it down so he won't forget. What this communicates is clear: *Message received, this is important to you as well as me, action to follow.* Imagine how it would improve communication and rapport if our bosses, managers, supervisors, and leaders did only that. How often have you talked to a supervisor and wondered if anything would ever come of it, or if they would even remember it, since they didn't write it down?

Another good reason to take notes: if there are issues— and any organization will have them—whoever has the best documentation wins. I learned that in the FBI and in my private consulting work over the last eighteen years. Working memory, as it's called, doesn't work perfectly. Humans get things wrong all the time. And none of us is immune to forgetting. It's hard to forget something that's staring at you in your journal or to-do list. Write it down to remind you to get it done, to inspire you, and to protect you if need be, but write it down.

I've found one more benefit to writing things down. Using available technology, I can now have real-time, face-to-face communications with clients around the world. Often the callers are stressed about a particular issue. After I hear what they have to say, I ask everyone involved to put their thoughts in writing. Not because I'm lazy and don't want to take notes. I am taking notes. But for clarity, I want everyone to think about what they're saying, what they saw or heard, and what they want the record to actually reflect.

Repeatedly, I've found that what they initially emphasized, upon reflection and with a little more critical thinking, changes—and always for the better. What they initially mentioned first now may come second. Other factors come to light. With less emotion and more thinking, the facts become more lucid.

Emotions affect our ability to observe. In our conversation, I allow my clients to air their emotions so that we—especially they—can see more plainly what the key issues are. Those show up in the written version. In the end, too, a written record of an incident may be needed, so why not do it as soon as possible?

This is especially important in human resource situations where tempers may be at issue, or when something has happened that's critical to the business. I find that by encouraging clients to immediately write down their thoughts and observations after airing the problem helps them to both calm down and gain greater clarity.

As a person or as a leader, we cannot communicate with clarity until we understand with clarity. To do that, we must be able to differentiate between what is emotional and what is factual; between what someone thinks and what someone knows or suspects. For that, writing things down is magical.

10. **Agree and add.** Decades ago, an instructor came to one of our seminars at Quantico to talk about establishing rapport. He had an interesting perspective, as he worked in the theater and, in particular, comedy. One thing he talked about was a technique he had learned in improvisational comedy: agree and add.

Basically, it works like this. The person says something: "This commute sucks!" To which you say: "It really sucks [agree . . . and then add:]—especially when there's an accident." With that single statement, you've let someone know that you're listening, you validate, and you get it. Or they say: "He's such a know-it-all." To which you reply: "He is, isn't he—always has to have the last word." Simple repetition of what was said, with something small added that lets them know you understand and are in sync. How much better this is than when someone replies, "Yeah," "Right," "Uh-huh," or simply nods. Sure, sometimes an affirming nod works fine. But for validating others' thoughts and feelings, agree and add works best.

Incidentally, this doesn't mean you can't disagree. If you're completely opposed to something someone says and find it objectionable, feel free to express that. But there are ways to do it with nuance. I call it the Agree, Add, Affirm Method. As before, you *agree* and *add* something—but then you *affirm* your own thoughts or convictions on the matter. It might sound like this: "Yes, commuting really sucks, especially in the winter." Then, after a few seconds, you affirm: "But to be fair, it's remarkable how they keep the roads open after a heavy snow." Or you could say: "I agree with you—the commute stinks and it's a big hassle, but it's certainly better than last year at this time."

Caring doesn't mean bowing to what everyone else says. There's a place for your own take. But for the sake of harmony, it's wiser to agree, add, and affirm.

I know wonderful, intelligent people who just don't get this and bring pleasant conversations to a halt by pedantically correcting a minor detail or by outright disagreeing. Conversations are so much more successful and collaborative when we allow everyone to feel they can talk and share ideas. We don't need to always correct or edit what others say. If you continually object to what people say, they'll eventually grow tired of interacting with you.

The Healer's Method

This final communication technique is one I've shared with clinicians over the years but have rarely mentioned in my writing. It's so important that I've given it a section of its own. I call it *The Healer's Method*, but it applies to a much broader range of situations than the name might suggest.

As a student of anthropology, I have examined the practices of shamans or healers throughout the world. When you think about it, good emotional and physical health is the ultimate state of comfort and well-being, and often what the shaman or healer does is more psychological than anything else. Through dances, incantations, animal sacrifices, physical manipulation of objects, laying on of hands, the power of suggestion, drugs, and of course the placebo effect, they provide comfort, and in some cases contribute to healing.

By studying these techniques that are seen in many cultures, and while working with clinicians to improve their communications skills, I was able to decode what the most effective healers do. In fact, those clinicians who consistently were rated highly by patients, where the patient felt that their health had improved under that clinician's care, were using the Healer's Method without realizing it.

The Healer's Method follows this sequence: Visual, Vocal, Verbal, Tactile.

1. **Visual.** Just as a mother—the first healer/helper/caregiver most of us know—enters the room and makes the baby happy just by coming into view, so clinicians who entered the room with their white lab coat on, stethoscope around neck or visibly displayed, received the highest ratings. Why? Because those are the accoutrements that we in the modern world associate with the healer—someone who makes people feel better. A doctor or a nurse is that archetypal figure. The clinician's smile, another powerful visual, makes the patient smile, something Mother Teresa of Calcutta practiced herself and advocated when she said, "We shall never know all the good that a simple smile can do."

2. **Vocal.** The visual is followed by the vocal—the tone of the healer's voice: pleasing, interested, engaged—that invites conversation and creates psychological comfort. Here's an example from a physician in Tampa, Florida, who allowed me to attend his morning hospital rounds: "How are you, Mrs. Garza? How's the shoulder?" The tone is comforting, not hurried, not indifferent—signaling genuine interest in her response.

3. **Verbal.** The doctor's words add to the therapeutic effect: caring, knowledgeable about the person's concerns, calling her by name. This doctor continued: "Do you have a little bit more movement today? Let me see you raise your arm."

He asked her with a smile, modeling the movement using his own arm for her to see. "This is wonderful progress," he said, examining her closely, validating her efforts, only then taking notes.

4. **Tactile.** Then this doctor took his patient's hand as you would your grandmother (palm up), not vertical as you would a business associate, and he wished her continued success. Still holding her hand, he gently patted her upper arm with his other hand. "I will see you again before I leave today," he promised, his hand firmly reinforcing his words; his smile causing her to smile in turn. Mrs. Garza, even though having discomfort, lavished praise on this doctor and when asked to rate her pain on a scale of one to ten after his visit she rated it as three where earlier she had rated it as a five.

I would argue, and many doctors I have interviewed agree, that the therapeutic effect begins not with the medicines they deploy, but rather with what is communicated verbally and nonverbally within the space of the interaction: the visual contact between themselves, the staff, and the patient and—very importantly—what the patient expects to see in the healing setting and in the image the healer projects. The tone of voice is key—caring, sincere—as are the words that explore, show interest, and encourage. Finally, touch, something our species needs, when properly applied, heals. As Helen Keller reminded us, "Paradise is attained by touch."

It's as simple as that. Not magical or mystical. Simply one human fully attuned to another and aware that communication is so much more than words—indeed, we influence each other visually, vocally, verbally, and finally with touch. We experience it first through loving parents whose mere presence, tone of voice, words, and caress can make us feel so much better. When we're boarding the plane and are greeted by the pilot, smartly dressed in uniform, with a warm smile and a friendly hello and perhaps a touch on the arm, she too is following the Healer's Method. She is there to provide that psychological comfort a first-time traveler may need. Just four easy steps that positively influence others: easy to replicate, profoundly powerful when properly applied.

We've covered much ground in this chapter. But the core message is this: exceptional people above all else strive to communicate, in their own way, that they care. For Director Freeh, it was getting up early and meeting his agents, literally, on the road—out of the meetings, out of the usual strict protocols, where he encouraged us to speak frankly.

By living a life of rectitude and being trustworthy, we lay the groundwork of credibility necessary for communicating that we care. By understanding the primacy of emotions and using it, along with nonverbal communication that inspires comfort and openness, to validate others and communicate authentically, we demonstrate that we care.

Caring inspires, renews, motivates, calms, and encourages. Each of us has this capacity. When others feel comfortable that we care, that is how, together, our communication moves from informational to transformational. That is how, together, we can move mountains.

CHAPTER 4

Action

MAKE IT TIMELY, ETHICAL, AND PROSOCIAL

———

By knowing and applying the ethical and social framework for appropriate action, we can learn, as exceptional people do, to "do the right thing at the right time."

Do your work and I shall know you.
—Ralph Waldo Emerson

"Stop those guys! They just robbed us!"

I don't remember hanging up the phone. It had been a quiet spring night at Richard's Department Store in Miami, where I was working after school during my senior year of high school. Graduation was coming up. I had football scholarships and college on my mind. In those few seconds, hearing my boss's voice, everything was about to change.

I sprang into action and rushed to block the robbers' exit. Seeing me trying to head them off, the two men split up and made for different exits. The one headed my way came for me without hesitation, lunging with the eleven-inch fishing knife he had used to rob the clerks in the back. I saw the glint of the blade and turned at the last moment. The knife sank twice into my left upper arm, severing (as I would later learn) the bicep, triceps, brachial artery, ulnar nerve, medial nerve, inferior cutaneous nerve, and the brachialis muscle. The severed muscles retracted by the force of the tendons and blood began to gush as I went down.

There was no pain at first. But then, as the muscles contracted even further, the pain was unbearable, contorting my body. Blood was pouring out so fast that the first person to get to me slid on the blood on the floor and fell down beside me. Fortunately, a police officer arrived, having responded to a silent alarm during the robbery. I was starting to pass out from the blood loss, but he wouldn't let me. He reached in so deep that his fingers disappeared into my open wound, effectively pinching the vessels shut. He saved my life.

The local papers said I was a hero, the politicians who stopped by the hospital said as much, and even then-president Richard Nixon took the time to write me a letter, thanking me for my "courageous actions."

This story has a hero, and it is not me. Here's what really happened: a boy of seventeen acted thinking it would help, and he failed.

I failed to stop the robbers. They got away, and the money was never recovered. I failed in that I burdened my family with the emotional toll of my three weeks in the hospital, the months of recovery afterward, and my uncertain future. When the twenty-three football scholarship offers vanished overnight, I wasn't sure if I'd be able to attend college that year at all. Certainly, it would not be on a football scholarship; my arm had required more than 150 sutures inside and out.

That is what happened. But even that isn't the point of the story. The point is this: action, even with the best intentions, brings no guarantees of success. What I learned that day in Miami was that you can do all the "right" things—rise above expectations, even follow the letter of the law—and still fail. That is the challenge of trying to prescribe specific actions. Perhaps that works fine in a factory, but not in real life.

When it comes to action in real life, those things that we must or should do in a moment in time cannot be governed by lines of code, bullet points, or checklists. At some point, in an instant, as Captain "Sully" Sullenberger did with his doomed aircraft, one has to commit to act: to take control of that plane, even with both engines out, and attempt to land it, based on the skills one has mastered—but there are no guarantees.

Theodore Roosevelt said, "In any moment of decision, the best thing you can do is the right thing. The worst thing you can do is nothing." Management guru Peter Drucker observed: "Management is doing things right. Leadership is doing the right things." No one would argue with these statements. But how to know the "right things" to do? What is appropriate action? It's a question we constantly confront as individuals, as parents, as citizens—and certainly as leaders—daily.

Our actions each day shape our lives: they build credibility or undermine it, win friends or make enemies, increase your speed to market or get you trampled in the dust.

How you choose to act matters, too. Do you act with joy, enthusiasm, diligence, care, and with others in mind? Only you can craft not just what you do, but how you do it.

If you're looking for the quickest route to influence others, look no further than action. Action has a weight all its own. These are the nonverbals that shout: *This is who I am, this is what is important to me, this is how I feel about myself and others.* Your actions, day in and day out, define you. Aristotle was right: "We are what we repeatedly do."

And so it bears asking: Do you control where you're headed in life, or is life running roughshod over you? The only way to make a difference in our lives and in our world is through our actions. Indeed, I would argue that character is the sum total of our actions—

what we do each moment of our lives and the effect our actions have on others.

Which brings us back to doing the right thing. It's easier said than done. No one's perfect. All of us have failed to take appropriate action at times—or we took the right action, but the results weren't what we expected. Exceptional people are no different. They act and sometimes they fail. That dichotomy—success or failure—isn't the full story when it comes to assessing action. Action, when purposed properly, has a unique power. Here is where we begin to discern what defines the actions of the exceptional.

In this chapter, we'll explore the ethical and social underpinnings of appropriate action. I'll share a protocol for decision-making around action that you can apply in all kinds of circumstances. It's a protocol in which the willingness to act, to be accountable, and to work in furtherance of others becomes paramount. Why? Because that is how exceptional people and worthy leaders act. In the process, you'll be setting the stage to truly differentiate yourself and achieve a level of influence most people only dream about.

Action Defines Who We Are

Every few days, a man in a horse-driven cart visited the small town in Cuba where I lived until the age of eight. At each house, he'd ask if they had any food to throw away—what some would call slop—so he could feed his pigs. This recycling system worked well: nothing went to waste. He'd been doing it for decades, and everyone just referred to him as *el guajiro* (literally a peasant farmer in Spanish).

The old man of course smelled not very pleasant, and his clothes were often dirty, but he always had a smile. I was glad to see him, as he let me pet *la yegua* (his mare) and sometimes even allowed me to sit on her so I could pretend to be an American cowboy.

Most vividly, though, I remember how my mother or my grandmother would go out in the hot Cuban sun to greet this weathered old man, carrying a glass and a jar of ice water on the serving tray reserved for our dinners. And it wasn't just any glassware: it was handblown and imported from Czechoslovakia.

I watched this happen so often that I finally asked my mother: "Why do we give *el guajiro* water with our best glassware, since we children are not allowed to use it ourselves except at dinnertime?"

"*Porque se lo merece*," she replied. Because he deserves it.

It was my first lesson in action as we'll be discussing it: action that is reliable, taken when needed, not just when convenient, to ameliorate; to value and care for others, whatever their status.

My mother and grandmother made sure that our guest, however humble, dirty, and smelly he might be, received our best.

Giving their best: that is the unwritten contract exceptional individuals live by.

Decades later, I brought this event up to my mom, looking for perhaps a deeper answer. "This is how I was reared," she replied. "That we have a responsibility to others, that we must care." As I often affirm, the true measure of a person is how they treat those who can do absolutely nothing for them. A lesson I learned from my mother at a very young age.

Our propensity for action has multiple roots. As Alan Jasanoff notes in his illuminating book *The Biological Mind*, how we act is based in part on biology, our gender identity, and our DNA, as well as on what is socialized into us by our parents, friends, schooling, and other institutions including religious organizations. I was lucky to have a loving, caring family, where the example of action on behalf of others was performed and reinforced repeatedly. Not all of us are so fortunate. Yet we have free agency and we have the capacity to act in furtherance of others: to be prosocial, humane, decent, and kind even when our background or upbringing has created obstacles for us. All that's needed is the will. And that is up to us.

There's an explicit yet unwritten social contract that is self-evident and self-validating: we will survive and thrive if we take care of each other. With rare exceptions, this social contract is found in every culture studied. Over millennia, our forebears proved it to each other, and in the last three hundred thousand or so years, *Homo sapiens* could not have survived without it. In fact, a reward mechanism for caring action is built into our neurocircuitry for the very purpose of survival. The powerful neurotransmitter and hormone oxytocin is released when we care for and bond with others. Dopamine, too, is released when we are thoughtful, kind, and generous to others. This helps explain why we bond to babies almost immediately and why when we help someone, we feel good afterward. As Ellen Galinsky reminds us in *Mind in the Making*, even babies are primed to help others, and in doing so there will be positive social consequences as well as beneficial physiological rewards.

Most of us honor that unwritten but vital contract, or try to at its most basic level. When someone is lost, we give directions; when someone falls, we help them up; when someone's down, we comfort them; when they're at their weakest, we give support. But what goes into our action decisions, especially when the circumstances are more dynamic or complicated? For starters, it depends on how much you care.

Action and Inaction Speak Loudly

You can claim to care, to love, to be this or that, but until there's proof—in the form of demonstrable behavior—those are empty words. Countless times, when my work in law enforcement required me to appear in court, I listened to people testify that the defendant was a good father, a good mother, a good son, a good neighbor. Then someone else would testify as to the person's actions, and the pleasing façade of "goodness" would come tumbling down.

When it comes to action, especially action that benefits others, several factors are in play—or should be—even before the decision of whether or not to act. They're important both in our private lives as well as in a business setting.

In Chapter 1, we discussed emotional balance as a key component of self-mastery. Before we can take wise action, we need a reality-based assessment of ourselves to know what our strengths and weaknesses are. Otherwise, it's all too easy to delude ourselves, thinking that we're prepared and able to act, and that the options we have chosen are faultless. We may be erroneous in our logic and thinking because we don't assess to find our own blind spots, we may fail to consider what others have to say, or frankly we may be too hardheaded or ignorant to know what is best—and so we fall victim to what's known as the *Dunning-Kruger effect*.

Researchers David Dunning and Justin Kruger discovered that underperforming individuals (read: lacking in self-mastery—self-awareness as well as actual capacity) "reach erroneous conclusions and make unfortunate choices, but their incompetence robs them of the ability to realize it." Their ill-deserved and often unjustified self-confidence leads them to "hold inflated views of their performance and ability." So, even before they act, they are primed to do the wrong things because they have no clue as to how inferior their thinking is. And because they have no realistic clue, they'll deem their actions appropriate even when they fail, because they lack the capacity to be introspective. It takes self-awareness and that higher component, self-mastery, to understand when we lack ability or expertise. In other words, the hallmark of good, intelligent decision-making is to "be good at knowing what we don't know" and likewise knowing what is not a good course to take—otherwise anything we decide to do seems okay.

The flip side, for some, is freezing in fear and failing to act. In both cases, self-mastery (Chapter 1) prepares us for possible actions to take based on reality and capability, observation (Chapter 2) allows us to understand the situation in context so we can act appropriately, and skillful communication (Chapter 3) allows us to give and receive the information and support needed to carry out the mission. The exceptional have all these capacities in their corner when contemplating action. They're especially crucial in business, where failure to act appropriately can catastrophically cripple an organization.

Need an example? The Boeing 737 MAX.

As I began to write this book, the Boeing corporation was being sued because they failed to care about crew and passenger safety when pilots complained about software issues that caused the Boeing 737 MAX plane to behave erratically in certain situations. Those planes were finally grounded after two planes crashed, killing more than 350 people. Boeing lost millions of dollars in revenue *each day* the planes were grounded and lost their customers' confidence as well.

When we don't care enough to overcome our fears to act, we may not investigate how the final product performs, what the customer thinks, or what the public might perceive. We don't change the diaper, don't take the child to see the doctor in time, don't clean the dishes, don't do what we're asked. We fail the fallen and injured and pretend everything's all right. We delay responding to the urgent needs of others. Failure to act equals failure to care.

Failure to act is defining, to be sure, but in the lowest of terms. Those who delay, deny, dither, procrastinate, miss opportunities, stick their head in the sand, or are bystanders to wrongdoing eventually pay a price. Failure to act by governments during the COVID-19 pandemic of 2019–2021 caused thousands of people to die needlessly.

On a personal level, the toxic residue to a child or a spouse from a failure to act may have immediate as well as long-term psychological effects, including frustration, distrust, withdrawal, even depression. Every day children lose trust in their parents, couples grow distant, customers take their business elsewhere, and people are voted out of office—because of failure to act.

I tell business leaders all the time: if you have someone working for you who doesn't care, you will pay the price, because they may do what's required of them, but not with enthusiasm, not with the same commitment as you, and likely not as competently or completely. Employ them if you wish, but don't expect them to carry their full weight or perform when you need them the most.

Doing the right thing is as much a function of *how* you do it as what you do. Attitude and demeanor are key nonverbals that speak louder than words. Don't you feel better when someone acts with diligence, meticulousness, thoroughness, attentiveness, and alacrity, compared to the same action performed with apathy, reluctance, haphazard effort, or even disdain?

What's interesting about this component is that it's entirely in our control, even when almost nothing else is. Yet few of us fully exercise this power or grasp its influence. I'm reminded of the example of Nelson Mandela in the previous chapter. In prison he was thwarted and obstructed in almost every way. Yet his attitude was within his control, and through his mind-set, and the actions stemming from it, he turned even his enemies into allies.

Only you can control how you'll act. But rest assured others will notice and will be influenced by you.

Does that mean you can't have a bad day? There will be times when we fail to act or to do so in time—and we'll have to deal with the consequences. But a bad day doesn't define us, though it can make us regret our actions or inactions and make others less willing to cooperate with us in the future. There may be fences to mend. Remember, it's what we do habitually that defines us. Life is a movie, not a photo fixed in time. What the exceptional do with a bad day is resolve to make the next day better.

A friend told me her father used to counsel her, "If you wait to make a decision until you have all the information you'd like to know, there's no decision left to make."

It's true we often have to make decisions when we don't know as much as we'd like before action must be taken. But the exceptional understand that there comes a moment when it's better to commit to action and deal with the outcome, whatever that may be, compared to the harm that will certainly be done by dodging, delaying, hesitating, or waiting to have all the *i*'s dotted and *t*'s crossed—or, for fear of failure, failing to act at all.

How do they weigh what to do? They draw on knowledge, history, precedent, study, observation, and validated personal experience. They are guided both by moral principles and by their understanding of what has worked for themselves and other extraordinary individuals in the past.

Because they have so much more information to rely on, they avoid the pitfalls of the Dunning-Kruger effect and can make better and faster decisions. In contrast, someone else would need to wait for all the ducks to be lined up, and by then their action, even if right, might be too late.

The Ethical Action Protocol

While it would be wonderful to come up with a formula for action that fits every circumstance, that is impossible. This is perhaps why the gold standard for the Ritz-Carlton Hotel Company is simply this: "We are Ladies and Gentlemen serving Ladies and Gentlemen." As their website says, "This motto exemplifies the anticipatory service provided by all staff members." Rather than a long list of things to do, this succinct mission statement gives us insight into their thinking. To serve ladies and gentlemen, you must know how to do so, you must observe and seek to anticipate what is needed, and your actions must be performed as a lady or as a gentleman would perform them—with care and respect. With this mind-set, the hotel has always stood for the epitome of good service—exceeding expectations and creating an incredible amount of psychological comfort for their guests.

So, if there's no master book of rules or procedures, and in the absence of a personal motto, then what do we do?

In my FBI career, decisions were often made simpler because of rigid boundaries of comportment. One merely had to ask, is it within the law? Is it ethical? Will it stand up to judicial scrutiny or Department of Justice guidelines? But in life, we don't always have those kinds of institutional criteria. The *Ethical Action Protocol* (a guide I developed in collaboration with Toni Sciarra Poynter for decision-making when there is doubt or uncertainty as to how to proceed) is a series of four questions that I've found useful in weighing the appropriateness of actions under consideration:

1. Do my actions and behavior build trust?
2. Do my actions and behavior add value?
3. Do my actions and behavior positively influence or inspire?
4. Are my actions and behavior prosocial?

These four questions may not all be relevant to every circumstance where action is needed. But over the decades, I've found them useful as a reference point, especially if there's time to think and prepare, or if a situation is particularly complicated or uncertain. Individually or together, depending on circumstances, they can serve as a framework for choosing what to do. Let's take a look at each one.

Do My Actions and Behavior Build Trust?

When I retired from the FBI, the future US Attorney for the Middle District of Florida, Brian Albritton, said something to me that still resonates: "Joe, you are going to be presented with many opportunities now that you've retired from the FBI. Always remember, your reputation is everything."

I had worked hard to establish trustworthiness at the Bureau. It had proven invaluable: when even criminals can rely on you, you know you've achieved it. I remember one suspect, as if testing my honesty, asked, "Am I going to jail?" "Of course you are, if I can prove you're guilty," I replied. "But then you knew that, didn't you?" "Well, at least you didn't try to bullshit me otherwise," he said. By answering him honestly, I demonstrated that I was trustworthy. Perhaps it was no coincidence that he later asked me to call his family to let them know he had been arrested. He didn't think his less-than-trustworthy friends would. I did reach out to his family, and they in turn helped me out with other matters.

On my own, retired from the FBI after twenty-five years, I felt I had to prove myself all over again. I no longer had those FBI credentials I could flash that said I was a representative of the United States, here under the authority of the attorney general. My current credentials as a civilian are the same as yours. What is that common credential that you and I carry? Demonstrable trustworthiness. That you and I are allowed into someone's home or into an office and have access to everything of value in those venues, from children to accounting books, is based on that credential—trust based on performance.

In business, trustworthiness and credibility amalgamate into your professional reputation. If you think people don't assess your professional reputation, you're deluding yourself. Whether they call for references, check out your social media, or informally call someone who knew you at your old job, people want to know what your reputation is. It matters.

Stephen R. Covey wrote, "If you want to be trusted, be trustworthy." What does trustworthiness look like on the ground? It's based on everything you've read thus far and this: we become trustworthy when we demonstrate consistently and unequivocally that we care about others, fulfill our obligations, and reliably act in furtherance of others.

Recall some moments in your life when someone let you down. When there was no action, or action was taken carelessly, reluctantly, too slowly, with indifference, or worse, with the intention to harm. Perhaps you feel an emotional or physical response just thinking about these disappointing experiences.

Now, recall when someone expedited your needs, made your life better by removing undue burdens, or made you feel special, cared for, or safer. You may feel warm inside just remembering. This, too, happens because of an action someone took—maybe not always perfectly, but *with an intent to care that you trusted*. This is what distinguishes the trustworthy. Decades on, I can remember with such clarity people I've met and worked with who never faltered, who could be counted on, who were reliable and consistent. How fondly they remain in my mind. What a gift it is to find perennially reliable individuals who consistently act in our best interest—individuals we can trust to care.

Do My Actions and Behavior Add Value?

Exceptional action doesn't just meet the needs of the moment. It seeks to improve, make better, augment, or elevate not just in the present but in the future. To add value to a situation or to an individual through action, the action must apply or infuse something of value—tangible or intangible. Perhaps it's insight, expertise, creativity, leadership, funding, energy, tenacity, or professional skills. Perhaps it's something physical that you can do for others that they can't do for themselves.

Exceptional individuals don't live by the self-serving and limiting concept of *quid pro quo* ("something for something"). They help and act because doing so is intrinsically rewarding. When I help a neighbor I've never met before lift something into her car, I don't expect anything in return. She may see me more kindly or appreciatively; it may make her consider me a reliable neighbor, but that's not why I do it. Whether I do it, you do it, or a company does it, goodwill has benefits, but they extend outward. As Adam Grant noted in his book *Give and Take*, it's the givers who in the end do best.

I vividly recall conducting a behavioral assessment for a client in New York. On each floor I visited, everyone kept saying, "Oh, you have to meet Henry." This went on for two days. But Henry was never around, it seemed, or was too busy. Finally on the third day, I said, "I'd love to meet Henry." People were surprised I hadn't. Now I was really curious. So Henry was officially summoned to meet with me.

Nothing remarkable, I thought on first impression. But then I thought about how everyone who mentioned him smiled when they did so. There was something here.

Henry was self-effacing, but he told me about himself. He had taught himself to work with computers, and he ran the IT department even though he was only a high school graduate. While we talked, various people walked by, and they all stopped to say hello to Henry. For everyone, he had a smile or a funny story.

When we were done, I understood why people had said "you have to meet" him. The value he added to that organization, beyond running the IT department, and helping anyone—including, as I learned, spouses at home who needed help setting up their latest Bluetooth-connected gizmo—was his sheer joy. He didn't just contribute his professional skills. He brought joy to his job, and he shared it with everyone. I'm willing to bet that "joy" wasn't anywhere in his job description—but Henry was doing it. The results were magnificent.

I got the impression that people sought him out regularly, as if they needed their daily dose of Henry. I was told when he was on vacation, people missed seeing him in the snack room. When I sat down for my final review with the three company executives after a week there, they all agreed, Henry was so much more than a technician. As the CEO noted, "My greatest fear is that one day he will leave. You are lucky if once in a few decades you find someone like that—just one." He was right.

Routine chores of life become pleasurable, even memorable, from such interactions. A colleague told me about a routine visit to her local pharmacy in search of a product she needed. As she scanned the shelves, a voice came from nearby: "Is there something specific you're looking for?" Yes, there was. Not only did the store clerk tell her where the product was, but she walked her to the right place. Once there, she pointed out the shelf signage indicating that two could be purchased for a discount, with use of the store rewards card.

My colleague didn't have a card and had no intention of getting one: "I'm a little intimidated by that stuff and I'm usually in a hurry, assume I'll run into problems, and don't want to spend the time." But she was tempted by the discount, because this product is sometimes hard to find. "In the most low-key way, the store clerk offered to go with me to the cashier when checking out and help me sign up—it's just a few questions, and then it's done. She was so relaxed and made it sound so easy. Before I knew it, I was signing up!"

The caring clerk stood nearby as the cashier started to ring up the purchases. That's when my colleague thought of an issue: she usually used the automated checkout because it was faster. She was worried about running into problems when trying to use the rewards card with the machine.

Now, incredibly, the cashier swung into caring action. Instead of just saying that the machine prompted customers to scan the card, "she offered to *walk me over there herself* and we'd do it together. And then she did!"

My colleague left with a good supply of what she was looking for, at a good price, feeling great about her experience with the staff at "her" store. The store made an extra product sale and added a customer to its mailing list. How is this not a win-win?

But it gets better. Later that day, a customer satisfaction survey arrived by email asking about her experience. My colleague gave glowing feedback and told the story in detail. Sometime after 9 P.M. that evening, she got a personal email from the store manager, thanking her for her feedback and sharing that the first helpful clerk had worked at the store for years and loves helping customers. He was still trying to figure out who the cashier was, but he said he had shared the story with everyone on the team, so they would know that their good work made a difference. He closed with a personal invitation to write him anytime with input and ideas, or to seek him out in the store.

As I've said: action has a weight all its own. What stories are your customers, colleagues, or friends telling about their experiences with you and your business? (What, you think they don't?)

There are many surprising ways like this that add value to the bottom line. Value can be enhanced by skills, of course, but upward valuation in quality is often tied not just to what we do, but *how* we do it, as discussed earlier—our attitude and demeanor. Going the extra mile, as they say, is really a personal choice. Commitment to excellence and pride in what you do are attitudes you can count on to bring value to all you do. They also inspire others to do the same. Dr. Martin Luther King Jr. said it eloquently: "If a man is called to be a street sweeper, he should sweep streets even as a Michelangelo painted, or Beethoven composed music, or Shakespeare wrote poetry. He should sweep streets so well that all the hosts of heaven and earth will pause to say, 'Here lived a great street sweeper who did his job well.'" Action as we define it—and as the exceptional apply it—is not just about doing our job. Action is taking things to that next level where we seek to add value to everything we do especially when it benefits others, whether they are aware of it or not.

Do My Actions Positively Influence or Inspire?

On May 27, 1992, in the city of Sarajevo, a mortar round descended on a group of people who had left their homes and braved sniper fire and shelling during the early stages of the Bosnian conflict, so they could buy bread from the only working bakery. The Bosnian conflict, which had already taken hundreds of lives, would be defined by cruelty, ethnic cleansing, inhumanity, and the most cowardly of acts. One of those acts of inhumanity would come to be reframed by the act of one man.

The mortar round landed at exactly 4:00 P.M. as the last rations of the day were being made available. It immediately killed twenty-two people, and more than one hundred were injured. Blood, human tissue, and brain matter spattered nearby buildings as high as the third floor. The smell of blood, explosives, burnt clothing, and human flesh permeated for days—a nauseating reminder of the trauma.

This act of mayhem—one of many, and by no means the last—was levied against a hungry, desperate, and beleaguered people who were being exterminated by mortar rounds, kidnappings, mass executions, or picked off one at a time by sniper fire.

Into the heart of this hell walked a man. Vedran Smailović had no weapon. He was not a soldier. He couldn't retaliate with skills of that kind. But he had two things going for him: he had been the principal cellist of the Sarajevo Opera Company—a distinguished opera house—and he cared.

He had to find a way to honor his fellow countrymen who twenty-four hours earlier had been killed or injured. And so this thirty-seven-year-old did the unthinkable, placing his life at risk, to venerate the dead and comfort the living. For the next twenty-two days, in remembrance of those killed, he took a chair to where the mortar round had left a crater, and there with cello in hand, wearing his performance tuxedo, Mr. Smailović played Albinoni's *Adagio in G Minor*, one of the most soulful pieces of music ever written, with the same fervor as if he were in a concert hall.

Why? Because it was what was needed. In the midst of unimaginable violence and death, one man cared deeply about his fellow citizens enough to act. He could do little but honor those he valued as best he could, using his skill as a musician. In doing so, he provided comfort and inspiration to an anxious and war-worn people.

Like all exceptional individuals, he asked himself: *What is needed right now? What can I do? How can I help?* A stirring song to ease the mind and the pain—this is what he gave.

Did his playing stop the Bosnian conflict? No. The war would continue for another three years. Did it save lives? Who can tell? But for about seven minutes each day, his music silenced terror and torment so that others might have a small respite. By playing with such love, devotion, and tenderness, he demonstrated in the midst of ruin and slaughter that humanity and kindness were still alive—and in that way, he gave his fellow citizens hope. In the process, quite unexpectedly, he also brought the attention of the world to the horrors that were taking place.

Reporters asked Mr. Smailović why he did it. His answer was simple: "I am a musician. I am part of this town. Like everyone else, I do what I can."

Doing what we can doesn't have to be heroic. Or even all that complicated. What are your circumstances? Can you make your world a little bit better? Can you pick up that garbage someone else threw out the car window near your home? Can you volunteer at the Y to help a child learn to read? Can you encourage someone in school not to quit? Can you smile at someone as they pass? Can you say to a colleague, "I can see you're busy, let me take care of this"? These are not heroic deeds. But there is always something more we can do to make the world better.

The influence of positive actions is doubled: not only do you have the potential to positively affect how others view you, but even better, you might influence positive attitude and action in others. Giving strength and succor to others lifts them toward finding those reserves in themselves. Positive actions for the benefit of others can help them to keep going even in dire situations, as Vedran Smailović found when he took up his cello and played his tribute to those who had fallen and for those who continued to endure.

Are My Actions and Behavior Prosocial?

All day long we do things necessary for our survival and well-being. But we're also presented with opportunities that affect others. When we act for the benefit of others, we are engaging in prosocial action.

Prosocial action is a step beyond caring. It is action to ameliorate. What a wonderful word *ameliorate* is. It means to make things better. That is what exceptional individuals do.

Exceptional individuals are attentive to their environment and to others—and without prompting, they seek to improve things. Not because they are ordered to or because it's their job, but because making things better matters to them.

Curtis Jenkins does that every morning when he gets behind the wheel of his yellow school bus, and no one has ever asked him to. His greatest satisfaction is not his paycheck, though I'm sure he appreciates that. No, his greatest satisfaction is to make life just a little bit better for each child who rides his bus to Lake Highlands Elementary in Dallas, Texas.

He knows their names. He also knows their birthdays, what they're interested in, what they've accomplished, who's struggling in what class, who needs a little more attention that day, who's having troubles at home, and who needs a little motivation or an extra smile. His job title is bus driver, with a duty to drive a bus safely and on time; that is all. But Mr. Jenkins is exceptional for those kids and that school because doing just enough to get the job done isn't good enough for him. He improves life for those children by being attentive to their needs and concerns. A word of encouragement here, a carefully crafted question there to let a shy girl speak up about her latest accomplishment, a little gift to inspire a budding writer.

If you ask the kids who ride his bus, they'll tell you the small gifts he carefully selects and gives to them are just the icing on the cake. What they look forward to is simply being in the presence of Curtis Jenkins. His smile, his caring comments, his interest, his vicarious joy when they're having a good day, and the love he has for each and every one of them—all demonstrate his genuine wish to make their lives better. Even more beautiful than the word *ameliorate* is seeing it in action. Curtis Jenkins practices it every day.

Exceptional individuals anticipate problems before they happen— or get worse. They grasp the implications of situations and emotional realities and seem able to penetrate to essences in understanding the concerns at hand, thus shaping an appropriate response. In the workplace, they don't need a Human Resources manual of dos and don'ts because their prosocial actions are rooted in respect for others and a desire to address their needs and aspirations—they are, in the full sense of the word, apperceptive. Just this precept applies: all action must be befitting of others. It is the very basis of ethics. When we say "he stepped up" or "she went above and beyond" about someone's performance at work, we're often praising the prosocial quality of their actions—the time, positive energy, and care they put in to produce a superior result that does the company proud. In a community, when we recognize the efforts of someone who tirelessly worked with the homeless shelter or animal rescue, with children who need help after school, or with the elderly or others in need, we are recognizing the prosocial actions of exceptional people.

Motives matter when it comes to defining prosocial action. We all know people who engage in seemingly prosocial action when they want or need something in return. Authentic prosocial action is performed without an agenda. Indeed, it's like a gift in which the gift is in the giving.

We don't always know the full effects of our prosocial actions—and it shouldn't really matter, because the reward is in the doing. It is one of life's beautiful mysteries that we have this capability at our disposal to employ in the world, with ripples of results extending, perhaps infinitely, we know not where. Maybe you remember someone who did something—a small thing or a large thing—that, for you, at that moment in your life, was transformative. For me, one such person was Mrs. Lightbourne.

Mrs. Lightbourne and her son, Michael, lived a few blocks from us. Her house, you might say, lacked curbside appeal and her furniture should have long ago been donated, but we neighborhood kids didn't care. What Mrs. Lightbourne had in abundance was love for all of us. That was what mattered. We all hung out at her house because it was a comfortable place where we could gather, laugh, and play. We didn't even have to knock. We were always welcomed and fed. Where she got the money to feed us, I don't know, because teenagers can eat a lot. She knew all of us inside out and she always knew what to say, what to ask, and how to make us smile.

In the months after I left the hospital following my stabbing, I struggled. I'd spent three weeks in the hospital and my recovery had been delayed due to nerve damage, blood loss, and infection. The pain in my arm, the inability to move my fingers in a coordinated fashion, missing the final months of my senior year of high school, the uncertainty about what my future would hold—including losing scholarship options—weighed heavily on me. For the first time in my life, I felt mentally down. My mind was foggy, I was losing interest in people and things. It was not a good time. Unbeknownst to me at the time, I was suffering the effects of post-traumatic stress disorder (PTSD), though no one called it that back then. The latent effect from this event, beyond this period of low-grade depression, was that for decades thereafter, just seeing a knife in the hand of someone in the kitchen caused me to shake and have panic attacks. I tried to pretend everything was okay, but it wasn't. *I* wasn't—how could I have been? I think some people around me picked up on that.

Mrs. Lightbourne had visited me in the hospital early on, but I hadn't seen her in a while. After I was released from the hospital, while still in recovery mode with daily visits to a physical therapist to work the arm and learn to use my fingers again, I tried to avoid everyone. But somehow, Mrs. Lightbourne was keeping track of me through my friends. The day before graduation she called and said get up, get out of the house, get some fresh air, and come over, I want to see you.

It brightened my day and in no time, we were catching up. She asked how I was and said that she'd heard I was not feeling well emotionally. I told her I had sort of withdrawn and that college now seemed only a dream as the scholarships had vanished and we had little money for school. We talked about how I would make up the work missed from school. *It would be a miracle if I graduated*, I thought. After a while and to my surprise she brought out some brownies, knowing they were my favorite. This story would have a great ending just here, with my favorite treat.

But that is not where it ended. Near the end of our conversation and after I had devoured most of the brownies, she went to her room and came out with a little box, about the size of a jeweler's box, wrapped in the same kind of tinfoil she used to cover the brownies. I told her that if it was money, I would not accept it. She said she had no money to give me, that it was just a little something for me to remember her.

I promised Mrs. Lightbourne I would honor her request that I not open the box until graduation morning. We hugged and talked some more, but not for very long as my arm was still in a sling, my left shoulder was still somewhat swollen, and I was feeling the discomfort of the stitches on the inside of the arm. While I was very curious as to what was in the box as I walked home, I left it alone as promised.

Graduation day came, and it was an exciting time as I was,

fortunately, able to complete my studies and graduate. There was the whirl of activity at my house as we got ready to head out to the ceremony. Just before we left, my mom asked if I had opened the box from Mrs. Lightbourne. I hadn't, so with everyone gathered, I did.

I peeled away the aluminum foil—which she had pleated to make it even more special—and the first thing we noticed was that the box itself was handmade from the remnants of a discarded shoebox, as some lettering was still visible. She had carefully cut the box down and folded and taped the cardboard to form a two-by-two-inch box. How long she worked at putting that together I can only guess, but I know it must have taken her a while.

When I opened the box, there, sitting on a small wad of cotton was a dime—all of ten cents. Next to it was a small folded piece of paper. On the paper was written: "If you ever need anything, don't hesitate to call." For those of you who are too young to remember, a dime back then was all you needed to make a phone call from a telephone booth.

My whole family stared at that dime in silence for several seconds. They then looked up at me, looked back at the dime, and then we all began to wipe away tears.

It was only a dime in a homemade box. Yet nearly fifty years later, this is the only gift I remember from my youth—the most valued and treasured. A reminder that not only did Mrs. Lightbourne care about me and was concerned, but by presenting it as she did, she demonstrated just how much she valued me. She had done what all exceptional people do—what each of us can do, even by the smallest of acts—she had assessed, in this case, my emotional needs and turned a mere transaction into something transformational by the value her actions expressed to me.

Ready for Action at the Exceptional Level

Imagine that you're thirty-three years old and a group of your colleagues from all over the nation, each with their own special interests, comes to you and says, in essence, "If you're not too busy, how about drafting a Declaration of Independence? We need you to put together something that lets the King of England know we have major issues being his subjects. Keep in mind it has to be perfectly argued so everyone (we hope!) will support it. Make sure to note clearly our justification and what we stand for—and though it's not found anywhere else on the planet, make a convincing case for this novel idea that 'all men are created equal.' Also, if it isn't too much bother, the document must set forth these ideas with such reasoned logic, stirring rhetoric, and moral justification that we will be compelled to sign it and live by its tenets, despite knowing that the moment we do so, we will be committing treason, a capital offense, against a sovereign. Oh, and one more thing: you have to write it with a feather quill (goose, swan, turkey—your pick), on animal parchment, keep mistakes to a minimum, and with perfectly legible penmanship so that it will be easy to read."

Who among us, at any age, would be up to such a challenge, then or now?

As it turned out, there was one person, but just one, who could fulfill those requirements in 1776. Only Thomas Jefferson, "the Sage of Monticello," could do it—because he was ready to act at an exceptional level. As Lincoln noted in 1859:

> *"All honor to Jefferson—to the man who, in the concrete pressure of a struggle for national independence by a single people, had the coolness, forecast, and capacity to introduce into a merely revolutionary document, an abstract truth, applicable to all men and all times . . ."*

Today, the Declaration of Independence is secured in the Library of Congress, encased in a bombproof transparent casing infused with argon gas that rests securely on a specially built titanium frame attached to an elaborate aluminum conveyor that can retract the near-holy document into a vault deep underground that can sustain,

I have been told on good authority, a nuclear attack on the nation's capital. There is no other document on planet Earth, or for that matter in the known universe, that is so revered and protected. And why? Because one person was ready to act at an exceptional level.

What prepared Jefferson to be able to write such a document—a death warrant for every signator, so exquisitely argued and eloquently written that it would affirm the resolve of those involved and stand the test of time to become a touchstone to others seeking to risk their lives to carve out their own freedom and equality?

He had that scaffolding of self-mastery that we've talked about, to be sure. But he had one thing more: he was ready for action at an exceptional level. How did he accomplish that? By one particular action he took each day.

We tend to think of action as being outward-facing—what we do out there in the world—perhaps a physical act. That might have been the case in an earlier century, but our actions today are mostly intellectually driven—for example, analyzing, ideating, and forecasting—for better problem-solving, decision-making, and innovation. For that, we need a daily dose of knowledge and information. Today, if we're to have any chance of success at all, action begins with what Louis Pasteur extolled: a "prepared mind."

Buckminster Fuller pointed out in 1950 that human knowledge doubled approximately every century up until the 1900s. By the end of World War II, knowledge was doubling every twenty-five years. Today, depending on what field you're in, knowledge is growing at a tsunami level of velocity and intensity. In nanotechnology, knowledge is doubling every two years. Medical knowledge is doubling every eighteen months according to some, or as often as every seventy-three days, by some authoritative estimates. Not in a specialty field? You're still not exempt: knowledge in general, according to the experts, is doubling every thirteen months, with some arguing that it may actually be doubling every twenty-four hours.

Just think about that—by this time tomorrow, the world's knowledge may have doubled. The only way to keep up is by doing what

Jefferson did every day. He stayed on top of current trends, novel ideas, philosophical thought, and technological and scientific advancements by reading daily—the best technology available in his time. Only by taking action to prepare his mind was he able to act at an exceptional level in the clutch: to bring all his knowledge to bear to make a quantum leap forward when nothing less would do.

If you want to act at an exceptional level and give yourself the best chance to compete effectively in any business, dedicate yourself to keeping up with knowledge, breakthroughs, trends, discoveries, and new ideas. Always important, it's now the new standard, as knowledge changes so fast that it's quickly obvious when you're not up to speed. As author Mary Renault said, "There is only one kind of shock worse than the totally unexpected: the expected for which one has refused to prepare."

When four-star marine general and former secretary of defense James Mattis was asked why he made the time to read each day, he replied, "Thanks to my reading, I have never been caught flat-footed by any situation, never at a loss for how any problem has been addressed (successfully or unsuccessfully) before. It doesn't give me all the answers, but it lights what is often a dark path ahead." This highly accomplished general, who went on to become President Trump's defense secretary, credits his leadership success not to his fighting skills as a marine, but to his "reading habits."

General Mattis noted that as a warrior, he could avoid mistakes others had made, having read about them. What for some were new tactics in the twenty-first century, he had already read about from writings in the third century or even from the time of the Peloponnesian War.

While heading Microsoft, Bill Gates would take "Think Weeks"—solo retreats where he read papers submitted by his employees on what they thought was trending in technology. And even though he is highly accomplished and one of the wealthiest men in the world he still reads exhaustively, as he often notes on social media. His example illustrates that the more responsibility we have for others—in

Gates's case, his business and philanthropic endeavors—the greater our responsibility to take action based on knowledge we actively accumulate as our personal well of wisdom.

How you get your daily dose of knowledge—what you read, listen to, or view, or what lectures, professional groups, or trainings you attend—is up to you. But to act exceptionally today, you must stay in step with information and knowledge (rules, laws, regulations, trends, inventions, circumstances, market forces, political realities and instability, changing expectations and demands, social movements, philosophical ideas) that is growing so quickly. It is the exceptional way.

Redefining Heroes

There are scores of books on Medal of Honor winners—people who placed their lives in danger for the benefit of others. If you read their stories closely, you'll find a striking similarity: not one of them set out to be a hero. Their actions became heroic due to one simple yet powerful catalyst: they cared. They cared for their comrades, their buddies, their fellow marines, the guy next to them wearing the same uniform, their "band of brothers." There's no hero gene in our DNA. No ON switch for heroic behaviors. The only requirement is that you care. It wasn't heroism that made me try to stop a pair of armed robbers. It was simply about caring—I didn't want someone else to get robbed or hurt. When you care, you have courage to act, not the other way around.

Caring can be defined as acting in ways that are prosocial, offered when needed the most, and intended to benefit, elevate, honor, or value others. In other words, we venerate others through our caring actions.

Exceptional caring is the mother of exceptional acts. It is what enables someone to sit down in the rubble of a war zone and play an elegy on their cello. It empowers us to blow the whistle on unprincipled actions. It elevates us to be someone who, in our own way, takes action to ameliorate—whether we're driving a bus, running a business, or leading a nation.

Most of us will never be called upon to do heroic things in the way that Medal of Honor winners are. Yet everyday life presents us with plenty of opportunities to take action, and at times to do something others might consider notable or extraordinary, perhaps even heroic. Sometimes it's what we do; sometimes—as the stories of Henry, Curtis Jenkins, and the staff at the local pharmacy reveal—it's how we do it. At those times, we will act depending on how much we care.

The more we live this commitment, the easier it becomes, until something transformative happens: we are the ones who become known for caring. Not because we say we care, but because of *what we do that shows we care.*

When we care, we positively shape how we're perceived—even when, as will happen at times, we fail. Our actions in furtherance of others can carry influence beyond what we can imagine. What that is, we may never know. The fact that we failed must not keep us from trying again. We must resolve to learn from those actions, not beat ourselves up or retreat because we failed. Basketball superstar Michael Jordan said: "I've missed more than nine thousand shots in my career. I've lost almost three hundred games. Twenty-six times I've been trusted to take the game-winning shot and missed. I've failed over and over and over again in my life. And that is why I succeed." He succeeded because in the end he cared: he practiced hard, he played hard, and he triumphed mightily even though he failed at times.

If you should fail, even as I failed that day at Richard's Department Store, remember these words that Theodore Roosevelt spoke to a graduating class of police officers in Paris at the Sorbonne, sixty-one years to the day before I was stabbed:

> *"It is not the critic who counts; not the man who points out how the strong man stumbles, or where the doer of deeds could have done them better. The credit belongs to the man*

who is actually in the arena, whose face is marred by dust and sweat and blood; who strives valiantly; who errs, and comes short again and again, because there is no effort without error and shortcoming; but who does actually strive to do the deeds; who knows the great enthusiasms, the great devotions; who spends himself in a worthy cause; who at the best knows in the end the triumph of high achievement, and who at the worst, if he fails, at least fails while daring greatly, so that his place shall never be with those cold and timid souls who know neither victory nor defeat."

I've always taken solace in those words. Though we may fail, at least we acted. Roosevelt's "great devotions and enthusiasms" are what today we call caring.

When it comes to human beings, only one thing matters—that you care and care deeply. Why this is so, and how to make caring a more intentional part of your life and interactions, is what the next chapter is about.

We started this chapter with the question of knowing how to act. If you care, you never have to worry about how you'll act. That decision has already been made. Then it's just a matter of unleashing the creativity, talents, passion, abilities, and skills you've carefully nourished in your mind and heart.

CHAPTER 5

Psychological Comfort

THE MOST POWERFUL STRENGTH HUMANS POSSESS

———

By grasping the foundational truth that what humans ultimately seek is psychological comfort, we can discover what exceptional people know: that whoever provides psychological comfort through caring wins.

> I believe that every human mind feels pleasure in doing good to another.
>
> —Thomas Jefferson

When the stock market collapsed in 2008, sending economies worldwide shuddering into near arrest and throwing millions into financial free fall, panicked investors turned to their financial advisers. The advisers were in a quandary because no one, and I mean no one, knew what would happen next. But they had to say something.

Most financial organizations went into overdrive, sending emails, scheduling conference calls, providing historical charts, graphs, and general bromides that basically stated, "We know things are bad, we have no answers, but based on our knowledge of history, there is hope." But that wasn't what individual investors needed. What they sought was something else.

Things were rough enough that financial institutions started contacting me, asking, "You're the communications expert—what can we do to satisfy and keep our clients and investors?" My answer was unequivocal: "Stop talking and start listening. What your clients need you to do is provide psychological comfort, not advice."

I was flown to New York to explain myself. They felt there had to be more to it than that. There wasn't, not at that crisis moment. After decades of observing human behavior in crisis situations, I learned that when things are really bad, we humans don't seek answers so much as psychological comfort.

These nervous executives weren't convinced at first. They'd worked hard and prepared all sorts of informational literature for their customers, as was their practice. It was how they thought they could "help."

Information is valuable, I acknowledged. But when we are scared, what we need is someone to be human and to just listen. I urged them to visit their major clients, and even to hug them if they needed it (some did). Above all, they needed to listen to people's fears. Humans gravitate to and will remain loyal to those who ultimately provide them with calm and assured psychological comfort.

So that's what these executives did. They stopped speculating and started listening. At a conference three years later when things were starting to turn around in the financial and housing markets, one of them came up to me and said, "You were right. We didn't know crap about what was going on, and our clients knew we didn't know. But they were grateful we were there for them, to listen to them."

It's been illuminating to see an even more striking replication of this phenomenon during the COVID-19 pandemic in 2020, which is ravaging the world as I write these words. In mere weeks, our lives and livelihoods have been so upended that many wonder whether social and working life will ever be the same. Early on, graphic photos from Milan and New York City morgues as well as the massive economic upheaval permeated the news, which was amplified on social media. There has been so much uncertainty about this virus, its scope, its deadliness, and how to avoid or treat it that almost every mental health professional I have talked to has mentioned the uptick in anxiety, tension, panic attacks, even domestic violence.

The more uncertain the times and the greater the stress, the more humans need psychological comfort. As the world copes with the social and economic fallout from this pandemic while anticipating ways to dampen or obliterate recurrences as they flare, we will see who among our leaders is better at mobilizing communities toward cohesive, prosocial action that will not only keep them safe from this virulent contagion, but also will provide psychological comfort.

While extraordinary events such as these attest to the need for psychological comfort, in truth, we need it every day. It is the culminating chapter in this book for two reasons. First, because caring is so singularly important that I want to leave you with it as the book's ultimate message. And second, because of the hundreds of books I've read on leadership and influence, they seem to have forgotten this reality: whoever provides psychological comfort wins.

It's one thing to understand this truth, but quite another to practice it actively as a matter of habit. Psychological comfort comes in many forms and varies under different circumstances. A calm, soothing voice can do the trick one minute; an approving glance, another. It could be a pat on the back, a kind word, an acknowledgment, a verbal validation of something long suppressed, a warm blanket, a cup of hot tea, a kiss on the forehead, a thank-you note, a smile, stepping forward to meet the new arrival, carrying a package for someone in need, asking if anything further is needed.

Psychological comfort takes many different guises. But to provide it, we must be prepared and willing. We must be able to observe or anticipate what is needed or what would contribute to the well-being of another and be ready to act on it. This is where the other four domains we've discussed—Self-Mastery, Observation, Communication, and Action—unite to form an elegant supportive structure and feedback system that will guide and direct you to fully develop and achieve the highest levels of influence, goodwill, and that most prized of attributes: trustworthiness. It begins and ends with the capacity to instill psychological comfort.

In this chapter, we'll look at the scientific underpinnings of psychological comfort and its primacy in our lives, and then at a model I've developed and have used successfully for many years to assess for and provide psychological comfort in real time, while working toward goals and objectives.

Psychological Comfort: A Primal Necessity

We are babies.

I'm sure you didn't anticipate reading those words in a book such as this. But our need to be comforted never leaves us.

Our quest for comfort begins at birth. Babies cry to express discomfort: they're cold, hungry, wet, or in pain. Our body systems are constantly making minute adjustments to keep us comfortable—cooling or warming us through sweat or shivering, to maintain homeostasis. Many of our nonverbal habits are rooted in our need for psychological comfort, from sucking our thumbs as babies to chewing gum vigorously as adults.

As we mature, our quest for comfort simply takes different forms. We trade the soothing safety of being rocked in a parent's arms or gently swaddled in a blanket for a warm hug or the comfort of a soft bed. We trade cooing noises, early smiles, and playful exchanges with our parents for the familiar tones of a loved one's voice and a welcoming face. We never lose our need to touch, to socialize, to engage, to have good times—it just looks different at each stage of life. Greetings from playmates are replaced with "likes" on social media. The beloved stuffed toy or raggedy pillow that accompanied us everywhere in childhood might today be a pet on our lap or within reach. We relax and nap on the couch instead of in a cradle.

We are a species that has devised innumerable ways to orchestrate contentment for our psychological comfort. From sipping morning coffee to surfing the web; from playing cards to binge-watching Netflix—we actively seek psychological comfort in its many forms. I do it every time I sit in the sun with a good book, headphones playing cello renditions of Ennio Morricone's voluminous works, as do you in your own unique way. And, if we choose, we can assist others in achieving it. In fact, if we are kind and generous, that's usually what we seek to do for others.

I define psychological comfort as a state of being where our biological, physical, and emotional needs are met or exceeded, and there is an absence of anxiety, apprehension, or fear that satisfies our needs and preferences, provides tranquility, or that allows us to enjoy a moment or an experience fully.

That is why we soothe the baby, massage our necks as we do our taxes, swing gently in a hammock, watch the sunset, hug our daughter in triumph after the soccer game, or practice what the Dutch call *niksen*—the art of doing nothing, according to behavior specialist Anne-Maartje Oud. It's also why we are constantly touching ourselves—stroking our chins, running our fingers through or twisting our hair, massaging our earlobes. These actions pacify and self-soothe, creating psychological comfort. Indeed, psychological comfort is so important to our species that after we die, loved ones may arrange that we be placed in a luxuriously padded coffin, often with a soft pillow to cushion our head. A purely symbolic gesture indicating how important psychological comfort is to us: to honor others, we provide them with comfort, even in death.

Psychological comfort drives many of our everyday choices. Did you ever wonder when you go to buy toothpaste why there's so much variety? After all, though some may have a little more of this or that, they're all basically the same. Still, I bet you're loyal to your brand. Just as you're loyal to a particular soap, deodorant, shampoo, or other product. How you got there, through trial and error, or perhaps at the insistence of your parents, is a testament to the human

need for what I call *preferred variability*. Preferred variability—
your choices in food, snacks, toiletries, footwear, and much else—
reflects the highly nuanced preferences you've developed over the
course of your life and gravitate toward for your personal psychological comfort.

Conversely, whenever psychological discomfort happens—and I
mean *whenever*—we may resist, turn away, or object. Resentment
builds, negative impressions are formed, and we may be disappointed at best, frustrated or angry at worst. Our aversion is swift
and consistent. Once again, we see the primacy and importance of
psychological comfort—and why it was left for last in this book.

Psychological comfort has physical and mental components. Both
need to be addressed. While it feels great to have clothes that fit well,
to live in a comfortable home, or to lie on a beach with warm, pow-
dery sand under our toes and diaphanous blue waters to delight our
eyes and soothe our bodies, there's more to life than physical comfort. If you're upset about how you're being treated at work or in a
relationship, none of those other things matter because there is no
psychological comfort.

When you hear that stress is a killer, it's not just a figure of speech.
Stress contributes to heart and vascular disease, eats away at our
immune systems, and much more. What is stress but the opposite of
psychological comfort?

The research is ample: we're healthier physiologically, psychologically, even cognitively when we have psychological comfort. We
perform better in almost all tasks, think better, and live longer,
healthier lives. Just the psychological comfort of having a pet will
increase our life expectancy by several years. Having a supportive
spouse or a partner has shown in repeated studies to expand our life
span. Having a hobby increases our longevity. Whether by focusing
our attention away from stressful matters through social interaction,
or through the power of touch and the release of oxytocin, all of
these contribute to a healthy life as well as a happy one.

Psychological comfort is about more than elevating our mood or satisfying our preferences. It forms the bedrock of our mental and physical health as well as our enduring relationships, and in no small way, as you will see, shapes how we view and navigate a dynamic and at times precarious world. Two classic experiments in particular drive home the importance and the power of psychological comfort.

The "Visual Cliff" Experiment

In the first experiment, a baby between the ages of nine and twelve months is placed on a table topped by a plexiglass sheet covering a checkerboard pattern visible beneath. As the baby crawls on the glass, attracted by a toy on the other side of the table, the baby comes to what appears to be a precipice. It's merely an optical illusion created by the researchers—at no time is the child in this experiment or in the countless others in danger. Approaching the precipice, the baby always stops—even at a young age they somehow know that a precipice is dangerous. The baby inches near the edge . . . then looks to find the mother's face where she waits at the other side of the table. If the baby's mother smiles and nods with confidence, encouraging the baby to go on, the child is far more likely to continue to crawl right over that perceived chasm. If the mother does not look, avoids making eye contact, or frowns at the baby (making a "fear face"), the child usually stops or turns back. By communicating non-verbally to the child that it is okay, the mother is imbuing the child with psychological comfort. And with that reassuring comfort, the child continues exploring.

Psychological comfort is so powerful that something as small as an encouraging look or a smile, even when we're very young, can help us summon the fortitude to do something we perceive as dangerous. Such is the influence our smile alone can have on others to overcome fear.

Our quest for comfort escalates in times of stress. Isn't that what we're seeking when our plane hits turbulence, luggage bins are flying open, people gasp at how violently the plane is shaking—and we look around for that calm and composed face of a flight attendant or a fellow passenger that says, *It's going to be okay*?

Sometimes it may be a difficult task that you aren't sure you can complete or that takes sacrifice. But the fact that others are rooting for you is what gets you through. That is what exceptional people do. They have the wisdom and capacity to lift us, inspire us. Somehow, they know precisely what is needed at that moment: those words, that reassuring look that in just a few seconds heartens us to push forward. It's no different from that baby looking to its mother to see if it is okay to cross the artificial "abyss."

Conversely, we can ruin someone's day, erode confidence, and negatively influence by failing to acknowledge or even smile at others. How many times have we sought an approving look or even just to be noticed by someone we love or respect or who is higher up in an organization, and they fail to provide it? Or worse, there's an expression of scorn, disdain, or a blank look of indifference, as though we're beneath notice. When you consider that we absorb these messages even as babies and toddlers, it gives one pause to think of the cumulative effects of the blank or careless looks someone might have received as a child, at home, in school, on the job. Who can measure the negative effects, the efforts stymied, the goals, projects, and dreams not pursued?

The "Still Face" Experiment

The second landmark experiment was done in the 1970s by Edward Tronick with pediatrician T. Berry Brazelton and is referred to as the "Still Face" experiment. A mother and a baby (they varied in age in multiple experiments) sit face-to-face in a room, playfully interacting. A few times the mother looks away and back, and each time she smiles and giggles, as does the baby. But then, on cue, the mother looks away, and this time when she faces the baby again, she has a "still face"—showing no reaction whatsoever to the baby.

From the baby's perspective, it's a *What happened?* moment. The baby looks at the mother, waiting for the expected smile or happy eyes (wide, engaging eyes). But there's nothing but a blank face. The baby keeps looking at first, then turns away, then looks back. The baby acts out to try to get a response, to no avail. At this point, some of the babies "kind of collapse," as Dr. Tronick reported, or lose "postural control"—in other words, their arms and legs flail. They may "look at the mother out of the corner of their eyes," as if suspicious, "but they don't turn to her," as they normally would. They become sad and "have a helpless look." It is wrenching to watch: in a matter of seconds, the babies become troubled, anxious, even inconsolable.

That a baby could pick up on emotions of the face at that early stage of development stunned the scientific community. This experiment showed that we are hardwired to look for these visual cues because they provide a very vital necessity—psychological comfort—and when it is not forthcoming, this negatively affects us. One could argue that these babies lose their trust of even their mothers when there is a lack of facial engagement.

As it is for babies, so it is for us. I have run this experiment in my classes over the last two decades and almost invariably, having been genial most of the seminar, when I turn and present a still face to an attendee, they almost always show signs of psychological discomfort, adjust themselves in their seats, become tense, and look around at others as if to validate or ask whether they did anything wrong. In an instant, the positive momentum in our interaction stops as they try to resolve what's gone awry—simply by several seconds' denial of the psychological comfort we derive from a normally responsive human face.

As convincing as these experiments are, perhaps the greatest evidence of the power of psychological comfort comes not from experiments but from the reality that orphaned children experienced under Nicolae Ceaușescu's regime in Romania in the 1980s and 1990s. A Soviet-styled government was indifferent to these children, and perennial mismanagement led to decades of chronic understaffing, lack of funding, corruption, malfeasance, inadequate nutrition, the absence of the most basic medical care. But the greatest damage was done by denying those children basic human contact—not a hug, not even a cursory human touch, no holding while crying.

Researchers found that the children, lacking any kind of psychological comforting, were underdeveloped, having to self-stimulate to the point where they would rock constantly, their arms flailing uncontrollably. As they grew up, they had little to no trust in other humans. Their brains were in a constant state of arousal as if in imminent danger—perceiving the world and adults as fear-inducing. Many never recovered even after being adopted, suffering neurological, learning, psychological, and adaptive problems, their brains permanently altered, unable to establish bonds or to trust.

No doubt this is extreme, but it makes the point. We humans need and thrive with psychological comfort. In its absence, we can become hesitant, fearful, or even damaged. When psychological comfort is temporarily or periodically disrupted, it can be forgiven and can even make us more resilient. But when this disruption is repeated (preoccupied parent, inattentive boss, institutional indifference) and prolonged, it can be psychologically wounding and destructive. Lack of caring in whatever form, over time, can be devastating—for children, families, organizations, and communities. The resulting psychological discomfort plays out as mistrust, apathy, failure to participate, unwillingness to step forward to help or take a stand, reluctance to get involved, even reluctance to vote.

Every day in the US and around the world children and adults are denied psychological comfort, be they in a war zone, or as refugees, or because of uncaring parents, employers, or city governments. The damage done is immeasurable. What exceptional individuals do is recognize that where others fail, they must prevail. They know it is up to them, that it is their duty to provide that psychological comfort, just as we would give water to the thirsty or oxygen to the ill.

Caring: The Bridge to Psychological Comfort

In previous chapters, we've discussed how the exceptional observe, communicate, and act with the intention to care—not to manipulate a certain result, but because they genuinely deeply care. What makes caring so pivotal? It is the catalyst that drives us to provide psychological comfort for others. When we care, the psychological comfort we provide is more timely, more plentiful, more noticeable, more meaningful, and more influential. I'm not talking here about institutional comfort—that we expect when we check into a clean and quiet hotel. I'm talking about person-to-person psychological comfort. This is the kind that has positive, even long-lasting effects.

We are primed to seek and receive this kind of comfort, and so it doesn't take a grand or expensive gesture—just the right one. Famed author and human rights advocate Aleksandr Solzhenitsyn wrote vividly of his dystopian incarceration during the Soviet era in *The Gulag Archipelago*. Mentally, physically, and spiritually he was worn down by backbreaking labor, the harshness of Siberian winters, the cruelty of guards, and starvation-level rations. His situation, like that of many political prisoners, was bleak, and he saw little reason to continue to live.

His desperation apparently did not go unnoticed. Solzhenitsyn writes that at the bleakest of his time there, when he felt all was lost, a skinny old prisoner unknown to him walked over and squatted down next to him. Without saying a word—as prisoners were forbidden to talk to each other—the man took a stick and traced in the dirt the sign of the Christian cross. He then got up and returned to his work, never saying a word or even looking at Solzhenitsyn.

From that simple cross in the dirt, Solzhenitsyn realized that he was not alone in his fight against the Soviet empire. Not alone in having a moral conscience. And it gave him hope. Even a symbol, provided at the right moment, can provide profound psychological comfort—in this case, as Solzhenitsyn said, motivating him to want to continue to "live another day."

How potent that story is. Perhaps in your life you've had someone say something to you at the right moment that made all the difference. As I described in the previous chapter, Mrs. Lightbourne's handwritten note, tucked alongside a dime in a humble cardboard box, certainly did that for me. I have a dear friend who, in her darkest hour of cancer treatment, was given hope by a doctor passing by who took a moment to say just the right thing at the right time—simply stopping to ask if she was okay as she sat quietly resting in a lobby chair before leaving the hospital. What is perhaps a small though well-intentioned act for one may be life enabling for another. That is often the minimum we can do for others—the right word at the right time. We must never hesitate to speak up and make life just a little bit better for others. But is there more?

Sometimes, caring spurs us to do things we never imagined, but they are immediately called for in order to provide psychological comfort.

While working on this book, I read about a child on the autism spectrum who became emotionally overwhelmed at the Universal Orlando theme park and had what his mother called an "autistic meltdown"—writhing on the ground as if in pain, "sobbing, screaming, rocking, hyperventilating, and truly struggling to breathe."

When an autistic child is overstimulated or is struggling, they act out in a way that for those who have never experienced it can be disturbing or even frightening. Usually, in these circumstances, there's not much we can do beyond being understanding. But one exceptional person, Jennifer Whelchel, a park-ride attendant, went further: she decided to provide psychological comfort.

Jennifer lay down on the floor next to the child in agony and allowed the boy to cry his heart out, all the while helping him to breathe more slowly. In lying down in harmony with him, she let everyone know that this was okay, and this was going to play out as it needed to play out, as the child needed it. And to those who dared gawk, who even thought to look twice, she asked them politely to move along and not to take pictures.

"She spoke to him so calmly, and while he screamed and sobbed, she gently kept encouraging him to let it all out." Within a short time, the boy began to calm down. He sat up, drank some water, and his emotional equilibrium was slowly restored. What did it take? Not someone scolding or dictating to him what to do, looking on judgmentally, or trying to ignore it—but someone who understood and who was willing to engage him by using her body language and her calming voice to provide much-needed psychological comfort.

There was no hurry to get this disturbance taken care of. There was only caring validation of the child's feelings of being emotionally overwhelmed.

To say this was extraordinary doesn't begin to cover it. You want to know what exceptional looks like? There it is, in the behavior of this gem of a human being. Selfless attention to others and providing psychological comfort immediately and efficiently when it is needed the most.

Are we all as prepared, observant, and ready to act as she was? And what if all leaders were like her? She's that and more. She is what I would call a person of consequence, a person who is worthy to lead. Not appointed to lead. Worthy to lead. How few of those there are.

Jennifer said later in an interview that "she wanted to be on his level to be able to connect with him, but also wanted to be sure he had his own space." Jennifer is not a special needs teacher. She has no training in psychology. She is the mother of two, had worked at Universal for about six years, and was to begin law school the next year. While she'd had sensitivity training, she had never done this before. Yet somehow, she recognized what to do to be effective, supportive, and nonconfrontational. She understood that autistic meltdowns happen, that they are not what most people think—a spoiled child throwing a fit—but that this was a transient emotional event that would pass, if given proper attention.

Why do acts like this make the news? Arguably because they're so rare. Only when we choose to make psychological comfort our default code of conduct, our *modus vivendi*, part of our character when it comes to others, can we truly call ourselves exceptional.

Jennifer needed no prompting; the catalyst to care was already active within her. She did what she thought needed to be done in that moment. Would you and I have done it the same way? Probably not. But that is the beauty of observing with situational awareness and seeking to communicate and act quickly and prosocially in a way that is sensitive to others' needs. Our response doesn't have to be perfect. It just has to ameliorate, in the view of the recipient. Humans don't seek perfection; they seek psychological comfort.

The exceptional learn to read the needs and preferences of others and adapt to contribute to psychological comfort. There are so many ways both large and small, as you've seen in this and in previous chapters. Empathy, humility, kindness, ethical comportment, proper decorum, honesty, generosity, stability, consistency, trustworthiness, an upbeat attitude, compassion, altruism, cooperation, magnanimity, even humor—all have their merits in contributing to psychological comfort. It's up to us to deliver how that will look.

Examples of providing extraordinary psychological comfort inspire us, but what about the everyday? How do we use the power of psychological comfort one-on-one, or in a small business gathering?

The Empathic Model for Social Interaction

As a young FBI agent, I was cautioned that the academy would teach me how to *do* my job—but that to *excel* at it, I'd have to master special skills on my own.

There was never any question of what my job entailed. I knew the goal was to get to the truth, get a confession, find the documents or the evidence, or obtain that small-but-all-important admission that would be helpful to the case. That required a skill set having nothing to do with how to gather evidence, apprehend a suspect, or conduct a SWAT operation. It was about succeeding in critical social interactions with the public, intense one-on-one interviews with criminals, often in dynamic situations where time was of the essence or it was difficult to establish rapport.

One capacity that served me well was my ability to assess others quickly, observing their needs, wants, desires, intentions, and particularly their concerns and fears. I was grateful for that and my early studies of nonverbal communication. I learned on the first day of work while responding to my first bank robbery in Phoenix, if you're slow to assess others, you miss opportunities you may never have again. That teller who seemed so nervous and so frightened of our agents asking questions was altogether too comfortable when she was robbed. Turns out, her boyfriend was the robber and she made sure she gave him really large bills. I missed that calmness on the tape, and so I conducted a less-than-stellar interview. I vowed never to miss that sort of cue again. Life doesn't wait for you to "get it." Life moves on, and quickly. We must be ready to observe and act.

As we explored in Chapters 2 and 3, observation and communication can help us answer important questions, if we take the time to ask them: Should I engage this person now, or should I wait? What signs suggest that they might be receptive or resistant? How do I deliver bad news? How do I validate their concerns and communicate that I screwed up but that I will fix things? How can I help us find common ground? How can I get my message across? How do I persuade them to invest in my idea or proposition? Did I say something that has turned them against me or made them suspicious? These are all valid questions that take place in business settings especially when we are dealing with people we are unfamiliar with.

Whether as an agent or as a businessperson, we all want to get to that transaction phase where the business gets done. But how do we get there?

Decades of assessing others, gauging how and when to interact, and building trust and rapport to positively influence and motivate people to cooperate with me led me to develop what I came to call the

Empathic Model for Social Interaction (EMSI). It's a simple, structured way to deal more effectively with people—those we know or those we don't.

The EMSI framework is a three-phase feedback loop that allows us to engage with others based on real-time observations rather than sticking to predetermined agendas. Too often, for example, even a seasoned salesperson is so focused on their "script" that they hope to cover that they're blind to what's happening right in front of them: that the person they're trying to engage is in a hurry, not in the mood, is losing interest, isn't impressed, or has already made up their mind.

In the FBI, I found the EMSI guide effective in establishing cooperation even with people who at first would have nothing to do with me. When I retired from the FBI, I found the model worked equally well in the business sector, where the better you can assess, adapt, and engage in real time, the greater your probability of successful transaction.

Empathic Social Interaction

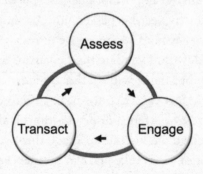

Copyright ©1984 Joe Navarro

Assess

Suppose you arrive at work and someone comes into your space and jumps right into: "Hi, this report came back—we have to add these last-minute budget projections and they need it by noon." Or you walk in the house after a long day and your mate or your child has a lot to say about something, and they need you to take care of it right away.

Life is full of these moments where the transactional dominates everything else. In essence this is the baseline of business ushered in by the industrial revolution, and in many places this practice still goes on.

But when it comes to influence, for the exceptional, there is a better way. I learned that in my work in the FBI early on. Solving a case is important, but how we get there can take many trajectories, and the most useful approach, I found, was a humanistic—that is, an empathic—one.

I quickly learned how critical it was to constantly assess each person I encountered or confronted so that I could communicate more effectively, because the success of my communication depended in large part on where they were psychologically. Stress, anxiety, fear, apprehension, distrust, or suspicion on the part of those being interviewed were detrimental to my ability to do my job. By caring enough to try to understand others, no matter how reprehensible their actions, I could open the possibility of establishing enough psychological comfort so that we could at least work together.

Time after time it was proven to me empirically that from within the space of psychological comfort, we are most productive and effective. It allows us to be in or as close to in synchrony as possible. As I often say, synchrony is harmony. We may not be in sync as to objectives, but if we can at least be in synchrony on an emotional level, then much more can be achieved.

Most people aren't interviewed by FBI agents. So they may feel intimidated, they may fear getting involved, they may worry how this might impact their job, what neighbors might think, or what this may do to their reputation at work. We assessed for these issues even in a brief encounter on a street corner. There was no point wasting our time or theirs if the person we were attempting to connect with was stressed, distracted, or hypersuspicious.

Once in the theater of the FBI interview room, one would think that getting to the facts is the most important issue. But for me, it was also important to assess for what was in the mind of the individual being interviewed at the moment, not just what they may have witnessed or participated in.

What did I assess for? Essentially the same things I assess for now: Who am I dealing with? Where are they emotionally? Are they stoic or talkative? What is their level of receptiveness? What is their background? What is their agenda? What do they want? Are they being reasonable? What do they fear? What do they know or not know? Is time of day a factor? Do we need a break? Do they want or need to talk about other things before we can circle toward my objective? As we converse, do I see changes in behavior that might indicate discomfort, dislike, hesitation, concern, or a wish to leave? Or do they seem more engaged, relaxed, less tense, more pensive, less combative, more cooperative?

Everything they did nonverbally or said, mattered. At each stage (initial greeting, notification of why they were being questioned, et cetera), I would gather as much information as I could through their words, hesitations, bodily reactions, how they positioned their hands (thumbs high/confident, thumbs low/less so) so I could then decide how to further engage them as I worked toward my objective (the transaction phase of the model): to get them to open up and talk to me or cooperate in some way.

In a business setting, the specific stakes and objectives may be different, but there's a fundamental similarity. Whether it's making a sale, negotiating a contract, or collaborating on a project or venture, the transaction won't happen unless there's opening up and cooperation between the parties. That can only happen through mutual understanding and respect. And *that* will only happen when there is psychological comfort.

Assessment is a continuous process of observation and situational awareness. You're ever vigilant for displays of comfort and, more importantly, discomfort, because these are very much revealed in real time. You're also looking for the nonverbals that reveal personal preferences (chooses a chair versus a couch), a comfortable personal distance (often farther away than we think), when there's a higher degree of comfort on their part (they lean back, stretch out arms, use their hands more, and in an open position), or the important social cues that demonstrate "turn yielding"—the intended opportunity given to you to speak your mind or, finally, to initiate the transaction phase.

For the exceptional, this assessment process continues throughout the encounter, right to the end. Never stop assessing, not even while you're saying good-bye. You never know what may be revealed even after a transaction is completed.

Key Questions for Assessment

Here are some things to consider and assess for before and during a meeting with others:

> **What do I know about them?** With social media, LinkedIn, Twitter, Facebook, YouTube, TikTok, you have many opportunities not only to see what someone looks like and to learn about their background, but also to observe and listen to them for the information we discuss in this book. You can pick up a lot from their podcasts, interviews, and videos, including talking style, subjects of interest, accomplishments, even personality. Information like this can help you to establish rapport more quickly if you know what to talk about and what to avoid, while observing for what may be characteristic displays of comfort or discomfort.

> **What's the meeting protocol?** When in doubt, I call ahead to determine how much time I can anticipate we'll have for the meeting. This is something I'll check on again once I arrive. I've found that office assistants, secretaries, even colleagues are more than willing to help. Knowing ahead of time where we'll be meeting (office, conference room, cubicle, public space, virtually) is also helpful. As I write this amid the COVID-19

pandemic, it's important to know what protocol is in place regarding mask-wearing. There are sometimes cultural protocols, too, to ascertain ahead of time.

> **What are their spatial needs?** Even before shaking hands (more about that below), one of our first responsibilities is to assess for the spatial needs of others. The moment someone violates our space, we become uncomfortable; it may even render us unable to remember what someone said. To protect against the negative impressions spatial violations leave, it is incumbent upon us to assess for spatial needs that are cultural (in some cultures people like to stand very close; you see that in the Caribbean); or it may be personal (I prefer to have people no closer than three feet). Then there's the situational factor: at a party I may tolerate someone standing closer, but not in a business meeting, and certainly not when I'm around strangers on the street. To maximize face time, we must be careful to not violate spatial needs.

One quick way to assess for spatial needs: When I shake hands (if the person is comfortable doing so—and that's easy enough to just ask—even flu season can be a reason why some people would rather not shake), I lean in, making sure that my torso is at least four feet distant, so each party is leaning forward and extending their arms about two feet or so. If the person smiles and retracts their hand after shaking and does not move, I then maintain that distance, as that is probably comfortable for them. If the person moves back a step, then I know they need that extra space, and I respect that. If they move closer, then I know that is their more favored distance. Spatial needs are crucial, including your own, so if *you* need to back up a little, do so.

Another spatial tip: from my own experience in creating comfort, I know that by just angling my torso away a bit, I can make others more comfortable. In other words, don't continue to stand directly in front of someone.

Keep in mind that as people converse, they may move around each other or closer to each other. Changes like these should be noted as part of assessing psychological comfort and for progress in establishing trust and rapport.

> **What else might be going on?** Continually assess for factors that may disrupt a person's comfort level. Look for the usual culprits: limited time, dislike of meetings, hunger, fatigue, even nicotine withdrawal. At a meeting once I noticed a man moving a lot in his chair. He seemed to be restless. At first, I thought it was simple fatigue, as we had all been at it for a while. Then I noticed the nicotine-stained fingers of his right hand and realized he needed and wanted a cigarette. I called a break.

Sometimes there's discomfort from an unknown event that may have happened earlier in the day and may have nothing to do with us, yet we can see it in others' faces. Maybe they're upset because they had a hard time finding the office. Travel, especially cross-country, can wear anyone out. Perhaps they were up all night with a sick child. Be sensitive and attentive.

Sometimes there's irritability around something that was said or done, unresolved past issues between the participants, or a real or perceived inconvenience.

Whatever the circumstance, always remember, our bodies reflect our moods in real time. Pay attention, be sensitive, don't hesitate to ask if a break is needed, if they need privacy to make a call, if the meeting needs to be cut short because a snowstorm is moving in fast and will affect travel, if food and refreshments are needed, or if there's anything you can do to assist or ameliorate the situation. Action has a weight all its own.

Sometimes all you can do is validate someone's discomfort or annoyance, but at least validation brings us closer at a subconscious level. Remember: to validate is to venerate.

> **What can I offer to foster comfort?** Never underestimate the primacy and appeal of simple hospitality. The act of offering something to drink, a comfortable place to sit, a moment to clear the mind, a place to charge a phone—these courtesies are so easy, and they count for so much. The need to transact should not in any way inhibit your duty to create psychological comfort through prosocial acts such as attentive hospitality.

Speaking of hospitality, remember that the environment you're in contributes to psychological comfort. Noisy, busy environments where there is no privacy can lead to meetings that are cut short, ill-remembered, or even avoided in the future. In business the higher the status of the individual, the more considerate we must be when it comes to meeting space.

Once you've made your initial assessment, don't assume it's all over. In the FBI, I never stopped assessing my interactions. It is no different in my business meetings: during the engagement phase, while our conversation is taking place, another one is happening in my mind: What am I seeing and hearing? How is this going? Are we making progress? Did something just change? Where are these questions headed? Why are the nonverbals of the CEO and CFO so different? What is *not* being said? Is this person relaxing more; are they more comfortable? Are we developing trust in each other? Are we more and more in synchrony? Is the subject causing tension? Should I bring up this other topic now? How did they react to my mentioning that fact? Do they have questions that are not being asked? Perhaps they'll open up more if I avoid direct eye contact (this works beautifully sometimes)?

Why go through all this? Because in the Bureau it was hammered into us: you have only one chance—do it right. In talking to many businesspeople around the world, I've found that the same is true in business. Often we only have one opportunity to properly engage a client, so we'd better get it right. How do we do that? By constantly assessing them to see what is taking place, what needs attention, what may present as an issue, and whether their interest level and inquisitiveness are growing or diminishing.

Engage

Read the three scenarios below and see if you can guess what they have in common:

> Steve Jobs, while still in high school, looked through the Palo Alto phone book and decided he would call Bill Hewlett, CEO

and cofounder of Hewlett-Packard . . . at home (amazingly, the number was listed). That led to an apprenticeship and access to some of the best engineers in the world.

> An FBI agent in Miami, upon learning that the wife of a suspect he had been investigating had been hospitalized, sent her flowers. That led to the suspect opening up a dialogue, which led to his cooperation with the FBI, exposing other criminals involved.

> Detective Mike Willet had been handed a case where the suspect had already been interviewed multiple times with no result. She alleged that her baby had been kidnapped in a mere twenty seconds or so after she exited her car in a store parking lot to go to the shopping cart area. When Deputy Willet got the case, he went and sat down next to the suspect on a bench in the hall. In silence, they both watched as people walked by. After a while he said, "Let's go find your baby." With that, the suspect got up and together they walked to Willet's car. As they pulled up to the stop sign to exit the sheriff's office parking lot, Willet asked, "Do I go left or do I go right?" "Go left," she said. And just like that, the suspect led him to where she had disposed of her baby, after which she confessed to killing her own child.

What do these disparate examples have in common? Inventive engagement. What is normally referred to as thinking outside the box is really nothing more than being creative bearing in mind circumstances, context, personality, or opportunity.

Jobs was looking for a way in to the tech industry and to apprentice himself with some of the finest engineers at HP. This was before internships and other ways for industries to recognize untried talent were widespread. Rather than take the traditional route of going through HR, Jobs found a way to engage the right person at the right time, and what a difference that made.

Often, a criminal knows that the FBI is after him. Mob boss John Gotti, according to one of my FBI colleagues, used to send sandwiches to the FBI agents surveilling him—his way of saying, "I know you're there." It's a game villains often play to let law enforcement know they are not scared. The Miami agent had interviewed his suspect and had been pursuing him for a long time. Then he found out the suspect's wife was sick. Suspect or not, we all know how worrisome it is when a loved one is ill. So he sent flowers. Engaging on that shared emotional level turned out to be a powerful way to open up communication.

Deputy Willet successfully engaged a suspect who'd been interviewed multiple times without success. Instead of bringing her into an interview room for the conventional sit-down, he met her right where she was, just sitting down next to her. Instead of trying to start a dialogue as might have been expected, he said nothing. Together, sharing the same vantage, they just watched the world go by for a while. Then, instead of coming at her with more questions, he voiced the totally unexpected—not a question, but rather suggesting taking some action together that she might not resist: "Let's go find your baby." It was a brilliant engagement strategy. When I asked Mike, "How did you know what to say or do?" he replied, "I didn't. All I knew was that everything everyone else had tried did not work." So he tried something different—inventive engagement.

I'm not suggesting that you try an unusual method of engagement just to be unusual. I am suggesting that before taking any action, before you move to transaction, you consider: What is the best way to engage this person at this moment in time?

Perhaps an initial reach-out by phone is the way to go, as Steve Jobs did. Maybe it's an introductory email. I personally always appreciate and answer a handwritten note. Or perhaps it's a quick look into an office to see if the manager is busy. As one very successful CEO with offices in seventeen countries told me, "When I started out and even now, I gave a lot of thought to how I would approach bankers when seeking to capitalize our various programs. I can tell you that no two approaches were the same, now or then. Invariably, what country we were in, their personality all played a role, even the time of day."

It's worth thinking in advance about what the other person's preferences or perspectives might be. I'm reminded of the time when agents showed up with doughnuts and coffee for a key interview at someone's home. Their host graciously invited them in, but when they offered the refreshments, he said (and I quote): "I am Chinese born. I drink tea, and we don't eat doughnuts." As the agents told me later with embarrassment, the interview went downhill from there, and we never got another chance to talk to him because of that. Engagement doesn't work unless it builds psychological comfort—theirs, not yours.

Engagement, not transaction, is the most important aspect of any interaction. How we choose to engage moment to moment—what we communicate, how we behave—is what solidifies relationships and ensures a successful transaction.

Before engaging, I often ask myself: *How do I want to come across in this scene at this very moment?* If I've done the work we've talked about in the previous chapters—exercised self-discipline to prepare assiduously for the meeting, cultivated my observation skills and situational awareness to allow me to respond in the moment, allowed my curiosity and empathy to flow toward this person, acted with rectitude to build a foundation of trust—then I rely on those solid foundations and know that I'll always be able to get the conversation off on the right foot by finding something to talk about or that we may have in common. Simply expressing gratitude for the opportunity to meet is often enough to get things off to a solid start.

So, if you have embraced and are practicing all the traits of exceptional individuals, don't worry about exactly what to say. You are already communicating positively through how you present, and your preparation ahead of time provides valuable confidence to convey your message.

Engagement, like assessment, is an ongoing process that we modify and adapt, based on what our assessments are telling us. While the conversation unfolds, if you're utilizing the traits of exceptional individuals, the circumstances will speak to you: This is how to best engage this particular individual who, by his or her nonverbals, is telling me that they may be pressed for time or are uncertain. This person likes to speak fast and doesn't engage in small talk, so let me jump right in. From my advance research I've learned that this group of investors only gives you a twenty-minute meeting, make the most of it because they cut it off abruptly and that's all you have—so I rehearse my talking points ten to fifteen times. If the way to gain access to this doctor is by being extra nice to the receptionist, then she, too, is my priority for rapport-building. A prospective client wants to know where my family is from; I will tell him. The client's phone just vibrated and her eyes have shifted twice to this annoyance—I'll ask her if she needs to take that call or message and suggest a short break if so. If someone needs water (has dry mouth, is swallowing to moisten mouth, is clearing their throat), I get it before they ask for it. I am there with an agenda to be sure, I am in the business of business, but I am also keenly aware and attuned to what is needed or how things are changing—because I am also in the people business.

During engagement, if I assess that others have any apprehension, I focus on inspiring trust through my posture, behavior, voice, tone, and actions. When I conducted interviews in the FBI, the main thing I focused on in the engagement phase was getting face time—the amount of time we would spend productively face-to-face. Increasing face time was paramount. Without it, there would be no transaction and no possibility for another meeting. If the other person felt comfortable, then they'd be more likely to want to spend more time with me or have me come back.

To optimize a positive first impression, after shaking hands I would maneuver so that I always stood at a slight angle, rather than directly in front of others. I would use a tone of voice that was lower than my usual speaking voice. And, as soon as was practical while standing, I would cross my legs. At a subconscious level, this relaxes people more than if you are standing with feet side by side. Concurrently, I would tilt my head—a slight canting and exposure of the vulnerable neck—to demonstrate I was listening and inquisitive. This tends to encourage people to open up. Foot crossing while standing and a slight head tilt are subtle subconscious cues that you can send out that encourage people to stay with you longer. Also, by smiling, relaxing my face, giving slight nods of concurrence when appropriate, I sought to create an environment where hopefully we could engage for a longer period of time, or at least encourage others to be receptive. I also recognized that when people stand at angles to each other, they are more likely to speak with each other longer. There is absolutely no difference in business—these small things make for longer as well as better engagements.

Keys for Positive Engagement

Here are some things you can do to facilitate comfort and enhance your engagement with others:

> **Mirror their behaviors.** If they want to stand and talk while leaning against a wall, do the same. If they have coffee, have one also, or at least something to drink. While sitting, you can subtly mirror their posture: Are they leaning forward, with hands on table? Leaning back with arms crossed, head tilted? It doesn't have to be identical, just similar.

> **Mirror their words.** If they say, "This is going to cause real problems," don't say, "We can work out the issues." Mirroring people's words ("problems," not "issues") contributes to harmony. If they're using sports terminology, resolve to work with that, even if it's not your forte. If they want to "hit it out of the park," "put some points on the board," "punt it" to another department, or make a "slam dunk"—those may be terms you have to employ also to let them know that you get it.

> **Adjust to their speech pace.** We can never match another person's speech pattern, but if someone likes to talk fast, make an effort to keep up with them. If they are slow and deliberate, don't talk too fast. This is a complaint I hear often about "fast-talking" people.

> **If you're using technical or professional terms or buzzwords, make sure that everyone understands what they mean.** Euphemisms or colloquialisms like "that has a lot of moving parts" or "you could hear crickets" or "that dog won't hunt" might not resonate with people from different regions or cultures. In New York you may hear the word *capiesce* [pronounced "kuh-*peesh*"], used to mean "do you understand?" I lived in Utah and Arizona for about ten years and I never heard it used once. Each generation has its own preferred words or trending words, too—be careful you don't fall into the trap of thinking everyone understands. Same goes for terms of art specific to particular industries.

> **Assess for the nonverbals of synchrony.** This is subtle, but if they are breathing and blinking at approximately the same rate as you, chances are you're in synchrony. This is good! If they're leaning back and spreading their arms out on the couch, these are positive signs, as is looking away as we talk and think—it means we're comfortable enough to freely look away from each other, as if with friends.

> **Don't let repetitive behaviors distract you.** Many people have them. I like to bounce my leg. Some people twirl pencils or do other things. It's how they soothe themselves and pass the time. But be careful when they begin to drum their fingers suddenly—it may be a sign of impatience or boredom—so watch for other clues to try and confirm.

> **Know when to wrap things up.** Be aware that when they're looking at the clock, their smartphone, or the exit repeatedly, or if their feet point toward the door—there may be other things on their agenda. If you see these behaviors or if you see their hands on their knees, it's probably time to wrap up the

meeting. Don't hesitate to ask, "How are we doing on time?" They will appreciate it.

A final, important caveat: dedicating yourself to fostering psychological comfort does not mean that you have to become a "yes person" or a sycophant. You can create an environment where there is psychological comfort with well-established and rigorous boundaries. Psychological comfort is an objective; it does not mean obsequiousness or subservience.

Transaction

During my FBI interviews, once I had figured out how to best engage the person and felt that they were more relaxed and receptive, only then did I transition to that critical phase of the transaction—in other words, why I was there and what I was interested in achieving. Deciding when to make this transition is no different in business meetings, difficult conversations, or when we meet someone for the first time.

For you, the transactional phase may be about what you're selling or promoting, or to interest someone in an opportunity. Whatever it is, there comes a point where you've established a degree of rapport, and it's time to act.

Exactly how you should go about this is as individual as the transactions themselves. But the foundations for exceptional individuals hold true: If you prepared carefully for the meeting, if you present yourself as well-mannered, well-intentioned, and responsive, chance will favor you. If you are energetic, respectful, and poised to interact and answer their questions, they will respect and appreciate you. If you can adjust and pivot depending on their reactions, they will recognize that you have social conscientiousness. If you do all these things, you will be perceived as trustworthy. It is by continually demonstrating your trustworthiness that you will encourage others to listen to you, accept you, and work with you to get things done.

But remember, just because you're in the transaction phase and are doing your presentation, that doesn't mean that you go dormant on observation. You are still monitoring how the other person is receiving and reacting to what you're saying.

People have told me, "I was trying to remember everything I wanted to say, but I got distracted because I had difficulty reading their reactions," or "There was so much going on I forgot to say" this or that. I know it's not easy. It has happened to me, too. That's why you have to practice and build your observational skills—so you can become at ease with focused assessment while you engage and transact, even in dynamic or distracting environments and situations.

Keys for Effective Transaction

Here are some of the factors I focus on during transaction:

> **Go a step beyond body language.** Keep assessing individuals' body language, but also be aware of distractions that are pulling them out of engagement. It could be text messages being received and answered (including their reactions to those messages). It could be room temperature (Are they taking off their jacket, rolling up their sleeves? Or the opposite: Wrapping their shawl around themselves or rubbing chilly arms?), time of day (Afternoon energy slump? Sun shining into their eyes?), or environmental noise (Can you close the door, step out for a moment to quietly ask others to tone things down a notch, or suggest the meeting be continued at a quiet café down the street?).

> **Note changes in word usage,** such as "the project" versus "our project" or other language that indicates that some reserve has crept in. If they say, "You said," be prepared to do more reengaging because this is usually a prelude to latent emotions behind some unresolved issue, such as: "You said we could close on the house June 1. What happened?" Just those two words let you know you have more engagement work and explaining to do. Similarly, "What about . . . ?" gives you a

hint that issues need to be resolved before the transaction can move forward.

> **If you see discomfort displays or signals that they've heard enough, don't just keep talking.** You want to keep the conversation going, but paradoxically, that means switching gears when you see nonverbals that say they've made up their mind (lips pursed fully forward or pursed and then quickly pulled dramatically to one side) or they have issues. Lip pursing, neck scratching, ventilating behaviors (pulling on shirt collar) or jaw shifting are hints that something's not right. They're your cue to pause and ask what they're thinking thus far, what issues may be of concern to them. Or you may wish to remain silent, let them fill the void. This gives them the opportunity to take the conversation in the direction they wish to pursue. When you see there are concerns, remember, those things you are observing are a means of communicating what they may be feeling without expressing it in words. Not hearing words of concern doesn't mean we ignore it. I like to address it right there and then, especially when I know time is limited. Why drag it out? Make it easy for them by saying, "Does this sound like something you would be comfortable with?" Most likely they will come back and say, politely, this is not for us or we want to go in another direction. And that's fine. Allow your gracious acceptance that this isn't working for them to save your reputation for another day.

> **Remember you're there to convey, not convince.** Address questions quickly, without hesitation. You're prepared, so you'll be comfortable with facts and details. Now is not the time to cajole or push. The exceptional never have to do that. Others' reception of your pitch or offer or ideas will be based on two things: how they feel about what is tendered, and how they perceive you. Presumably your products and services speak for themselves.

> **Don't fight the tyranny of indifference.** What happens if no matter what you have done they seem indifferent or distracted or perhaps emotionally they are not in a good place? It's best to

walk away and return another day. As I often warn executives, "Don't waste your best lines when it's the worst of times." Wisdom is knowing what to say that matters and when to say it. That is what exceptional individuals do.

> **No matter what happens, remain confident in who you are.**
  At this point, you have done all you can. Your message is strong, you are prepared, you radiate enthusiasm, congeniality, and trustworthiness. You got here through self-mastery, observation, and utilizing your best communication skills. The rest is up to them.

The Attenuation of Fear: A Duty the Exceptional Embrace

When I was assigned to the San Juan, Puerto Rico, office of the FBI, we dealt with terrorist groups, bank robbers, kidnappers, carjackers, killers and rapists on the high seas, and drug traffickers. Investigating them or even arresting them did not bother me. But during that time, I discovered quite by accident something that scared the heck out of me.

It happened one day when the Special Agent in Charge of the San Juan FBI Office "volunteered" me (read: I was ordered to go because no one else wanted to do it) to take the FBI SWAT Rappel Master Course. This is a course where you not only learn how to rappel but also are certified to teach it to others.

That moment, rappelling off buildings and mountainsides became my future reality. That moment, I also realized how afraid I was of heights. Not "concerned." Not having "issues" or "challenges." Jelly-kneed, gut-clenching, little-kid scared.

I had rappelled down the side of a sloping mountain in Provo, Utah, not far from Robert Redford's Sundance. But what awaited me was way different. Rappelling down the side of a building under tactical conditions and wearing a Kevlar helmet, gas mask, a canteen, heavy body armor including a ceramic plate, a medical kit with two 500 ml bags of Lactated Ringer's solution, slinging an MP-5 submachine gun, four extra magazines, plus a SIG Sauer 226 semiautomatic pistol with two extra magazines, two stun grenades, and a heavily ruggedized Motorola encrypted radio, while using night-vision goggles to enter an eighth-story window at night with a titanium breaching tool is not fun. Looks good on television . . . not fun.

But it was a done deal. So I kept my mouth shut and off I went with a lump in my throat and fear in my gut, just hoping I'd make it through somehow.

At the Rappel Master School in Quantico, we spent the first two days tying knots and learning about our equipment. I was pathetically glad for this time to try to build some kind of confidence in our gear, while we learned eighteen different knots. We had to be able to tie each one with our eyes closed, even while submerged in water at night. These we would use to secure our lines. There's nothing quite like being sixty feet up and an instructor says, "Would you go off the side of a building with the way that line is secure?" Or how about out of a helicopter, forty feet above a pitching deck? It makes you think.

On the third day, we climbed the six-story rappel tower where we had to master going over the side quickly and efficiently. For several days we practiced going down facing up in the traditional style; then in the Australian commando style facing down, using just a simple carabiner or D ring to control the descent, all the while simulating tactical conditions where we had to stop on our way down, secure ourselves temporarily to do a dynamic entry (crash through a window) or—if need be in hostage rescue situations—quietly take out a sentry with a suppressed pistol or throw in a stun grenade.

I was surprised, once I had confidence in my own knot tying, that I was not as scared as I thought I would be. The instructors had a lot to do with that. Over the next week, we progressed in our rappelling and window entries with greater confidence. We even rappelled off the eleven-story Jefferson building at Quantico, which was tension-producing, both because of the height and because we did it in the middle of a thunderstorm. I was a little scared, but it was manage-able. Sometimes that's what attenuating fear is about: validating the fear and then managing it through step-by-step repetition and struc-tured practice.

By the beginning of the second week, we had learned how to tie ourselves off, tie on to another person's rappel harness, and do a rescue by actually cutting off their rope so that they become part of our rig and we are now rappelling and controlling not just our own descent but also that of another 190-pound SWAT operator pre-tending to be injured while we apply first aid, who is just as scared (or more) than we are and counting on us to get both of us down safely.

I still had a twinge of fear every time I went over the side of the tower at ever more blistering speeds (to ensure we did not make a tar-get for snipers). Something in the subconscious, especially the limbic system, always wants you to make sure you don't go over that wall. But at least my fear wasn't hobbling me. It had become manageable. Yet we had one more task to complete: the mountain-climbing phase of training that was required for us to graduate from the program the following week.

The foul weather that had persisted for a week followed us to Sen-eca Rocks, West Virginia, where we would meet our final challenge. This was not a scenic moment. This was a mountain that first had to be climbed, in full SWAT gear, and then rappelled down—with a body rescue, in the rain, with lightning storms nearby, high winds, and periodic hail.

We hadn't even started climbing and already we were soaked. Our equipment and clothing, already heavy, were made heavier by the rain. Our climbing shoes were standard SWAT boots that weren't designed for climbing. We couldn't even see the top of the moun-tain, obscured by low clouds. Flashes of lightning lit clouds in the distance, with the thunderous crack of superheated air around each strike.

That we would fall was certain. It was built into the program.

The question was how far, from what altitude, and would we get hurt? The ambulance parked at the base of the mountain was not there for decoration.

Full-blown fear returned. I felt it, and I could see it on the faces of others.

Fear and psychological comfort have a parallel relationship in humans. The more we have of the former, the more we need of the latter. In a way, fear is psychological discomfort on steroids.

Indeed, fear causes us to seek psychological comfort at all costs. A famous example of this dynamic can be found in psychologist Harry Harlow's "monkey experiments," in which baby monkeys raised with two surrogate "mothers"—one made of wire that provided their food, and one that didn't provide food but was soft and cuddly—chose the cuddly mother when they were frightened or stressed. It wasn't that the baby monkeys wanted something soft; it was that something soft provided psychological comfort for their fears. As it is for primates, so it is for humans. We attach to whomever provides the most psychological comfort—in relationships, in love, in anything that involves human interaction and connection.

Think about the times your parents, teachers, coaches, even workmates helped you through a crisis caused by fear. Perhaps it was going to a new school, or maybe you were up against bigger players in a game, or you had to perform a task where your learning curve was steep and failure was not an option if you wanted to advance. How fortunate we were when someone stepped up and engaged us, seeing what we needed: an encouraging word, an emotional boost, a kind and more experienced voice guiding us in the right direction. When we're in the grip of fear, we are that frightened young monkey needing something reassuring to grab on to, or that baby on the precipice in the visual cliff experiment—as I was, facing that mountain.

This is where the worthy leader must step in and use their presence, guidance, influence, and prestige to lead others away from fear. Leaders fail us when they miss the mark on attenuating fear. That is the one mark that exceptional individuals never miss, because they know how destructive and toxic fear can be.

Most people don't like to think about their fears, much less talk about them. Yet fear in all its manifestations is ever-present. In many ways, it is the great disruptor: the odious, oppressive inhibitor that keeps us from fulfilling our potential.

Fear can drive us as almost nothing else can—and not in good directions. It can hobble us from living a full life. It leads us to make poor decisions. It results in inaction, avoidance, procrastination, dishonesty, cover-ups, aggression, cruelty, even inhumanity.

Fear inhibits and paralyzes us to the point where we don't want to commit to the relationship, apply to the program, start that business, go after that job, get on the plane, deal with that person, or want those people moving into our neighborhood or working alongside us. We might have all kinds of reasons and explanations besides fear, but that's what it is. The human brain actually only focuses on one thing: Is this a threat to me? If it is a threat, it can initiate a graduated cluster of survival responses, including the *freeze, faint, forgo, flight, fight*, or *forget* response. These fear-driven behaviors are useful for survival, but they do not help us live a healthy, vibrant life.

In studying hundreds of books on leadership and management, I was astonished to find that fear is not talked about. It is in this book because, now more than ever, it needs to be called out as the weapon of mass destruction that it is, and for the threat it poses. Fear can be inhibiting, even disastrous, for a person, an organization, or a nation.

What drove the actions of Stalin, Mussolini, Hitler, Pol Pot, Slobodan Milošević, and others? What allowed them to hurt so many people through pogroms and genocide? They were masters at the propagation of fear. They used the primal, galvanizing force of fear to move the masses as pawns to support their causes and carry out their hideous crimes. Unfortunately, fear is a very persuasive way to get people to come together.

All hatred is based on a foundation of fear. No one is born hating this or hating that. But you can be taught to fear and hate. You can even be taught to fear a skin color, and in doing so you can come to hate others who may have lighter or darker skin.

As Eric Hoffer reminded us in *The True Believer* after examining the effects of fascists and Nazis after World War II, "Passionate hatred can give meaning and purpose to an empty life." People who fear seek out others who also fear, and together they support each other in hate. It's something that malignant potentates and leaders have excelled at, from Bosnia to Rwanda where ethnic fears festered into genocide in the past thirty years—something I thought I would never see again in my lifetime. Every genocide I have studied started with fear and was transformed into hatred with rhetoric and vitriol.

US history teaches us that fear unites—and what we fear can all too easily turn into hatred. When allowed to thrive, fear can have devastating consequences. What do you think lynchings in the South after the Civil War were all about? It was fear of emancipated blacks. There was a time when in New York City and Boston there were posted signs on businesses that said, "Irish need not apply." They, too, were feared. The Chinese Exclusion Act of 1882 was based on fear of the West Coast being transformed by an abundance of Chinese workers. Fear of Jews drove US authorities to reject the entry in 1939 of more than nine hundred Jewish passengers on the MS *St. Louis*, sometimes referred to as the *Voyage of the Damned*. The ship had to return to Europe and many of the passengers were later killed in concentration camps.

No one is immune to fear and its toxicity. Franklin Delano Roosevelt is considered one of the greatest US presidents. He led us through the Great Depression with his historic words: "We have nothing to fear but fear itself," and then guided us through World War II. But he did not follow his own advice. After the 1941 attack on Pearl Harbor by the Imperial Japanese Navy, he yielded to fear and xenophobia, incarcerating and relocating more than 120,000 Japanese Americans merely because they had Japanese ancestry.

No such efforts were made to incarcerate those of German or

Italian ancestry in the United States, even after German U-boats repeatedly sank Allied shipping, including the famous incident of the USS *Reuben James*, sunk by a German U-boat in 1941, killing 115 Americans. Moreover, pro-Nazi supporters had regularly gathered in large rallies on the East Coast—the most famous rally being the 1939 gathering of twenty-two thousand members of the German American Bund, a pro-Nazi group, which had rented out New York City's Madison Square Garden for the occasion. Somehow, that was okay, even when they displayed their allegiance to Adolf Hitler. But it was not okay to have Japanese ancestry. That is the danger of fear when not attenuated by leaders.

More recently, it is fear that is driving the rise of right-wing extremism in the United States and in other countries around the world. Fear of change, fear of minorities, fear of people of color, fear of losing out, fear of losing jobs to migrants, fear of being killed by refugees, et cetera. Today it is the fear of Muslims, Mexicans, of refugees from Latin America. Tomorrow, who knows? What we do know is that history has taught us all too well what happens when we stoke the embers of fear. Where fear is propagated, it must be extinguished.

This is why it is the responsibility of the exceptional individual and the worthy leader to look for fears, real or imagined, and assuage them—at work, in the home, in the community, or wherever they exist.

Fear can do another horrific thing, which researchers learned when studying the orphaned children in Romania. Deprive children of psychological comfort, keep them in a state of constant limbic arousal or fear, and they will fail to develop mentally, their neural networks too busy mistrusting, too fearful, to develop cognitively.

Even adults are affected when their brains are continually hijacked by fear, apprehension, and mistrust. I've interviewed enough victims of abuse to know how they can be intellectually overwhelmed, unable to think or remember clearly, and disinterested in life while in the grip of fear.

We often define leadership as taking charge, setting a course, having an idea or a vision. We forget that one of the most important responsibilities of a leader is to deal with the anxieties and fears that befall all of us. To pull aside the blinding curtain of irrationality and put things in perspective, remind us of our clearer vision, and encourage our better, braver selves. To not give irrational fear more oxygen or let it hobble, hurt, distract, divide, or destroy us.

A person, group, or nation that lives in fear is forever constrained by those fears.

Ameliorating fear in oneself and in others is the work of the exceptional. It is a responsibility absolutely required of our leaders, but one also shared by you, me, and every person in our human family, for our collective betterment. Because fear only stands down by concerted effort, whether exerted from within or with the help of others.

We stood there as the rain poured down, surreptitiously glancing at one another. Reading the fear. Fearing the fear. We all kept looking up at that rain-soaked mountain, shaking our heads. Fear had its crushing, immobilizing grip on us.

At the very instant that the treacherous thought crossed my mind: *I could go back to my office right now and still get paid the same—* Matt, one of the instructors who had been working with me, walked over.

"What do you fear, Joe?" Matt asked point-blank, no messing about, as I looked at that wet and windswept mountain.

Talk about an insightful engagement strategy. I cannot remember another time in my adult life, before or since, that another man asked me that question. Maybe he was a master at assessing; I don't know. But he knew I wanted this. The question we had to get at was: How, in my head, was I going to achieve it?

"I'm scared of screwing up or falling down, I guess," I said, unsure, checking my pockets for the fifth time for all my gear and the reassurance of a small jar of peanut butter in my climbing pants that would be all I would eat that day. Perhaps what I wanted to say was, *I fear falling and dying.* Hell, I feared even saying that. But I think he understood.

"You won't screw it up too badly." He smiled. "You know what to do. More importantly, *I* know you know what to do. And if you do screw something up, so what? We have you on a safety line. If you fall, at most you'll fall five or six feet. Look, you can stay down here and join them," he said, pointing to a few agents who had refused to go up the mountain, "and I won't say another word. Or you can climb, one step at a time. Just know this, Agent Navarro," he said, engaging me with a little more formality to get my attention, "I would not let you go up there if I didn't think you could do it." He squeezed my shoulder, smiled, turned and walked away.

I did go up that mountain. It took almost five hours, as we also rehearsed rescues along the way. I did slip and fall a few feet, just enough to remember the falling sequence: Yell, "FALLING!"; protect the head and neck with your arms; use the legs to keep off the wall; recover in position to continue; check on those below you; exhale; let the person on the safety rope (the belay person) know you're ready to climb once more; stretch your arms to release the lactic acid; continue the climb. And I did. Slowly, cautiously, sometimes ungracefully, I continued to climb and got to the top in time to welcome my teammates who were having even more difficulties as a result of the high winds and the unforgiving routes they had been given. We were wet, our equipment was soaked and heavy, some people's boots had fallen apart, everyone had bruises on their hands and arms, we were shaking—but we made it.

There was the personal triumph of climbing a mountain, of conquering a fear, and the delight of being able to eat a jar of peanut butter with wrinkled, cold, wet, filthy fingers because the spoon had fallen out when I fell. But the best part, the unexpected gift I received, was to watch the sun finally break through the overcast and illuminate a breathtakingly verdant valley others pay to see. And what really topped it off, as the sun moved the clouds out, was watching a military jet, a Grumman EA 6B Prowler, doing a low pass through the valley below us: yes, we were looking down on him, close enough to see a crew of four and even the pilot's kneeboard; that's how low and close he was to us. Managing that fear allowed me to see something I will never forget, now forever etched in my mind. It also taught me a lesson I cherish: our responsibility to each other when we sense that others may be experiencing fear.

Life is hard enough with all its moments where fear can paralyze us. We don't need people who encourage or stoke fear. It is the person who conquers their own fear or helps others to overcome fear to whom we owe our admiration. To be counted among those few we call exceptional requires that they prioritize the attenuation of fear as a duty. When the stock market plummets, when yet another hurricane ravages the Gulf of Mexico region, when a pandemic threatens a way of life, it is that person—that woman, that man, alone or in concert with others—who rises to quell fear whom we will long honor and cherish.

What would the world look like if we didn't have those stalwarts, those individuals who every day provide psychological comfort and work hard to assuage fear? Our lives are made so much better because they are there, humble though they may be—perhaps a grandmother, an auntie, a teacher, a trusted friend, even a kind stranger—who lived by this simple creed to provide psychological comfort and to diminish fear.

But as with all things prosocial, the ability to ameliorate or dispel fear depends on us individually. It depends on how well-prepared we are and on our will to act. It requires the introspection and self-awareness that come through self-mastery, so we have the courage of our convictions and the clarity to recognize fear when we see it. It demands that we observe and discern what is needed and when, so that we can communicate or act prosocially.

When we minimize fear and increase psychological comfort, we are helping others to reach and exercise their full potential. We are providing that bedrock that underlies happiness—and that allows us to conquer those mountains that get in our way.

Fear has a purpose—it is there principally to help ensure our survival. But fear does not allow us to thrive. Only psychological comfort can help us there. The exceptional individual understands this and works to better our lives by (1) minimizing the fears that can cripple us and (2) maximizing the psychological comfort that allows us to enjoy life and flourish.

And so, we come to this point where we must self-analyze. Every one of us—as a parent, as an employee, a manager, an executive, a CEO, a sales associate, a military leader, a health worker, a first responder, a citizen—must ask ourselves: If these two objectives are the highest measure of an exceptional person, how do I stack up? Do I seek to fulfill them full-time, sometimes, or rarely? Have I made them a priority, and if not, why not?

These are sobering questions, but that is where we are today, In the twenty-first century, in a more enlightened world, this is the new platinum standard: How much are we contributing to psychological comfort and ameliorating fear?

Two powerful concepts, just two, but as I look back on five decades of studying exceptional individuals, these are what stand out. They are what can really make a difference in a life. Resolve to do them and your life will not just be better, it will be nobler, and those around you will thank you.

And then—but only then—you can join the ranks of the exceptional.

Final Thoughts

Who are we, if not measured by our impact on others? That's
who we are! We're not who we say we are, we're not who we
want to be—we are the sum of the influence and impact that
we have, in our lives, on others.

—Carl Sagan

We began this book with a question: What makes people exceptional? Now that we've journeyed far into that inquiry, you may
naturally be asking yourself: *Am I exceptional?* Before you answer,
ponder this: How would an exceptional individual answer?

When I've asked myself *that* question, I've backed away from answering. My weaknesses are a frequent-enough reminder that there's
always more work to be done. And in the end, perhaps it's not for us
to say, but rather others.

If so, then what question should we be asking? What would the
exceptional ask? It might be: *What have I learned so far, and what
more can I do?*

Exceptional individuals don't stop to laud themselves or post their
achievements for the day on LinkedIn. They're too busy trying to
improve on what they've achieved. They may celebrate hard-won

progress, but then they keep going. Becoming exceptional is a life-long journey, not a tournament to win.

Isn't this what attracts us to exceptional individuals, and why they stand out? Because they never give up on themselves or on what they can do each day to make life just that little bit easier and better for themselves or for others?

Making life easier. Sounds simple. A violin with its four strings and a bow appears simple—but the execution of a world-class performance . . . not so simple. So it is with becoming exceptional. What it takes is the same for everyone: rigorous discipline, dedication, practice, but most of all an appreciation for what it takes.

Exceptional individuals are made, not born. And that's a good thing—because that puts this level of excellence within reach of you and me. However humble our beginnings, we can take command of ourselves—becoming caring and responsible stewards of what we learn, think, know, say, and do—and then extend our stewardship into the world so others, too, can benefit.

Through our intellectual and emotional mastery, we can be counted among the stalwarts—individuals others can always rely on. Through our actions, we demonstrate that we care, earning respect and trust. We teach, inspire, and lead by example. As stewards, we strive, work, seek, act, learn, refine . . . but we don't ever settle or consider the work to be done.

Stewardship doesn't stop at some magical finish line. Life has no such finish line. Stewardship is nurtured, shared, passed down from one to the next. It happens through these Five Domains that we learn, model, and bequeath to others in the great circle of human life:

> Through *self-mastery* we harness the internal resources to execute our aims, and aim ever higher.

> Through *observation* we come to know what is needed to ameliorate situations and relationships.

> We establish and nourish relationships through our ability
> to validate and *communicate* what matters most in a timely
> manner.

> All these hone our capacity to choose the prosocial *actions* that
> convert our positive intentions into something tangible and
> thus transformative.

> The ultimate result: the attenuation of fear and the creation of
> *psychological comfort*—that most precious gift humans seek,
> and our greatest strength for influencing others.

When the Five Domains all operate in harmony, they create something greater than the sum of their parts: the exceptional individual. The domains work together to prime and prepare you to perform more fully and with greater enlightenment, so you can positively influence the world around you. They are self-reinforcing: through practicing them, you sharpen your capacity to exercise self-mastery, to observe and analyze acutely so that timely and effective action can take place. This is how exceptional individuals learn from life: by doing. That accrued wisdom in turn makes for a more worthy life—and makes you more worthy to lead others.

Becoming exceptional is not out of our hands, but rather is entirely up to us and within our power. It starts the moment we systematically begin to adopt and exercise the behaviors and attitudes that will help us nurture and grow these characteristics. As we know: to be exceptional, one must do exceptional things. As with anything worthwhile, it requires effort—but the benefits are, without hyperbole—positively life-changing.

You now have a road map where accountability, authenticity, transparency, trust, resilience, conscientiousness, empathy, and civility all come together, not as separate practices you need to keep track of, but as part of an integrated, workable model for living a successful, principled life. Those valued qualities associated with the highest ideals of humanity, courage, inventiveness, leadership, humility, compassion, and wisdom now don't seem so out of reach. We can be successful and humane; caring while still having high expectations of others; ambitious and innovative yet attentive and prosocial. We are not without guidance here. We have a viable template for achievement as well as a philosophy for living as stewards. It is up to you.

Of course, we're human, and at times we'll slip, take a step back, or pause. But getting back on track begins with a single step. Being exceptional isn't about being perfect. It's about working to be better at the things that matter the most, for ourselves and others. And though we may be a work in progress, with plenty of room for improvement and refinement, the reward merits our continued best efforts.

Start now, today. Don't wait another minute—begin your personal quest. You now have what is required. Explore, learn, question, travel, be inquisitive, meet new people, seek new knowledge, innovate, help those who are challenged or fearful, provide that all-powerful psychological comfort to others, relish the opportunities to improve your positive influence—and never end your striving.

I wish you well on this path. As it unfolds, take time, now and then, to look back and see how far you've come. You will be forgiven if you smile, for there will be many who will be smiling back in gratitude. A "well done" is in order for a life better lived, for a destiny better crafted. Then continue on and rejoice. Because this is your accomplishment, your legacy, the one that matters the most—your exceptional journey.

Acknowledgments

At the end of every writing excursion, after I exhale, I have the opportunity to reflect on the many people who helped me along the way. To my wife Thryth, I say thank you for your loving support, encouragement, and patience with me. To my daughter Stephanie, who is my biggest cheerleader, and to my family near and far I say thank you with a bowed head.

Within my being resides an exquisite labyrinth of teachings my parents imbued me with. Though they be far from me now, they are two exceptional individuals who, through their example and the choices they made, molded me into what I became. I am forever indebted.

I would not have attempted this project if not for knowing that Toni Sciarra Poynter would join me in this endeavor. As my writing partner, she has guided, cautioned, and reminded me of so many things while opening my mind to different perspectives. Without her insights, probing questions, generosity, and writing and editing skills, this work simply would not have been possible as she has stuck with and seen the evolution of my thoughts and ideas since inception—almost twelve years ago now. Thank you, Toni; you are unequaled.

Steve Ross (SteveRossAgency.com), my literary agent and friend, whose wisdom I have admired for so long, was, as always, instrumental in launching this project and for that I am so grateful. Steve is a writer's dream—he opens doors just when they seem shut.

To Nick Amphlett, my editor at HarperCollins, thank you for nearly a decade of collaboration. Nick shares my enthusiasm and vision, and with his kind guidance and gentle prodding has proved himself insightful, supportive, and above all caring. Nick is such a pleasure to work with and I am so grateful that he championed this effort.

My gratitude of course extends to Liate Stehlik, publisher, and Ben Steinberg, associate publisher at HarperCollins, for being supportive of my work over the years. It is a pleasure to say that Harper-Collins holds the majority of my literary collection and they are part of the reason.

No book can come to life without the precious work of others such as production editor Andrea Molitor and copyeditor Laurie McGee, who so diligently worked to help this manuscript into its final shape. Thank you both. Bianca Flores in publicity has come through for me once more to get the word out and crafted a campaign worthy of her efforts. The work of Kayleigh George behind the scenes in marketing is so much appreciated, as is the work of the cover designer Rich Aquan. To Cathy Barbosa-Ross, who for over a decade handled foreign sales and translations, I thank you once more. Well done and hearty thanks to you all.

As a writer I take my responsibility to inform seriously and cautiously. I have tried to be clear in my thoughts and words, but if there are any faults or mistakes, they rest with me alone.

—Joe Navarro, Tampa, Florida

It is always a privilege to work with Joe Navarro. Joe, thank you for inviting me on this journey with you, and for bringing your all to our work together. You relish grappling with ideas, "can't wait to" dive into the next draft, and your perspectives—right down to the level of your word choices—push my thinking in new directions. Our conversations on the phone and on the page always go somewhere interesting. It has been wonderful to see you evolving your ideas in this book with time. I hope they will be as helpful and inspiring to others as they have been to me.

To Nick Amphlett: Thank you for the perceptiveness, respect, and enthusiasm you brought to the editing process. Those qualities together are essential in an editor and keenly appreciated at the point when a manuscript, the repository of much thought and effort, is delivered into the hands of another. Your notes led to seeing and framing material in new ways. Thank you.

To Steve Ross, our agent: your astute insights informed this project at critical points, and your advocacy saw it through. Thank you, Steve.

I thank my sister Leslie for always listening, no matter what kind of sense I might (or might not) have been making. Love and thanks to Dona, Fern, and Mackenzie for encouragement and diversion, whenever needed.

My husband, Donald, continues to be supportive in countless ways. You understand the creative process, and for that—and our many conversations about the art and craft of it all—I am so fortunate. On the ground, this translated into dinners you uncomplainingly made, served, and cleaned up; good humor when chores weren't done; and tolerance when conversations went unremembered and plans were disrupted by deadlines. Above all, thank you for being the good soul that you are.

—Toni Sciarra Poynter, New York, New York

Bibliography and References

Abitz, Damgaard, et al. 2007. "Excess of Neurons in the Human Newborn Medi-odorsal Thalamus Compared with That of the Adult." *Cerebral Cortex* 17(11): 2573–2578. Accessed March 20, 2020.

Aburdene, Patricia. 2007. *Megatrends 2010: The Rise of Conscious Capitalism.* Charlottesville, VA: Hampton Roads Publishing Company, Inc.

Ackerman, J. M., et al. 2010. "Incidental Haptics Sensations Influence Social Judgments and Decision." *Science* 328(June 25): 1712–1714.

Adlaf, Elena W., et al. 2017. "Adult-Born Neurons Modify Excitatory Synaptic Transmission to Existing Neurons." *eLife.* 2017; 6 doi:10.7554/eLife.19886.

Adler, Ronald B., and George Rodman. 1988. *Understanding Human Communication.* New York: Holt, Rinehart and Winston.

Agha, R. A., and A. J. Fowler. 2015. "The Role and Validity of Surgical Simulation." *International Surgery* 100(2), 350–357. doi:10.9738/INTSURG-D-14-00004.1. https://www.ncbi.nlm.nih.gov/pmc/articles/PMC4337453/. Accessed August 25, 2019.

Alessandra, Tony, and Michael J. O'Conner. 1996. *The Platinum Rule: Discover the Four Basic Business Personalities and How They Can Lead You to Success.* New York: Hachette Book Group.

Allen, David. 2001. *Getting Things Done: The Art of Stress Free Productivity.* New York: Penguin Books.

Allport, Gordon. 1954. *The Nature of Prejudice.* Cambridge, MA: Addison-Wesley.

Ariely, Dan. 2016. *The Hidden Logic That Shapes Our Motivations.* New York: Simon & Schuster/TED.

Arthur, W., and W. G. Graziano. 1996. "The Five-Factor Model, Conscientiousness, and Driving Accident Involvement." *Journal of Personality* 64(3): 593–618.

Azvolinsky, Anna. 2018. "Free Divers from Southeast Asia Evolved Bigger Spleens." *The Scientist*, April 19. https://www.the-scientist.com/news-opinion/free-divers-from-southeast-asia-evolved-bigger-spleens-30871. Accessed August 29, 2019.

Babiak, Paul, and Robert D. Hare. 2006. *Snakes in Suits: When Psychopaths Go to Work.* New York: Regan Books.

Bacon, Terry R., and David G. Pugh. 2003. *Winning Behavior: What the Smartest, Most Successful Companies Do Differently.* New York: AMACOM.

Baer, Drake. 2014. "This Personality Trait Predicts Success." *Business Insider,* April 30. https://www.businessinsider.com/conscientiousness-predicts-success -2014-4. Accessed August 10, 2020.

Bahrampour, Tara. 2014. "Romanian Orphans Subjected to Deprivation Must Now Deal with Dysfunction." *The Washington Post.* January 30. https://www .washingtonpost.com/local/romanian-orphans-subjected-to-deprivation-must -now-deal-with-disfunction/2014/01/30/a9dbea6c-5d13-11e3-be07-006c 776266ed_story.html. Accessed July 19, 2020.

Bailey, Melissa. 2016. "5 Bizarre, Low-Tech Tools Surgeons Have Used to Practice Human Operations." *Business Insider* (www.businessinsider.com), January 25. https://www.businessinsider.com/low-tech-surgeons-training-2016-1. Accessed August 25, 2019.

Baker, L. M., Jr., et al. 2008. "Moving Mountains." In *Harvard Business Review on The Persuasive Leader,* 51–66. Boston: Harvard Business School Publishing.

Ball, Philip. 2004. *Critical Mass: How One Thing Leads to Another.* New York: Farrar, Straus and Giroux.

Barraza, Jorge A., and Paul J. Zack. 2009. "Empathy Toward Strangers Triggers Oxytocin Release and Subsequent Generosity." *Annals of the New York Academy of Sciences* 1667, no. 1 (June): 182–189.

Begley, Sharon. 2004. "Racism Studies Find Rational Part of Brain Can Override Prejudice." *Wall Street Journal,* November 19, B1.

Bergland, Christopher. 2017. "How Do Neuroplasticity and Neurogenesis Rewire Your Brain? New Research Identifies How the Birth of New Neurons Can Reshape the Brain," in *Psychology Today* blog. February 6, 2017. https://www.psychologytoday.com/us/blog/the-athletes-way/201702/how-do -neuroplasticity-and-neurogenesis-rewire-your-brain. Accessed March 4, 2020.

Bertrand, Marianne, and Sendhil Mullainathan. 2004. "Are Emily and Greg More Employable Than Lakisha and Jamal?" *American Economic Review* 94:991– 1013.

Boorstin, Daniel J. 1985. *The Discoverers: A History of Man's Search to Know This World and Himself.* New York: Vintage Books.

Borunda, Alejandra. 2020. "We Still Don't Know the Full Impacts of the BP Oil Spill, 10 Years Later." *National Geographic,* April 20. https://www .nationalgeographic.com/science/2020/04/bp-oil-spill-still-dont-know-effects -decade-later/. Accessed September 3, 2020.

Boston Globe, The. 2002. *Betrayal: The Crisis in the Catholic Church, by the Superb Investigative Staff of the Boston Globe.* New York: Little, Brown and Company.

Campbell, Joseph. 1973. *The Hero with a Thousand Faces.* New Jersey: Princeton University Press.

Campbell, Joseph, Bill D. Moyers, and Betty S. Flowers. 1991. *The Power of Myth.* New York: Anchor Books.

Campos, Joseph, Mary D. Clinnert, et al. 1983. "Emotions as Behavior Regulators in Infancy: Social Referencing in Infancy." In *Emotion: Theory, Research, and Experience,* edited by Robert Plutchik and Henry Kellerman, 57–86. New York: Academic Press.

Canadian Museum of History. 2020. *The Maya Calendar.* https://www.history museum.ca/cmc/exhibitions/civil/maya/mmc06eng.html. Accessed September 1, 2020.

Carnegie, Dale. 1936. *How to Win Friends and Influence People.* New York: Kingston Press.

Catlette, Bill, and Richard Hadden. 2001. *Contented Cows Give Better Milk: The Plain Truth About Employee Relations and Your Bottom Line.* Germantown, TN: Saltillo Press.

Chamberlain, Andrew. 2017. "What Matters More to Your Workforce Than Money." *Forbes,* January 17. https://hbr.org/2017/01/what-matters-more-to -your-workforce-than-money. Accessed May 17, 2020.

Champy, James, and Nitin Nohria. 2000. *The Arc of Ambition: Defining the Leadership Journey.* Chichester, West Sussex, England: John Wiley and Sons Ltd.

Chokshi, Niraj. 2020. "Boeing 737 Max Is Cleared by F.A.A. to Fly Again." *New York Times,* November 18. https://www.nytimes.com/2020/11/18/business /boeing-737-max-faa.html?campaign_id=60&emc=edit_na_20201118& instance_id=0&nl=breaking-news&ref=headline&regi_id=55934149& segment_id=44807&user_id=a3c307e02448124bd26ace3907d12532. Accessed November 24, 2020.

Christensen, Clayton M., James Allworth, and Karen Dillon. 2012. *How Will You Measure Your Life? Finding Fulfilment Using Lessons from Some of the World's Greatest Businesses.* New York: HarperCollins Publishers.

Churchill, Winston S. 1976. *The Second World War: The Gathering Storm.* Boston: Houghton Mifflin.

Cialdini, Robert B. 2008. "Harnessing the Science of Persuasion." In *Harvard Business Review on the Persuasive Leader,* 29–51. Boston: Harvard Business School Publishing.

Coan, J. A., H. S. Schaefer, and R. J. Davidson. 2006. "Lending a Hand: Social Regulation of the Neural Response to Threat." *Psychological Science* 17:1032–1039.

Coffey, Wayne. 2020. "Novak Djokovic Out of U.S. Open After Hitting Lineswoman with Tennis Ball." *USA Today,* September 6. https://www.usatoday .com/story/sports/tennis/open/2020/09/06/novak-djokovic-us-open-default -disqualified/5735697002/. Accessed September 7, 2020.

Collier, Peter. 2016. *Medal of Honor: Portraits of Valor Beyond the Call of Duty.* New York: Artisan.

Collins, Jim. 2001. *Good to Great: Why Some Companies Make the Leap . . . and Others Don't.* New York: HarperCollins Publishers.

Conti, G., and J. J. Heckman. 2014. "Understanding Conscientiousness Across the Life Course: An Economic Perspective." *Developmental Psychology* 50:1451–1459.

Cossar, Rachel. 2020. *When You Can't Meet in Person: A Guide to Mastering Virtual Presence and Communication.* Amazon: Kindle.

Covert, Jack, and Todd Sattersten. 2011. *The 100 Best Books of All Time: What They Say, Why They Matter and How They Can Help You.* New York: Portfolio.

Covey, Stephen M. R. 2006. *The Speed of Trust: The One Thing That Changes Everything.* New York: Free Press.

Covey, Stephen R. 2004. *The 7 Habits of Highly Effective People.* New York: Free Press.

Coyle, Daniel. 2010. *The Talent Code: Greatness Isn't Born. It's Grown.* London: Arrow Books Ltd.

Coyle, Daniel. 2018. *The Culture Code: The Secrets of Highly Successful Groups.* New York: Bantam Books.

Csikszentmihalyi, Mihaly. 1990. *Flow: The Psychology of Optimal Experience.* New York: Harper and Row Publishers.

Csikszentmihalyi, Mihaly. 1996. *Creativity.* New York: HarperCollins Publishers.

Cuddy, Amy. 2015. *Presence: Bringing Your Boldest Self to Your Biggest Challenges.* New York: Little, Brown and Company.

Davidson, Richard J. with Sharon Begley. 2012. *The Emotional Life of Your Brain: How Its Unique Patterns Affect the Way You Think, Feel, and Live, and How You Can Change Them.* New York: Hudson Street Press.

De Becker, Gavin. 1997. *The Gift of Fear.* New York: Dell Publishing.

Densen, Peter, MD. 2011. "Challenges and Opportunities Facing Medical Education." *Transactions of the American Clinical and Climatological Association* 122:48–58. https://www.ncbi.nlm.nih.gov/pmc/articles/PMC3116346/. Accessed November 24, 2020.

Dinich, Heather. 2018. "Power, Control and Legacy: Bob Knight's Last Days at IU." ESPN, November 29. https://www.espn.com/mens-college-basketball/story/_/id/23017830/bob-knight-indiana-hoosiers-firing-lesson-college-coaches. Accessed July 28, 2019.

Dreeke, Robin. 2011. *It's Not All About Me: The Top Ten Techniques for Building Quick Rapport with Anyone.* Amazon: Kindle.

Dreeke, Robin. 2017. *The Code of Trust: An American Counter Intelligence Expert's Five Rules to Lead and Succeed.* New York: St. Martin's Press.

Drucker, Peter F. 2002. *The Effective Executive.* New York: HarperBusiness Essentials.

Duhigg, Charles. 2014. *The Power of Habit: Why We Do What We Do in Life and Business.* New York: Random House Publishing.

Ekman, Paul. 1975. *Unmasking the Face.* New Jersey: Prentice Hall.

Ekman, Paul. 1982. *Emotion in the Human Face.* Cambridge: Cambridge University Press.

Ericsson, K. Anders, Ralf T. Krampe, and Clemens Tesch-Römer. 1993. "The Role of Deliberate Practice in the Acquisition of Expert Performance." *Psychological Review* 100(3):363–406.

Ericsson, K. Anders, and Robert Pool. 2016. *Peak: Secrets from the New Science of Expertise.* New York: Houghton Mifflin Harcourt Publishing.

Etcoff, Nancy. 1999. *Survival of the Prettiest: The Science of Beauty.* New York: Anchor Books.

Ferrazzi, Keith. 2005. *Never Eat Alone.* New York: Random House, Inc.

Frank, Anne with Otto M. Frank, ed. 1997. *The Diary of a Young Girl: The Definitive Edition.* New York: Bantam.

Friedman, H. S., and M. L. Kern. 2014. "Personality, Well-Being, and Health." *Annual Review of Psychology* 65:719–742.

Fronk, Amanda K. "Killer Season." 2019. *BYU Magazine* 73(1): 11.

Galinsky, Ellen. 2010. *Mind in the Making: The Seven Essential Life Skills Every Child Needs.* New York: HarperCollins Publishers.

Gallace, Alberto, and Charles Spence. 2010. "The Science of Interpersonal Touch: An Overview." *Neuroscience and Biobehavioral Reviews* 34:246–259.

Gallo, Carmine. 2011. *The Innovation Secrets of Steve Jobs: Insanely Different Principles for Breakthrough Success.* New York: McGraw Hill.

Gallo, Carmine. 2014. *Talk Like TED: The 9 Public Speaking Secrets of the World's Top Minds.* New York: St. Martin's Press.

Gardner, Howard. 1993. *Multiple Intelligences: A Theory in Practice.* New York: Basic Books.

Gates, Robert M. 2014. *Duty: Memoirs of a Secretary at War.* New York: Random House.

Gates, Robert M. 2016. *A Passion for Leadership: Lessons on Change and Reform from Fifty Years of Public Service.* New York: Random House.

Gibbens, Sarah. 2018. "'Sea Nomads' Are First Known Humans Genetically Adapted to Diving." *National Geographic,* April 19. https://news.nationalgeographic.com/2018/04/bajau-sea-nomads-free-diving-spleen-science. Accessed August 28, 2019.

Givens, David G. 2005. *Love Signals: A Practical Guide to the Body Language of Courtship.* New York: St. Martin's Press.

Givens, David G. 2013. *The Nonverbal Dictionary of Gestures, Signs and Body Language Cues.* Spokane: Center for Nonverbal Studies. http://www.center-for-nonverbal-studies.org/6101.html.

Gladwell, Malcolm. 2002. *The Tipping Point: How Little Things Can Make a Big Difference.* New York: Little, Brown and Company.

Gladwell, Malcolm. 2005. *Blink: The Power of Thinking Without Thinking.* New York: Little, Brown and Company.

Gladwell, Malcolm. 2009. *What the Dog Saw: And Other Adventures.* New York: Little, Brown and Company.

Goldstein, Noah, Steve J. Martin, and Robert B. Cialdini. 2008. *Yes!: 50 Scientifically Proven Ways to Be Persuasive.* New York: Free Press.

Goleman, Daniel. 1995. *Emotional Intelligence.* New York: Bantam Books.

Goleman, Daniel. 2006. *Social Intelligence.* New York: Bantam Books.

Goleman, Daniel. 2013. *Focus: The Hidden Driver of Excellence.* New York: HarperCollins Publishers.

Goodall, Jane. 2002. *My Life with Chimpanzees.* New York: Byron Preiss Publications, Inc.

Goodall (van Lawick), Jane. 1971. *In the Shadow of Man.* New York: Dell Publishing.

Gottfried, Sophia. 2019. "*Niksen* Is the Dutch Lifestyle Concept of Doing Nothing—And You're About to See It Everywhere." *Time.* July 12. https://time.com/5622094/what-is-niksen/. Accessed August 1, 2020.

Grant, Adam. 2014. *Give and Take: Why Helping Others Drives Success.* New York: Penguin Books.

Greene, Melissa Fay. 2020. "The Romanian Orphans Are Adults Now." *The Atlantic.* June 23 (July/August Issue). https://www.theatlantic.com/magazine/archive/2020/07/can-an-unloved-child-learn-to-love/612253/. Accessed July 28, 2020.

Greene, Robert. 2004. *The 48 Laws of Power.* New York: Viking Penguin.

Greene, Robert. 2012. *Mastery.* New York: Viking Penguin.

Groll, Elias. 2015. "Shinzo Abe Regrets But Declines to Apologize for Japan's WWII Actions; The Japanese Leader Is Trying to Overhaul His Country's Constitution to Allow for a More Assertive Military." *Foreign Policy*, August 14. https://foreignpolicy.com/2015/08/14/shinzo-abe-regrets-but-declines-to-apologize-for-japans-wwii-actions/. Accessed June 11, 2020.

Grove, Andrew. 1999. *Only the Paranoid Survive: How to Exploit the Crisis Points That Challenge Every Company.* New York: Currency and Doubleday.

Haidt, Jonathan. 2006. *The Happiness Hypothesis: Finding Modern Truth in Ancient Wisdom.* New York: Basic Books.

Hardach, Sophie. 2020. "Do Babies Cry in Different Languages?" *New York Times*, April 4. https://www.nytimes.com/2020/04/15/parenting/baby/wermke-prespeech-development-wurzburg.html. Accessed September 1, 2020.

Hardy, Benjamin. 2016. "23 Michael Jordan Quotes That Will Immediately Boost Your Confidence." *INC.*, April 15. https://www.inc.com/benjamin-p-hardy/23-michael-jordan-quotes-that-will-immediately-boost-your-confidence.html.

Harlow, H. F., and R. R. Zimmerman. 1959. "Affectional Responses in the Infant Monkey." *Science* 130:421–432.

Harrell, Keith. 2005. *Attitude Is Everything.* New York: HarperCollins Publishers.

Hartman, Steve. 2019. "A School Bus Driver's Special Delivery." *CBS Sunday Morning*, May 26. https://www.cbsnews.com/video/a-school-bus-drivers-special-delivery/?ftag=CNM-0010aab6i&linkId=68113756&fbclid=IwAR0e0a3EF3KP0BLaFwCCpYyI_jOUi86B3BWDHpSJVkUg8sscTNXVuAckbWs. Accessed June 12, 2019.

Harvard Health. 2019. "The Power of the Placebo Effect: Treating Yourself with Your Mind Is Possible, But There Is More to the Placebo Effect Than Positive Thinking." *Harvard Health Publishing-Harvard Medical School*, May. https://www.health.harvard.edu/mental-health/the-power-of-the-placebo-effect.

Harvard University. 2007. "Project Implicit." https://implicit.harvard.edu/implicit.

Heathfield, Susan M. 2019. "10 Tips to Promote Creative Thinking." *The Balance Careers*, May 8. https://www.thebalancecareers.com/promote-creative-thinking-1918766. Accessed November 26, 2020.

Hebl, Michelle R., and Laura M. Mannix. 2003. "The Weight of Obesity in Evaluating Others: A Mere Proximity Effect." *Personality and Social Psychology Bulletin* 29:28.

Hewlett, Sylvia Ann. 2014. *Executive Presence.* New York: HarperCollins Publishers.

Hoffer, Eric. 2010. *The True Believer.* New York: Harper Perennial.

Hotz, Robert Lee. 1999. "Mars Probe Lost Due to Simple Math Error." *Los Angeles Times,* October 1. https://www.latimes.com/archives/la-xpm-1999-oct-01-mn-17288-story.html. Accessed September 3, 2020.

Hsieh, Tony. 2010. *Delivering Happiness: A Path to Profits, Passion, and Purpose.* New York: Business Plus.

Huffington, Arianna. 2014. *Thrive.* New York: Harmony Books.

Ingersoll, Geoffrey. 2013. "General James 'Mad Dog' Mattis Email About Being 'Too Busy to Read' Is a Must-Read." *Business Insider.* May 9. https://www.businessinsider.com/viral-james-mattis-email-reading-marines-2013-5.

Isaacson, Walter. 2003. *Benjamin Franklin: An American Life.* New York: Simon & Schuster.

Isaacson, Walter. 2017. *Leonardo Da Vinci.* New York: Simon & Schuster.

Jacobs, Charles S. 2009. *Management Rewired: Why Feedback Doesn't Work and Other Surprising Lessons from the Latest Brain Science.* New York: Portfolio.

Jasanoff, Alan. 2018. *The Biological Mind: How Brain, Body, and Environment Collaborate to Make Us Who We Are.* New York: Basic Books.

Journal of Neurosurgery Publishing Group. 2017. "JFK's Back Problems: A New Look." *ScienceDaily.* July 11. www.sciencedaily.com/releases/2017/07/170711085514.htm. Accessed August 2, 2019.

Kahneman, Daniel. 2011. *Thinking, Fast and Slow.* New York: Farrar, Straus and Giroux.

Kennedy, John F. 2003. *Profiles in Courage.* New York: Harper.

Klein, Allison. 2019. "An Autistic Boy Had a Meltdown at a Theme Park, and an Employee's Simple, Soothing Act of Solidarity Went Viral." *The Washington Post.* June 7. https://www.washingtonpost.com/lifestyle/2019/06/07/theme-park-employee-lay-down-ground-next-an-autistic-boy-having-meltdown-her-act-solidarity-went-viral/. Accessed June 26, 2020.

Knapp, Mark L., and Judith A. Hall. 2002. *Nonverbal Communication in Human Interaction,* 5th ed. New York: Harcourt Brace Jovanovich.

Kobayashi, Kenji, and Ming Hsu. 2019. "Common Neural Code for Reward and Information Value." *Proceedings of the National Academy of Sciences* 116(26): 13061–13066. doi:10.1073/pnas.1820145116.

Kolenda, Nick. 2013. *Methods of Persuasion: How to Use Psychology to Influence Human Behavior.* Boston: Kolenda Entertainment, LLC.

Kruger, Justin, and David Dunning. 1999. "Unskilled and Unaware of It: How Difficulties in Recognizing One's Own Incompetence Lead to Inflated Self-Assessments." *Journal of Personality and Social Psychology,* December.

La Ruina, Richard. 2012. *The Natural.* New York: HarperCollins Publishers.

LeDoux, Joseph E. 1996. *The Emotional Brain: The Mysterious Underpinnings of Emotional Life.* New York: Touchstone.

LeDoux, Joseph E. 2002. *Synaptic Self: How Our Brains Become Who We Are.* New York: Penguin Books.

LeGault, Michael R. 2006. *Th!nk: Why Crucial Decisions Can't Be Made in the Blink of an Eye*. New York: Threshold Editions.

Lejeune, Erich J. 2006. *Live Honest-Become Rich!* Heidelberg, Germany: Goyal Publishers.

Lemov, Doug. 2010. *Teach Like a Champion. 49 Techniques That Put Students on the Path to College*. Hoboken, NJ: John Wiley & Sons, Inc.

Leonard, George. 1992. *Mastery: The Keys to Success and Long-Term Fulfilment*. New York: Plume.

Library of Congress. 2010. Jefferson's Library. August 3. https://www.loc.gov /exhibits/jefferson/jefflib.html. Accessed March 15, 2020.

Linden, David J. 2011. *The Compass of Pleasure: How Our Brains Make Fatty Foods, Orgasm, Exercise, Marijuana, Generosity, Vodka, Learning and Gambling Feel So Good*. New York: Penguin Group.

Lipman-Blumen, Jean. 2005. *The Allure of Toxic Leaders: Why We Follow Destructive Bosses and Corrupt Politicians—and How We Can Survive Them*. New York: Oxford University Press.

Lloyd, Robin. 1999. "Metric Mishap Caused Loss of Nasa Orbiter." *CNN/Tech*. http://www.cnn.com/TECH/space/9909/30/mars.metric.02/. Accessed January 1, 2021.

Logan, Dave, John King, and Halee Fischer-Wright. 2008. *Tribal Leadership: Leveraging Natural Groups to Build a Thriving Organization*. New York: HarperCollins.

Lutz, Eric. 2019. "Reefer Madness: Elon Musk's Viral Blunt-Smoking Photo Comes Back to Haunt Him." *Vanity Fair*, March 8. https://www.vanityfair .com/news/2019/03/reefer-madness-elon-musks-viral-blunt-smoking-photo -comes-back-to-haunt-him. Accessed July 28, 2019.

Macias, Amanda. 2018. "The Extraordinary Reading Habits of Defense Secretary James Mattis." *CNBC*, September 15. https://www.cnbc.com/2018/09/13 /defense-secretary-james-mattis-extraordinary-reading-habits.html.

Maguire, Daniel C., and A. Nicholas Fargnoli. 1991. *On Moral Grounds: The Art and Science of Ethics*. New York: Crossroad Publishing.

Manchester, William, and Paul Reid. 2012. *The Last Lion: Winston Spencer Churchill: Defender of the Realm, 1940–1965*. New York: Little, Brown and Company.

Mandela, Nelson. 1995. *Long Walk to Freedom: The Autobiography of Nelson Mandela*. New York: Back Bay Books.

Mandino, Og. 1968. *The Greatest Salesman in the World: You Can Change Your Life with the Priceless Wisdom of Ten Ancient Scrolls Handed Down for Thousands of Years*. Hollywood, FL: Fredrick Fell Publishers.

McCormack, Mark H. 1989. *What They Still Don't Teach You at Harvard Business School*. New York: Bantam.

McCullough, David G. 2016. *The Wright Brothers*. New York: Simon & Schuster.

Medina, Jennifer, Katie Benner, and Kate Taylor. 2019. "Actresses, Business Leaders and Other Wealthy Parents Charged in U.S. College Entry Fraud." *New York Times*, March 12. https://www.nytimes.com/2019/03/12/us/college -admissions-cheating-scandal.html. Accessed July 29, 2019.

Mlodinow, Leonard. 2012. *Subliminal: How Your Unconscious Mind Rules Your Behavior.* New York: Random House.

Murphy Jr., Bill. 2018. "Want to Live Longer? A Neuroscientist Says These Surprising Daily Habits Make It Much More Likely. 'I have no explanation for it,' said the lead researcher. But she's certain it works." *Inc.* February 21. https://www.inc.com/bill-murphy-jr/want-to-live-much-longer-a-neuroscientist-says-these-surprising-daily-habits-make-it-much-more-likely-youll-live-past-90.html. Accessed April 12, 2020.

Nadler, Amos, and Paul J. Zack. 2016. "Hormones and Economic Decisions." In *Neuroeconomics,* edited by Martin Reuter and Christian Montag, 41–66. New York: Springer.

Navarro, Joe. 1984. *An Ethologist's Codex: Observations on Human Behavior.* Unpublished manuscript (Navarro Collection).

Navarro, Joe. 2009. "The Key to Understanding Body Language." *Psychology Today,* October 28. https://www.psychologytoday.com/us/blog/spycatcher/200910/the-key-understanding-body-language. Accessed September 2, 2020.

Navarro, Joe. 2017. *Three Minutes to Doomsday; An FBI Agent, A Traitor, and the Worst Breech in U.S History.* New York: Scribner.

Navarro, Joe. 2018. *The Dictionary of Body Language: A Field Guide to Human Behavior.* New York: HarperCollins Publishers.

Navarro, Joe, with Marvin Karlins. 2008. *What Every BODY Is Saying: An Ex-FBI Agent's Guide to Speed-Reading People.* New York: HarperCollins Publishers.

Navarro, Joe, with Toni Sciarra Poynter. 2014. *Dangerous Personalities.* New York: Rodale.

Neffinger, John, and Matthew Kohut. 2013. *Compelling People: The Hidden Qualities That Make Us Influential.* New York: Hudson Street Press.

Nelson, Charles A., et al. 2014. *Romania's Abandoned Children: Deprivation, Brain Development, and the Struggle for Recovery.* Boston: Harvard University Press.

Odobescu, Vlad. 2015. "Half a Million Kids Survived Romania's 'Slaughterhouses of Souls.' Now They Want Justice." *The World.* December 28. https://www.pri.org/stories/2015-12-28/half-million-kids-survived-romanias-slaughterhouses-souls-now-they-want-justice. Accessed May 26, 2020.

Oud, Anne-Maartje, and Joe Navarro. 2020. "Conducting Difficult Interviews or Conversations." *Psychology Today Blog,* February 1. https://www.psychologytoday.com/us/blog/spycatcher/202002/conducting-difficult-interviews-or-conversations. Accessed January 1, 2021.

Panksepp, Jaak. 1998. *Affective Neuroscience: The Foundations of Human and Animal Emotions.* New York: Oxford University Press.

Peale, Norman Vincent. 1952. *The Power of Positive Thinking.* Englewood, NJ: Prentice-Hall.

Peale, Norman Vincent. 1967. *Enthusiasm Makes a Difference.* Englewood, NJ: Prentice-Hall.

Peale, Norman Vincent. 1976. *The Positive Principle Today.* Englewood, NJ: Prentice-Hall.

Peters, Gerhard, and John T. Woolley, eds. 1962. "Remarks at a Dinner Honoring Nobel Prize Winners of the Western Hemisphere," American Presidency Project, April 20, 1962. Accessed 2014.

Peters, Thomas J., and Robert H. Waterman Jr. 1982. *In Search of Excellence.* New York: HarperCollins Publishers.

Pine, B. Joseph, and James H. Gilmore. 1999. *The Experience Economy: Work Is Theatre and Every Business is a Stage.* Boston: HBS Press.

Pinker, Steven. 2002. *The Blank Slate: The Modern Denial of Human Nature.* New York: Penguin Books.

Podles, Leon J. 2008. *Sacrilege: Sexual Abuse in the Catholic Church.* Baltimore: Crossland Press.

Post, Stephen. 2008. *Why Good Things Happen to Good People.* New York: Broadway Books.

Povoledo, Elisabetta. 2020. "It's Never Too Late to Pursue a Dream, a Graduate Says. He Can Back It Up." *New York Times*, August 5. https://www.nytimes .com/2020/08/05/world/europe/italy-graduate-96.html. Accessed August 20, 2020.

"Questionable Behaviour: Companies Are Relying More and More on Psychometric Tests." 2020. *The Economist*, November 5. https://www.economist .com/business/2020/11/05/questionable-behaviour?utm_campaign=editorial -social&utm_medium=social-organic&utm_source=twitter. Accessed November 10, 2020.

Rao, Srikumar S. 2010. *Happiness at Work: Be Resilient, Motivated, and Successful—No Matter What.* New York: McGraw Hill.

Ratey, John Jay. 2001. *A User's Guide to the Brain: Perception, Attention, and the Four Theaters of the Brain.* New York: Pantheon Books.

Reed, Anika. 2019. "British Airways Apologizes to Travelers After Flight Lands 525 Miles Away from Destination." *USA Today*, March 25. https://www .usatoday.com/story/travel/news/2019/03/25/british-airways-flight-lands -525-miles-away-destination-scotland-london-germany/3267136002/. Accessed September 3, 2020.

Roberts, Andrew. 2010. *Hitler and Churchill: Secrets of Leadership.* London: Weidenfeld & Nicolson.

Roberts, Andrew. 2018. *Churchill: Walking with Destiny.* New York: Viking.

Robinson, Greg. 2001. *By Order of the President: FDR and the Internment of Japanese Americans.* Cambridge, MA: Harvard University Press.

Roosevelt, Theodore. 1910. *"The Man in the Arena."* Speech, at the Sorbonne in Paris, France, on April 23, 1910. Accessed January 1, 2021 from the *Theodore Roosevelt Center at Dickinson State University.* https://www.theodore rooseveltcenter.org/Learn-About-TR/TR-Encyclopedia/Culture-and-Society /Man-in-the-Arena.aspx.

Ryu, Jenna. 2020. "Lea Thompson Supports Brad Garrett's Claim Staff Members 'Were Treated Horribly' by Ellen DeGeneres." *USA Today*, July 31. https://www.usatoday.com/story/entertainment/celebrities/2020/07/31/ellen -degeneres-brad-garrett-calls-mistreatment-common-knowledge/5554831002/. Accessed August 3, 2020.

Sagan, Carl, and Ann Druyan. 1996. *The Demon-Haunted World: Science as a Candle in the Dark.* New York: Ballentine Books.

Sanders, Betsy. 1995. *Fabled Service.* San Francisco: Jossey-Bass Publishers.

Sanders, Robert. 2018. "Enlarged Spleen Key to Diving Endurance of 'Sea No-

mads.'" *Berkeley News*, April 19. https://news.berkeley.edu/2018/04/19/enlarged
-spleen-key-to-diving-endurance-of-sea-nomads/.

Sandle, Tim. 2018. "Knowledge Doubles Almost Every Day, and It's Set to Increase." *Science Digital Journal*, November 23. http://www.digitaljournal
.com/tech-and-science/science/op-ed-knowledge-doubles-almost-every-day
-and-it-s-set-to-increase/article/537543. Accessed November 19, 2020.

Schilling, David Russell. 2013. "Knowledge Doubling Every 12 Months; Soon to
be Every 12 Hours." *Industry Tap*, April 19. https://www.industrytap.com
/knowledge-doubling-every-12-months-soon-to-be-every-12-hours/3950.
Accessed November 7, 2020.

Segev, Tom. 1999. *One Palestine Complete: Jews and Arabs Under the British
Mandate*. New York: Henry Holt & Co.

Seidman, Dov. 2007. *How: Why How We Do Anything Means Everything . . . In
Business (and in life)*. Hoboken, NJ: John Wiley & Sons, Inc.

Seligman, Martin E. P. 1990. *Learned Optimism*. New York: Alfred Knopf.

Shane, Scott. 2010. *Born Entrepreneurs, Born Leaders: How Your Genes Affect
Your Work Life*. New York: Oxford University Press.

Shankman, Peter, and Karen Kelly. 2013. *Nice Companies Finish First: Why Cut-
throat Management Is Over—and Collaboration Is In*. New York: Palgrave
MacMillan.

Shiel, William C. Jr., M.D. 2019. "Medical Definition of Synapse." MedicineNet
(www.medicinenet.com). https://www.medicinenet.com/script/main/art.asp
?articlekey=9246. Accessed August 25, 2019.

Silver, Katie. 2014. "Romania's Lost Generation: Inside the Iron Curtain's Orphan-
ages." *ABC Radio National*, June 23. https://www.abc.net.au/radionational
/programs/allinthemind/inside-the-iron-curtain's-orphanages/5543388. Accessed February 9, 2020.

Simmons, Annette. 2006. *The Story Factor: Inspiration, Influence, and Persuasion Through the Art of Story Telling*. Cambridge, MA: Basic Books.

Slater, Robert. 1999. *Jack Welsh and the GE Way*. New York: McGraw Hill.

Smith, Robert. 2009. *The Leap: How 3 Simple Changes Can Propel Your Career
from Good to Great*. New York: Penguin Books.

Sobel, Dava. 2000. *Galileo's Daughter: A Historical Memoir of Science, Faith,
and Love*. New York: Penguin Putnam, Inc.

Solzhenitsyn, Aleksandr I. 1973. *The Gulag Archipelago* (1st ed., trans.). New
York: Harper & Row.

Sorce, James F., et al. 1985. "Maternal Emotional Signaling: Its Effects on the
Visual Cliff Behavior of One-Year-Olds," *Developmental Psychology* 21(1):
195–200.

Sorensen, Ted. 2009. *Kennedy: The Classic Biography*. New York: Harper Perennial.

Statt, Nick. 2018. "NASA Is Currently Conducting a Workplace Culture and
Safety Review of Boeing and Spacex, Due in Part to Musk's Behavior." *The
Verge*, November 29. https://www.theverge.com/2018/11/19/18118769/elon
-musk-smoke-weed-nasa-admin-jim-bridenstine-workplace-culture-review.
Accessed August 11, 2020.

Stavrova, Olga. 2019. "Having a Happy Spouse Is Associated with Lowered Risk of Mortality." *Psychological Science*; 095679761983514 DOI: 10.1177 /0956797619835147. Accessed June 19, 2020.

Steiner-Adair, Catherine, and Teresa H. Baker. 2013. *The Big Disconnect*. New York: HarperCollins Publishers.

Stone, Douglas, Bruce Patton, and Sheila Heen. 1999. *Difficult Conversations*. New York: Penguin Books.

Sullenberger, Captain Chesley B., III, and Jeffrey Zaslow. 2010. *Highest Duty: My Search for What Really Matters*. New York: William Morrow.

Sullenberger, Captain Chesley B., III, and Jeffrey Zaslow. 2016. *Sully: My Search for What Really Matters*. New York: William Morrow.

Sutton, Robert I. 2007. *The No Asshole Rule: Building a Civilized Workplace and Surviving One That Isn't*. New York: Hachette Book Group.

Thompson, Terri, et al. 2012. "Victims of Lance Armstrong's Strong-Arm Tactics Feel Relief and Vindication in the Wake of U.S. Anti-Doping Agency Report." *New York Daily News*, October 26. https://www.nydailynews.com /sports/more-sports/zone-lance-armstrong-bully-downfall-article-1.1188512. Accessed July 29, 2020.

Tough, Paul. 2013. *How Children Succeed: Grit, Curiosity, and the Hidden Power of Character*. New York: Mariner Books.

Tracy, Jessica. 2016. *Take Pride: Why the Deadliest Sin Holds the Secret to Human Success*. New York: Houghton Mifflin Harcourt.

Tronick, Ed. 2007. *Still Face: The Neurobehavioral and Social-Emotional Development of Infants and Children*. New York: W. W. Norton and Company.

Trout, Jack, and Rivkin, Steve. 2000. *Differentiate or Die: Survival in Our Era of Killer Competition*. New York: John Wiley & Sons.

Underhill, Paco. 2009. *Why We Buy: The Science of Shopping*. New York: Simon and Schuster Paperbacks.

van Baaren, Rick B., et al. 2006. "Mimicry for Money: Behavioral Consequences of Imitation." *Journal of Experimental Social Psychology* 39:393–398.

Van Edwards, Vanessa. 2017. *Captivate: The Science of Succeeding with People*. New York: Portfolio.

Vedantam, Shankar. 2010. *The Hidden Brain: How Our Unconscious Minds Elect Presidents, Control Markets, Wage Wars, and Save Our Lives*. New York: Spiegel & Grau.

Vuori, Tim O., and Quy N. Huy. 2015. "Distributed Attention and Shared Emotions in the Innovation Process: How Nokia Lost the Smartphone Battle." *Administrative Science Quarterly*, 1–43. http://www.enterprisegarage .io/2015/12/case-study-how-nokia-lost-the-smartphone-battle/. Accessed August 3, 2020.

Walker, Rob. 2008. *Buying In*. New York: Random House Publishing Group.

Watson, Lillian Eichler. 1988. *Light from Many Lamps: A Treasury of Inspiration*. New York: Touchstone.

Watzlawick, Paul. 1974. *An Anthology of Human Communication*. Palo Alto, CA: Science and Behavior Books.

The Week. 2020. "The Impeachment Battle over Witnesses." January 31, Page 4.

The Week. 2020. Quote by Mary Renault. November 27, Page 19.

Weisfield, G. E., and J. M. Beresfor. 1982. "Erectness of Posture as an Indicator of Dominance or Success in Humans." *Motivation and Emotion* 6(2):113–131.

Welch, Jack, and John A. Byrne. 2001. *Jack: Straight from the Gut.* New York: Warner Business Books.

Wilson, Timothy D. 2002. *Strangers to Ourselves: Discovering the Adaptive Unconscious.* Cambridge, MA: Harvard University Press.

Wiseman, Richard. 2009. *59 Seconds: Change Your Life in Under a Minute.* New York: Anchor Books.

Wolfe, Ira. 2004. *Understanding Business Values and Motivators.* Atlanta: Creative Communications Publications.

Yahr, Emily. 2020. "The Downward Spiral of Ellen DeGeneres's Public Persona: A Complete Guide." *The Washington Post,* August 3. https://www.washington post.com/arts-entertainment/2020/08/03/ellen-degeneres-show-reputation/. Accessed August 3, 2020.

Young, Janette. 2018. "Four Ways Having a Pet Increases Your Lifespan." *The Conversation,* January 17. https://theconversation.com/four-ways-having-a-pet -increases-your-lifespan-88640. Accessed July 22, 2020.

Index